# The Ultimate
# *Summer*
# *Snack*
## Book

# The Ultimate

# *Summer Snack*

## Book

## Featuring 340 tempting summer dishes

PUBLISHED BY
SALAMANDER BOOKS LIMITED
LONDON

# A SALAMANDER BOOK

Published by Salamander Books Limited
8 Blenheim Court
Brewery Road
London N7 9NT

© Salamander Books Ltd, 1999, 2000

ISBN 1 84065 087 7

1 2 3 4 5 6 7 8 9 10

All correspondence concerning the content of
this volume should be addressed to
Salamander Books Ltd.

Printed in Spain

## CREDITS

Project managed by Charlotte Davies
Recipes by Meg Jansz and Lorna Rhodes
All photography by Ken Fields, except
pages 80-141 by Philip Wilkins

Filmset: SX Composing, England
Colour separation: P&W Graphics Pte, Ltd,
    Singapore

When making any of the recipes in this book,
you should follow either the metric or Imperial
measures, as these are not interchangeable.

# CONTENTS

# SALADS

This section contains five chapters of varied salad recipes to suit all tastes and occasions. Along with substantial main-course salads, lighter salads for eating as starters or on the side are also included, as well as a selection of fruit salads to round off a meal. All the serving sizes recommended in the recipes are for side salads, starters or light lunches, unless otherwise indicated as main-course meals. Some of the recipes are adaptations of traditional salads, while others are innovative and totally original creations.

Every civilization has eaten some mixture of raw indigenous vegetables as a health-giving part of its diet. Salads were originally the edible parts of various herbs and plants seasoned only with salt – the Latin word 'sāl', from which the word 'salad' derives.

As time progressed, the composition of salads became more varied. As early as 1699 in England, John Evelyn's *Acetaria* described 'Sallets' as 'a composition of Edule Plants and Roots of several kinds, to be eaten raw or green, blanched or candied, simple and serfe, or intermingled with others according to the season'. Evelyn recommended that the ingredients of a salad be carefully selected to complement and balance each other.

*Acetaria* distinguishes between simple and combined salads, however it is in classic French cooking where this distinction has evolved fully. French salads are traditionally of two types: a simple salad of tossed lettuce or another single vegetable, usually served after the main course, and a more complex combination salad, served as a separate hors d'oeuvre or even a light main course in itself.

It is the combination salad that has developed in the United States of America into the increasingly popular main-course salad, which now features extremely diverse ingredients, including meat, seafood, cheese, nuts and grains.

Although many salads contain these rather calorific ingredients, salads are fundamentally healthy because their basic ingredients are raw vegetables or fruits with their inherent vitamins and minerals intact.

## CHOOSING AND STORING INGREDIENTS
Using raw ingredients as the basis of your dish means that good quality is essential! For salad-making, always choose the best and freshest ingredients available. Although most fresh produce is now found, at a price, on supermarket shelves year-round, for quality and value buy produce during its growing season.

Fresh young asparagus in early summer, sun-ripened strawberries a little later on and crisp seasonal lettuce will always taste better than their forced greenhouse counterparts. The availability of root vegetables, grains, dried fruits and nuts in all seasons does enable you to make tasty salads throughout the year.

Once you have bought your ingredients, store them carefully. Salad vegetables should always be kept in a cool, dark place, preferably in a refrigerator. This will keep them firm and fresh. Fresh herbs last best in the refrigerator, either sprayed with water and placed in a polythene bag or standing in bowls of water.

**RIGHT:** Look for the freshest ingredients for your salads: ripe fruits, crisp lettuces and herbs, and any unusual colours or varieties.

Nuts are an excellent source of fibre and add crunch to salads. However, their shelf-life is relatively short because they have a high oil content, and can turn rancid. Buy nuts in small quantities, store them in airtight containers and use them quickly.

## DRESSINGS

Dressings are an integral part of any good salad. They should always work together with the tastes of the salad ingredients, without being overpowering.

In vinaigrette dressings, the recommended proportions are 3 parts oil to 1 part vinegar or citrus juice. However, you should experiment and alter proportions to suit you own tastes.

Many different oils are readily available. The most popular, olive oil, is used in many classic European recipes and is a monounsaturate, generally accepted as lower in cholesterol than, for example, the more exotic nut oils. For the health-conscious, use light olive oil.

The dressings in this book use traditional oils, such as olive and sunflower, as well as more unusual newcomers, such as hazelnut, walnut, chilli and sesame oils. You may like to prepare your own flavoured oils by adding some dried chillies, garlic, or herb sprigs to a bottle of oil. If you do this, allow the flavours to develop for at least two weeks.

## PREPARATION

Always ensure that all vegetables are washed before using. Washed salad leaves should be dried before dressing is added. The leaves will be crisper and the dressing will coat the leaves well. The best and quickest way to dry leaves is in a salad spinner, but a clean, dry linen towel can also be used to pat leaves dry.

If using nuts, toast them in advance as this enhances their flavour. Dressings can also be made in advance and set aside for their flavours to develop and create a stronger taste. However, dressings should be added to the salad just before serving to prevent leaves from becoming soggy. An exception is with pasta, grain and rice salads, where adding the dressing to the warm, cooked base ingredient allows the ingredient to absorb the flavours without affecting the look of the salad.

## PRESENTING YOUR SALAD

The visual appeal of food is a vital part of its enjoyment, so it is worth spending time on attractive presentation. Even the simplest side salad can be made decorative by careful slicing, an imaginative combination of colours and the arrangement of the ingredients on the plate. Not all salads need to be tossed; you can arrange the ingredients on the plate, then pour or drizzle the dressing over.

Garnishing your salad before serving will also enhance its visual appeal. Garnishes can vary from a single sprig of a herb to chopped herbs sprinkled over the salad, to a single extra ingredient from the salad, such as a prawn in its shell or a spring onion tassel.

Finally, cooking and eating should be fun! Enjoy preparing and eating the salads on the following pages, but do be flexible too and experiment with the almost infinite variety of beautiful and delicious ingredients available.

**RIGHT:** This Three-Melon Salad (see page 66) shows how simple melon balls can look stunning. Decorative shapes for fruits and vegetables can be cut using a canelle knife, zester or peeler.

# ALL-AMERICAN SALADS

This chapter includes classic favourites, such as the Waldorf Salad and the Caesar Salad, the stylish salad invented in 1924 by Caesar Cardini, which is usually finished with a flourish at your table in good restaurants. Also featured are salads that reflect the ethnic diversity of America, such as German Hot Potato Salad, and the wide range of ingredients available, such as the Lobster & Avocado Salad.

## CLASSIC COLESLAW

225 g (8 oz) white cabbage
175 g (6 oz) carrots
3 sticks celery
2 small shallots, peeled
45 ml (3 tbsp) snipped fresh chives

### DRESSING
90 ml (6 tbsp) mayonnaise
45 ml (3 tbsp) soured cream
15 ml (1 tbsp) white wine vinegar
15 ml (1 tbsp) water
2.5 ml (½ tsp) sugar
Salt and ground black pepper

Shred the cabbage finely. Peel the carrots and grate them coarsely. Slice the celery thinly and chop the shallots very finely. Place in a large bowl and add the snipped chives.

Place the dressing ingredients in a separate bowl and whisk well to combine. Pour over the vegetables and toss to coat. Refrigerate for at least 1 hour before serving to allow flavours to develop.　　SERVES 6

## FRUIT & NUT SLAW

100 g (4 oz) red cabbage
100 g (4 oz) white cabbage
4 spring onions
1 carrot
2 red apples
100 g (4 oz) Brazil nuts, halved
60 ml (4 tbsp) raisins
15 ml (1 tbsp) chopped fresh parsley, to garnish

### DRESSING
150 ml (10 tbsp) mayonnaise
30 ml (2 tbsp) water
2.5 ml (½ tsp) sugar
30 ml (2 tbsp) lemon juice
Salt and ground black pepper

Shred the two cabbages finely. Slice the spring onions thinly, and peel and shred the carrot. Quarter and core the apples and slice them thinly. Place the prepared vegetables and fruit in a bowl with the nuts and raisins.

Place all the dressing ingredients in a bowl and whisk well to combine. Pour the dressing over the prepared ingredients in the bowl and toss well to combine. Refrigerate for 1 hour to allow flavours to develop. Serve garnished with chopped parsley.　　SERVES 6

**TOP:** Fruit & Nut Slaw
**BOTTOM:** Classic Coleslaw

# PRAWN & COTTAGE CHEESE SALAD IN CAPSICUM CUPS

350 g (12 oz) cottage cheese
30 ml (2 tbsp) chopped fresh dill
175 g (6 oz) cooked, peeled prawns
100 g (4 oz) seedless green grapes
1 large shallot
Salt and ground black pepper
1 medium red pepper
1 medium green pepper
100 g (4 oz) crisp lettuce leaves
½ quantity Classic French Dressing (see page 74)
4 small cooked prawns in the shell and dill sprigs,
to garnish

Place the cottage cheese, dill and prawns in a mixing
bowl. Wash and halve the grapes and chop the shallot
finely. Add the grapes and shallot to the bowl and season the mixture well. Mix gently to combine.

Halve the peppers lengthways, keeping the stalks
intact. Remove the cores and seeds and discard. Toss
the washed and dried lettuce leaves in the dressing and
divide between four plates. Spoon one-quarter of the
cottage cheese and prawn mixture into each pepper
half. Place a filled pepper on each plate with the lettuce. Garnish each serving with a whole prawn and dill
sprigs and serve at once.                SERVES 4

# COBB SALAD

*This salad has been made with blue Brie instead of
Roquefort for a unique variation on an old favourite.
You may, of course, prefer to substitute Roquefort
or another blue cheese for the Brie in the recipe.*

4 hard-boiled eggs
225 g (8 oz) blue Brie cheese
225 g (8 oz) cooked, skinless, boneless
chicken breast
12 rashers smoked streaky bacon
6 tomatoes
12 stuffed green olives
12 stoned black olives
350 g (12 oz) iceberg lettuce, shredded
Blue Cheese Dressing, made with blue Brie
(see page 76)

Shell and slice the hard-boiled eggs. Slice the blue Brie
into long thin slices. Cut the chicken into thin strips.

Cook the bacon under a preheated hot grill for
about 10 minutes, turning halfway through, until it is
crispy. Allow to cool, then snip into bite-sized pieces.

Cut the tomatoes into quarters, remove the seeds
and chop the flesh roughly. Halve the olives.

Divide the shredded lettuce between four plates.
Arrange the prepared ingredients in rows on top of
the lettuce. Spoon one-quarter of the dressing on to
each salad and serve immediately.

SERVES 4 AS A MAIN COURSE

**RIGHT:** Prawn & Cottage Cheese Salad
in Capsicum Cups

# CAESAR SALAD

2 large slices, day-old white bread
120 ml (8 tbsp) olive oil
2 cloves garlic, crushed
1 Cos lettuce
8 anchovy fillets
50 g (2 oz) Parmesan cheese, grated

### DRESSING
1 large egg
1 clove garlic, crushed
5 ml (1 tsp) Dijon mustard
150 ml (¼ pint) extra virgin olive oil
30 ml (2 tbsp) white wine vinegar
Salt and ground black pepper

Prepare the croûtons. Remove crusts from the bread and discard. Cut the bread into small cubes. Heat half the oil and garlic in a frying pan, add half the cubed bread and fry over a medium heat for 2-3 minutes until golden. Remove with a slotted spoon and drain on absorbant kitchen paper. Repeat with the remaining oil, garlic and bread.

Wash and dry the Cos lettuce and tear into 5-cm (2-inch) pieces. Place in a large serving bowl. Drain and rinse the anchovies and snip finely. Add to the lettuce with half the Parmesan.

Make the dressing. Place the egg in a food processor with the garlic and mustard. With the motor running, pour the oil on the egg in a thin steady stream until a thick emulsion is produced. Add the vinegar, salt and pepper and blend again briefly.

To serve, pour the dressing over the salad and toss gently. Sprinkle over the remaining Parmesan and scatter over the croûtons. Serve at once.  SERVES 4

*Variation: Chopped crisply cooked bacon can be added to this salad for a tasty alternative.*

# WESTERN SALAD

2 large slices, day-old white bread
Corn oil for deep-frying
1 Cos lettuce
25 g (1 oz) rocket leaves
175 g (6 oz) blue cheese, such as Stilton, cubed
25 g (1 oz) Parmesan cheese, grated
30 ml (2 tbsp) snipped fresh chives

### DRESSING
1 egg
2 cloves garlic, crushed
150 ml (¼ pint) corn oil
30 ml (2 tbsp) lemon juice
Salt and ground black pepper

Prepare the croûtons. Remove crusts from the bread and discard. Cut the bread into small cubes. Heat the oil for deep-frying. When it is hot enough (a cube of bread dropped into the oil sizzles at the surface), fry the bread in batches for about 30 seconds until golden. Remove with a slotted spoon and drain on absorbant kitchen paper.

Make the dressing. Cook the egg in boiling water for 2 minutes to lightly soft boil it. Then spoon the soft egg into a food processor and add the garlic. With the motor running, pour the oil on to the egg in a steady stream to produce a creamy dressing. Add the lemon juice and seasoning and blend again briefly.

Wash and dry the Cos lettuce and tear into bite-sized pieces. Place in a salad bowl with the washed rocket. Add the cubed blue cheese and Parmesan.

To serve, pour over the dressing and toss gently. Scatter over the croûtons and snipped chives and serve at once.                    SERVES 4

**TOP:** Caesar Salad
**BOTTOM:** Western Salad

## WALDORF SALAD

250 g (9 oz) fennel
30 ml (2 tbsp) lemon juice
2 red apples
100 g (4 oz) red lettuce leaves, such as oak leaf
or lollo rosso
50 g (2 oz) walnut pieces, toasted
50 g (2 oz) raisins
Fennel fronds, to garnish

### DRESSING
90 ml (6 tbsp) mayonnaise
30 ml (2 tbsp) walnut oil
30 ml (2 tbsp) lemon juice
Salt and ground black pepper

Reserve the fennel fronds and slice the fennel bulb thinly. Place in a bowl with the lemon juice, tossing gently to coat. Quarter and core the apples and slice them. Add the apples to the bowl with the fennel and toss to coat with lemon juice.

Wash and dry the lettuce. Line a shallow serving dish with the leaves. Place the dressing ingredients in a bowl and whisk well to combine.

Just before serving, drain the fennel and apple and add to the bowl of dressing along with the walnuts and raisins. Toss to combine and spoon the salad on to the bed of lettuce. Garnish with the fennel fronds and serve at once. SERVES 4-6

## SWEDISH SALAD

175 g (6 oz) celery
225 g (8 oz) cooked beetroot
2 Cox's apples
50 g (2 oz) walnut halves, toasted
100 g (4 oz) radicchio leaves

### DRESSING
90 ml (6 tbsp) mayonnaise
30 ml (2 tbsp) lemon juice
30 ml (2 tbsp) soured cream
Salt and ground black pepper

Slice the celery thinly on the diagonal. Cut the beetroot into wedges. Peel and core the apples and slice them. Place the celery, beetroot and apple in a large bowl. Reserve a few walnuts for garnish and add the rest to the bowl.

Place the dressing ingredients in a bowl and whisk to combine. Pour the dressing over the prepared ingredients. Toss well to mix and set aside.

Wash and dry the radicchio leaves and tear them in half. Line a salad bowl with the leaves and spoon the tossed salad into the centre. Garnish with the reserved walnuts and serve at once. SERVES 4-6

**TOP:** Swedish Salad
**BOTTOM:** Waldorf Salad

## FLORIDA PRAWN SALAD

20 cooked king prawns in the shell
4 pink grapefruit
450-g (1-lb) piece Galia melon
225 g (8 oz) iceberg lettuce
20 ml (4 tsp) fresh chervil leaves

### DRESSING

90 ml (6 tbsp) grapeseed oil
90 ml (6 tbsp) mayonnaise
30 ml (2 tbsp) champagne vinegar
45 ml (3 tbsp) water
1 shallot, finely chopped
15 ml (1 tbsp) crushed dried pink peppercorns
Salt and ground black pepper

Peel 12 of the prawns and halve each prawn lengthways. Keep 8 prawns whole, for garnishing. Peel the grapefruit and cut in between the membranes to produce segments.

Using a melon baller, scoop balls from the melon flesh. Wash and dry the lettuce and tear the leaves into bite-sized pieces.

Place the ingredients for the dressing in a bowl and whisk together to combine.

To assemble the salads, divide the lettuce between four plates. Arrange the prepared prawns, grapefruit segments and melon balls on the plates, spoon the dressing over the four salads and scatter over the chervil leaves. Garnish each plate with 2 whole prawns and serve at once. SERVES 4 AS A MAIN COURSE

## CHEF'S SALAD

30 ml (2 tbsp) vegetable oil
350 g (12 oz) raw, skinless, boneless pieces
turkey breast
Salt and ground black pepper
100 g (4 oz) honey-roast or smoked ham
225 g (8 oz) Gruyère or Emmental cheese
4 small tomatoes
4 hard-boiled eggs
350 g (12 oz) iceberg lettuce
Thousand Island Dressing (see page 76)
Parsley sprigs, to garnish

Heat the oil in a heavy-based frying pan. Season the pieces of turkey breast with salt and pepper and add to the pan. Cook over a high heat for 10 minutes, turning occasionally, until the turkey is golden on the outside and cooked through. Remove and set aside to cool.

Slice the ham into long strips. Using a swivel vegetable peeler, slice the cheese very thinly. Cut the tomatoes into wedges and shell and slice the eggs. Shred the lettuce finely. When the turkey has cooled, slice it into neat pieces.

Assemble the salads. Divide the shredded lettuce between four large plates. Arrange equal amounts of turkey, ham, cheese, tomato and egg on each plate. Spoon a little dressing into the centre of each salad and garnish with parsley. Serve at once, passing extra dressing separately. SERVES 4 AS A MAIN COURSE

**RIGHT:** Florida Prawn Salad

## SWEET POTATO SALAD

900 g (2 lb) sweet potatoes
225 g (8 oz) carrots
1 green pepper
60 ml (4 tbsp) torn coriander leaves
Salt and ground black pepper

### BUTTERMILK HERB DRESSING

90 ml (6 tbsp) buttermilk
60 ml (4 tbsp) mayonnaise
15 ml (1 tbsp) finely chopped fresh coriander
15 ml (1 tbsp) snipped fresh chives
Salt and ground black pepper

Preheat the oven to 180°C (350°F, Gas mark 4). Bake the sweet potatoes for about 40 minutes until tender. Remove from the oven and set aside to cool. When cool, peel off the skin and cut flesh into large dice.

Peel the carrots and slice them thickly. Blanch in boiling, salted water for 2-3 minutes, then drain and refresh in cold water. Halve the pepper, remove the core and seeds, and dice the flesh.

Place the dressing ingredients in a bowl and mix to combine. Place the sweet potato, carrot, pepper and torn coriander in a bowl, season well and pour over the dressing. Toss gently to combine. Refrigerate the salad for 2 hours before serving to allow the flavours to develop. SERVES 4-6

## GERMAN HOT POTATO SALAD

450 g (1 lb) waxy potatoes
30 ml (2 tbsp) vegetable oil
225 g (8 oz) smoked back bacon, rinds removed and diced
1 small red onion
20 ml (4 tsp) chopped fresh sage

### DRESSING

90 ml (6 tbsp) mayonnaise
30 ml (2 tbsp) milk
30 ml (2 tbsp) soured cream
10 ml (2 tsp) coarse-grain mustard
Salt and ground black pepper

Place all the dressing ingredients in a bowl and mix well to combine. Set aside.

Peel the potatoes and cut into chunks. Cook the potatoes in boiling, salted water for about 8 minutes until tender. Drain and keep warm.

While the potatoes are cooking, heat the oil in a frying pan and fry the bacon for 8-9 minutes until crisp. Keep warm.

Dice the onion finely. Place the onion, hot potatoes and bacon in a mixing bowl with the sage. Pour over the dressing, toss well and serve the salad warm. SERVES 4

**TOP:** German Hot Potato Salad
**BOTTOM:** Sweet Potato Salad

## CHICKEN, GRAPE & HAZELNUT SALAD

450 g (1 lb) cooked chicken breasts
225 g (8 oz) black grapes
60 ml (4 tbsp) skinless hazelnuts, toasted
Salt and ground black pepper
225 g (8 oz) watercress
Fresh tarragon leaves, to garnish

### DRESSING

2 spring onions
90 ml (6 tbsp) mayonnaise
60 ml (4 tbsp) cream cheese
90 ml (6 tbsp) water
Salt and ground black pepper

Remove the skin from the cooked chicken and discard. Cut the meat into bite-sized chunks and place in a large mixing bowl.

Wash the grapes, halve them and remove the pips. Add the grapes to the chicken along with the toasted hazelnuts. Season with salt and pepper and mix gently to combine.

Prepare the dressing. Chop the spring onions finely and place in a bowl. Add the remaining dressing ingredients and mix well. Pour the creamy dressing over the chicken and toss gently to coat.

Discard the tough stalks from the watercress. Wash and dry the watercress.

To serve, arrange a bed of watercress on a platter and spoon the chicken mixture into the centre. Garnish with tarragon and serve at once. SERVES 4

## ASPARAGUS & EGG SALAD

450 g (1 lb) fresh asparagus stalks
4 hard-boiled eggs
225 g (8 oz) sliced pastrami

### BUTTERMILK DRESSING

60 ml (4 tbsp) buttermilk
60 ml (4 tbsp) olive oil
30 ml (2 tbsp) white wine vinegar
10 ml (2 tsp) coarse-grain mustard
Salt and ground black pepper

Cut the tough ends off the asparagus stalks and, using a potato peeler, peel the green skin from the asparagus stalks, stopping just below the tips. Blanch the asparagus in boiling, salted water for 2-3 minutes until just cooked. Drain and refresh in cold water.

Shell the eggs and slice each egg into 4-6 wedges. Place the ingredients for the Buttermilk Dressing in a bowl and whisk to combine.

To serve, arrange the asparagus, egg wedges and sliced pastrami on four serving plates. Drizzle some dressing over each portion and serve at once.

SERVES 4

**RIGHT:** Chicken, Grape & Hazelnut Salad

# LOBSTER & AVOCADO SALAD

2 small boiled lobsters
8 asparagus stalks, preferably white
1 large, ripe avocado
20 ml (4 tsp) lemon juice
100 g (4 oz) mixed lettuce leaves
Tarragon sprigs, to garnish

### DRESSING

30 ml (2 tbsp) olive oil
60 ml (4 tbsp) sunflower oil
30 ml (2 tbsp) tarragon vinegar
10 ml (2 tsp) finely chopped shallot
20 ml (4 tsp) chopped fresh tarragon
10 ml (2 tsp) Dijon mustard
5 ml (1 tsp) sugar
Salt and ground black pepper

Prepare the lobsters. Twist off the claws and crack them. Either leave the claws ready for eating or remove the flesh. For each lobster, gently separate the tail from the head and body. With sharp scissors cut down the length of the underside of the tail. Bend apart so the meat becomes free and remove the vein. Remove the flesh and slice into thick discs.

Cut the tough ends from the asparagus and slice each stalk in half lengthways. Blanch in boiling, salted water for 2 minutes. Drain and refresh under cold water. Peel the avocado, halve and slice the flesh thickly; then place in a bowl with the lemon juice.

Wash and dry the lettuce. Place the dressing ingredients in a bowl and whisk to combine.

To assemble, toss the lettuce with half the dressing and divide between two plates. Arrange the lobster, asparagus and avocado on each bed of lettuce. Spoon the remaining dressing over the salads, garnish with tarragon and serve at once.

SERVES 2 AS A MAIN COURSE

# CRAB LOUIS SALAD

350 g (12 oz) fresh crabmeat
1 onion
100 g (4 oz) celery
12 stuffed olives
Salt and ground black pepper
Pinch of cayenne
100 g (4 oz) iceberg lettuce
Celery leaves, to garnish

### DRESSING

60 ml (4 tbsp) mayonnaise
60 ml (4 tbsp) cream, very lightly whipped
60 ml (4 tbsp) chilli sauce
1 small green chilli, seeded and chopped
60 ml (4 tbsp) fresh chervil leaves
Salt and ground black pepper

Place all the dressing ingredients in a bowl and mix well to combine. Refrigerate while preparing the salad to allow the flavours to develop.

Flake the crabmeat and place in a mixing bowl. Peel the onion and grate coarsely. Wash the celery and slice thinly on the diagonal. Halve the olives. Add the ingredients to the crabmeat and season with salt, pepper and cayenne. Add the dressing and toss well.

Wash and dry the lettuce. Divide the lettuce between four plates and spoon one-quarter of the crab salad on to each plate. Garnish with celery leaves and serve at once.                    SERVES 4

**TOP:** Crab Louis Salad
**BOTTOM:** Lobster & Avocado Salad

## WILD RICE SALAD WITH SCALLOPS

225 g (8 oz) mixed long-grain and wild rice
2 spring onions
2 large carrots
½ red pepper
½ orange pepper
30 ml (2 tbsp) pumpkin seeds
450 g (1 lb) large scallops with corals
45 ml (3 tbsp) vegetable oil

### DRESSING

Grated zest of 1 lime
60 ml (4 tbsp) lime juice
90 ml (6 tbsp) sunflower oil
1 large clove garlic, crushed
20 ml (4 tsp) chopped fresh flat-leaved parsley
Pinch of sugar
Salt and ground black pepper

Cook the rice in boiling, salted water according to the instructions on the packet. Drain and refresh in cold water. Set aside.

Slice the spring onions into long, thin strips. Peel the carrots and, using a vegetable peeler, peel the carrots into long ribbons. Blanch the carrot ribbons in boiling, salted water for about 1 minute. Drain and refresh in cold water.

Remove the cores from the peppers and dice the flesh finely. Toast the pumpkin seeds under a hot grill for 2 minutes until pale golden. Remove the seeds and allow to cool.

Separate the scallop corals from the whites. Cut each scallop white into quarters and halve the corals. Heat half the oil in a frying pan and sauté the whites, stirring frequently, for about 3 minutes. Remove the scallops from the pan. Add the remaining oil to the pan and sauté the corals for 3 minutes. Remove the corals from the pan.

Place the ingredients for the dressing in a screw-topped jar and shake well to mix. Pour half the dressing over the rice and toss gently to coat. Place the rice in a serving dish.

Mix together the remaining ingredients, except the pumpkin seeds, and pour over the remaining dressing. Toss gently and spoon over the rice. Scatter over the pumpkin seeds and serve at once.     SERVES 4-6

## BLACK-EYED SUSAN SALAD

4 grapefruit
4 dates
40 g (1½ oz) pecan nuts
175 g (6 oz) mixed lettuce leaves, to include rocket, Cos and lamb's lettuce
Classic French Dressing (see page 74)

Using a sharp knife, peel the skin and white pith from the grapefruit and cut between the membranes to produce segments.

Remove the stones from the dates and slice the flesh into long segments. Cut the pecan nuts lengthways into quarters. Wash and dry the lettuce and tear large leaves into bite-sized pieces.

To serve, toss the lettuce with half the dressing and divide between four plates. Arrange the grapefruit in a spoke-like pattern over the lettuce and arrange the dates and pecan nuts in the centre. Spoon the remaining dressing over the salads and serve at once.

SERVES 4

**TOP:** Wild Rice Salad with Scallops
**BOTTOM:** Black-eyed Susan Salad

# EUROPEAN SALADS

*The surprisingly diverse flavours and ingredients of this small continent feature in the recipes in this chapter. Along with Caponata from Sicily, with its colourful variety of vegetables, and the French Salade Niçoise, with its Mediterranean taste, are the German Kartoffelsalat and the Norwegian Herring & Dill Salad, with their subtler, northern flavours.*

## GREEK SALAD

350 g (12 oz) feta cheese
4 plum tomatoes
½ cucumber
1 small purple onion
16 oil-cured Greek olives
Oregano sprigs, to garnish

### HERB DRESSING
90 ml (6 tbsp) extra virgin olive oil, preferably Greek
30 ml (2 tbsp) white wine vinegar
45 ml (3 tbsp) chopped fresh oregano
1 large clove garlic, crushed
Pinch of sugar
Salt and ground black pepper

Place all the dressing ingredients in a screw-topped jar and shake well to combine. Chill until required.

Cube the feta cheese and cut the tomatoes into wedges. Place in a large salad bowl.

Halve the cucumber and dice. Peel and thinly slice the onion. Add the cucumber and onion to the salad with the olives. Pour over the dressing and toss well. Serve at once.       SERVES 4

## TOMATO SALAD WITH HALLOUMI & ROCKET

8 small, ripe plum tomatoes
100 g (4 oz) halloumi cheese
2 spring onions
150 g (5 oz) rocket leaves
12 black olives

### DRESSING
90 ml (6 tbsp) extra virgin olive oil
30 ml (2 tbsp) red wine vinegar
30 ml (2 tbsp) chopped fresh oregano
Salt and ground black pepper
Pinch of sugar

Wash the tomatoes and slice thickly. Cut the halloumi cheese into thin strips. Shred the spring onions into long, thin strips.

Wash and dry the rocket and tear any large leaves into bite-sized pieces; then line a serving plate with the leaves. Arrange the tomatoes and cheese on the bed of rocket and scatter over the spring onions and olives.

Place the dressing ingredients in a screw-topped jar and shake well to combine. Spoon the dressing over the prepared salad and serve at once.       SERVES 4-6

**TOP:** Greek Salad
**BOTTOM:** Tomato Salad with Halloumi & Rocket

## FRENCH FRISEE SALAD WITH GARLIC CROUTONS

175 g (6 oz) frisée lettuce

**GARLIC CROUTONS**

4 cloves garlic, crushed

90 ml (6 tbsp) extra virgin olive oil

Salt and ground black pepper

75 g (3 oz) crustless white bread

**ROQUEFORT DRESSING**

45 ml (3 tbsp) corn oil

45 ml (3 tbsp) mayonnaise

30 ml (2 tbsp) white wine vinegar

30 ml (2 tbsp) water

2.5 ml (½ tsp) Dijon mustard

Few drops Worcestershire sauce

Salt and ground black pepper

100 g (4 oz) Roquefort cheese

Prepare the croûtons. Preheat the oven to 180°C (350°F, Gas mark 4). Place the garlic, oil and seasoning in a large bowl and mix well. Cut the bread into 1.5-cm (½-inch) cubes and add to the bowl. Toss well to coat. Transfer the bread to a baking sheet and bake on the top shelf of the oven for about 15 minutes until golden. Remove and set aside.

Place all the dressing ingredients, except the cheese, in a bowl and whisk to combine. Mash the cheese with a fork and add it, a little at a time, to the dressing, whisking well between each addition.

Wash and dry the frisée lettuce and tear into bite-sized pieces. Place in a bowl with half the croûtons, pour over the dressing and toss until evenly coated with dressing. Serve the salad at once with the remaining croûtons scattered over the top.     SERVES 4

## SALADE NICOISE

198-g (7-oz) can tuna in oil, drained and flaked

100 g (4 oz) fine French beans

100 g (4 oz) baby broad beans

6 anchovy fillets

½ cucumber

4 tomatoes

20 black olives

3 hard-boiled eggs, shelled

Chicory leaves, to serve

**DRESSING**

90 ml (6 tbsp) French olive oil

30 ml (2 tbsp) white wine vinegar

1 clove garlic, crushed

5 ml (1 tsp) Dijon mustard

45 ml (3 tbsp) chopped flat-leaved parsley

Salt and ground black pepper

Place the dressing ingredients in a screw-topped jar and shake well to combine. Set aside.

Place the flaked tuna in a mixing bowl. Halve the French beans and blanch them in boiling, salted water with the broad beans for 3 minutes until just tender. Drain and refresh in cold water.

Cut the anchovy fillets into small pieces and slice the cucumber into batons. Cut the tomatoes into wedges. Add beans, anchovy, cucumber and tomato to the tuna along with the olives. Pour over the dressing and toss the salad gently.

Wash and dry the chicory and line a serving dish with the leaves. Spoon the prepared salad into the centre. Cut each egg into quarters and add to the salad. Serve at once.     SERVES 4

**TOP:** French Frisée Salad
**BOTTOM:** Salade Niçoise

## WARM CHICKEN LIVER, SUN-DRIED TOMATO & PASTA SALAD

225 g (8 oz) dried pasta shapes
60 ml (4 tbsp) olive oil
3 shallots, sliced
2 cloves garlic, crushed
450 g (1 lb) chicken livers, trimmed
Salt and ground black pepper
8 halves sun-dried tomatoes in oil, drained and sliced
100 g (4 oz) frisée lettuce, washed and torn into bite-sized pieces

### DRESSING

60 ml (4 tbsp) oil from sun-dried tomatoes
60 ml (4 tbsp) olive oil
60 ml (4 tbsp) balsamic vinegar
60 ml (4 tbsp) chopped fresh parsley
10 ml (2 tsp) Dijon mustard
Salt and ground black pepper

Place all the dressing ingredients in a screw-topped jar and shake well.

Cook the pasta in plenty of boiling, salted water for about 10 minutes or until 'al dente'. Drain the pasta and immediately toss it with the prepared dressing while still warm. Set aside.

Heat the oil in a large frying pan and sauté the shallots and garlic for 1 minute until softened. Add the chicken livers, season well and sauté for a further 4-5 minutes until browned on the outside and just cooked in the centre. Transfer the chicken livers to the bowl of pasta. Add the sun-dried tomatoes and toss well to combine. Serve the warm salad immediately, on a bed of frisée lettuce.                SERVES 6

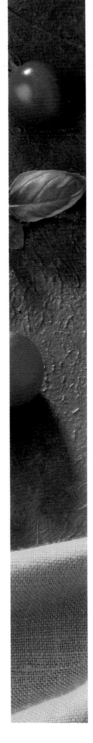

## SMOKED DUCK & PESTO PASTA SALAD

100 g (4 oz) dried pasta shapes
175 g (6 oz) cooked, smoked duck breast
12 cherry tomatoes
60 ml (4 tbsp) pine nuts, toasted
175 g (6 oz) mixed salad leaves
Basil sprigs, to garnish

### PESTO DRESSING

60 ml (4 tbsp) pesto sauce
90 ml (6 tbsp) vegetable oil
30 ml (2 tbsp) red wine vinegar
Salt and ground black pepper

Place all the dressing ingredients in a bowl and whisk to combine.

Cook the pasta in plenty of boiling, salted water for 8-10 minutes or until 'al dente'. Drain the pasta and immediately toss it with the prepared dressing. Set aside.

Slice the duck into thin strips and halve the cherry tomatoes. Add to the bowl of pasta along with the pine nuts. Toss well.

Wash the lettuce leaves and tear large leaves in half. Line a serving bowl with the lettuce and spoon the pasta salad into the centre. Garnish with basil and serve at once.                SERVES 4

**RIGHT:** Smoked Duck & Pesto Pasta Salad

## AVOCADO, MOZZARELLA & BAKED TOMATO SALAD

*The baked tomatoes in this salad take a long time to cook and, for convenience, can be prepared the day before and stored in an airtight container in the refrigerator until required.*

150 g (5 oz) mini mozzarella cheeses
2 ripe avocados
15 ml (1 tbsp) lemon juice
Basil leaves, to garnish

### BAKED TOMATOES

6 small, ripe plum tomatoes
Olive oil to drizzle
A little caster sugar
Sea salt and ground black pepper

### DRESSING

120 ml (8 tbsp) extra virgin olive oil
30 ml (2 tbsp) balsamic vinegar
60 ml (4 tbsp) torn basil leaves
Salt and ground black pepper

Prepare the baked tomatoes. Preheat the oven to 100°C (200°F, Gas mark ¼). Blanch the tomatoes for 20 seconds in boiling, salted water to loosen their skins. When cooled, peel off the skin, halve, and scoop out the seeds. Place cut-side down on a greased baking sheet. Drizzle each tomato with a little olive oil and sprinkle with a little sugar, salt and pepper. Bake for 1 hour. Turn over, drizzle with a little more oil and bake for a further hour. Remove and allow to cool.

Slice the mini mozzarella into thick slices. Peel and stone the avocados and slice the flesh. Sprinkle the avocados with lemon juice.

Mix together the dressing ingredients. To serve, arrange the tomatoes, cheese and avocado on four plates. Spoon dressing over each salad, garnish with basil and serve at once. SERVES 4

## ROCKET, BACON & AVOCADO SALAD

12 rashers rindless, streaky bacon
2 small avocados
15 ml (1 tbsp) lemon juice
175 g (6 oz) rocket leaves
90 ml (6 tbsp) finely grated Parmesan cheese
Ground black pepper
Italian Balsamic Dressing (see page 74)

Place the bacon rashers under a preheated hot grill and grill for about 8 minutes, turning halfway through cooking, until crisp and golden. Remove and drain on absorbent kitchen paper. When cool, snip the bacon into bite-sized pieces with kitchen scissors.

Peel and stone the avocado and cut the flesh into chunks. Place in a bowl with the lemon juice. Wash and dry the rocket leaves and place in a salad bowl. Add the bacon, avocado and 60 ml (4 tbsp) of the Parmesan. Add some black pepper and pour over the prepared dressing. Toss the salad gently and serve with the remaining Parmesan sprinkled over the top. SERVES 4

**TOP:** Avocado, Mozzarella & Baked Tomato Salad
**BOTTOM:** Rocket, Bacon & Avocado Salad

## CAPONATA

*This salad is best made a day in advance and stored
in the refrigerator to allow the flavours to develop.*

90 ml (6 tbsp) extra virgin olive oil
I red onion, sliced into rings
2 cloves garlic, sliced into slivers
I large aubergine
2 ripe beef tomatoes
2 courgettes
2 yellow peppers
30 ml (2 tbsp) sun-dried tomato paste
Salt and ground black pepper
30 ml (2 tbsp) red wine vinegar
30 ml (2 tbsp) chopped fresh flat-leaved parsley
15 ml (I tbsp) chopped fresh thyme
16 small black olives
8 anchovy fillets
2 Little Gem lettuces, washed and separated
into leaves
Flat-leaved parsley sprig, to garnish

Preheat the oven to 180°C (350°F, Gas mark 4). Heat
half the oil in a large, heavy-based, ovenproof saucepan. Add the onion and sauté for 2 minutes. Stir in the
garlic and sauté for a further minute. Set aside.

Cut the aubergine into 1.5-cm (½-inch) cubes. Peel
and seed the tomatoes and cut into large dice. Slice
the courgettes. Cut the peppers into 1.5-cm (½-inch)
cubes. Add the vegetables to the pan.

Stir the sun-dried tomato paste into the pan and
season the vegetables well. Cook over a low heat for 5
minutes, then cover the pan and transfer to the oven.
Bake for 40 minutes.

Place the remaining olive oil in a screw-topped jar
with the vinegar, parsley, thyme and seasoning. Shake
well to combine. Cut each anchovy fillet into four.

Stir the dressing, anchovies and olives into the
warm vegetables. Allow to cool.

Just before serving, line a dish with the lettuce
leaves. Using a slotted spoon, spoon the caponata on
to the lettuce. Serve garnished with parsley sprigs.
SERVES 4

## ORANGE &
## PURPLE ONION SALAD

6 large oranges
I large purple onion
12 black olives (optional)

**POPPYSEED DRESSING**
90 ml (6 tbsp) extra virgin olive oil
30 ml (2 tbsp) fresh orange juice
15 ml (I tbsp) white wine vinegar
7.5 ml (1½ tsp) clear honey
10 ml (2 tsp) poppyseeds
Salt and ground black pepper

Peel the oranges using a small sharp knife, taking care
to remove all the white pith. Slice the oranges thickly
and arrange them in overlapping circles on a shallow
serving plate.

Slice the purple onion into thin rings. Arrange the
onion on top of the oranges and scatter over the black
olives, if desired.

Place the dressing ingredients in a screw-topped jar
and shake well to combine. Spoon the dressing over
the salad and serve at once. SERVES 4-6

**TOP:** Caponata
**BOTTOM:** Orange & Purple Onion Salad

# GREEN LENTIL SALAD

175 g (6 oz) Puy lentils, soaked for 1 hour
1 orange pepper
1 red pepper
3 spring onions
100 g (4 oz) Escarole lettuce leaves
Oregano sprigs, to garnish

### DRESSING
60 ml (4 tbsp) yoghurt
30 ml (2 tbsp) olive oil
45 ml (3 tbsp) chopped fresh parsley
45 ml (3 tbsp) chopped fresh oregano
1 large clove garlic, crushed
1.25 ml (¼ tsp) paprika
Salt and ground black pepper

Place all the dressing ingredients in a bowl and whisk to combine. Set aside.

Drain the soaked lentils and place in a saucepan of fresh water with a little salt. Boil the lentils gently for about 20 minutes or until tender, then drain. While still warm, toss the lentils with the dressing to allow the flavours to absorb. Set aside.

Halve the peppers and remove the cores and seeds. Grill under a preheated hot grill for about 10 minutes until the skins are charred. Remove and cover the peppers with damp absorbant kitchen paper to make them easier to peel. Once cool, peel off the skins and slice the flesh into thin strips. Chop the spring onions finely and add to the lentils along with the peppers. Toss well. Wash and dry the lettuce leaves and serve the salad on a bed of Escarole lettuce, garnished with oregano sprigs. SERVES 6

# TURKISH SALAD

*Labna balls are strained yoghurt balls preserved in oil. Herbs are sometimes added to the oil. They are available in jars from good continental delicatessens.*

2 courgettes
½ onion
8 labna balls in oil, drained
6 artichoke hearts in oil, drained
1 Cos lettuce
60 ml (4 tbsp) finely diced red pepper

### DRESSING
30 ml (2 tbsp) oil from the jar of labna balls
30 ml (2 tbsp) extra virgin olive oil
30 ml (2 tbsp) lemon juice
2.5 ml (½ tsp) ground cumin
1.25 ml (¼ tsp) chilli powder
Salt and ground black pepper
Pinch of sugar

Place all the dressing ingredients in a small saucepan. Whisk to combine and heat the dressing very gently to warm it.

Using a vegetable peeler, peel long ribbons of courgette. Slice the onion very thinly. Place the courgette ribbons and sliced onions in a bowl, pour over the warm dressing and toss gently to combine. Set aside.

Halve the labna balls and the artichokes. Wash and dry the lettuce and tear the leaves into bite-sized pieces. Divide the lettuce between four plates. Add the labna balls and artichoke hearts to the courgettes and onions, and toss gently to coat with the dressing. Divide the mixture between the plates. Sprinkle one-quarter of the diced red pepper over each salad and serve at once. SERVES 4

**RIGHT:** Turkish Salad

## GREEK PEACH & GRILLED GREEN PEPPER SALAD

4 green peppers
2 large, ripe peaches
175 g (6 oz) feta cheese
12 calamata olives

### CUMIN DRESSING

10 ml (2 tsp) cumin seeds
120 ml (8 tbsp) olive oil
45 ml (3 tbsp) white wine vinegar
Salt and ground black pepper
Pinch of sugar

Halve the peppers lengthways and remove the cores and seeds. Place them cut-side down on a baking sheet and grill under a preheated hot grill for 8-10 minutes or until the skins are charred. Remove and cover the peppers with damp absorbant kitchen paper to make them easier to peel. Once cool, peel off the charred skins and slice the flesh into thick strips.

Halve and stone the peaches and slice the flesh thickly. Cut the feta into small cubes. Place the peppers, peaches, feta and olives in a mixing bowl.

Make the dressing. Dry-roast the cumin seeds in a frying pan for about 1 minute, until they begin to pop and their aroma is released. Transfer to a bowl with the remaining dressing ingredients and mix well.

Pour the dressing over the salad ingredients and toss gently. Refrigerate for 1 hour before serving.

SERVES 4

## SPICED RICE SALAD

100 g (4 oz) brown long-grain rice
100 g (4 oz) white long-grain rice
50 g (2 oz) fresh dates
75 g (3 oz) dried apricots
50 g (2 oz) shelled pistachio nuts
60 ml (4 tbsp) snipped fresh chives
Coriander sprigs, to garnish

### DRESSING

75 ml (5 tbsp) pistachio or corn oil
45 ml (3 tbsp) lime juice
45 ml (3 tbsp) chopped fresh coriander
2.5 ml (½ tsp) chilli powder
Salt and ground black pepper

Place all the dressing ingredients in a screw-topped jar and shake well to combine.

Cook the two types of rice in separate saucepans of boiling, salted water, following the cooking instructions on the packets. Once cooked, drain and mix the warm rice with the dressing. The rice will absorb the flavour of the dressing. Set aside.

Remove the stones from the dates and cut the flesh into long slivers. Cut the apricots into quarters. Add the dates and apricots to the rice along with the pistachios and chives. Toss well. Serve the salad at room temperature, garnished with coriander sprigs.

SERVES 4

**TOP:** Spiced Rice Salad
**BOTTOM:** Greek Peach & Grilled
Green Pepper Salad

# NORWEGIAN HERRING & DILL SALAD

450 g (1 lb) baby new potatoes
4 pickled herrings
2 small shallots
12 chicory leaves, preferably red
1 soft lettuce heart

### DRESSING

90 ml (6 tbsp) sunflower oil
60 ml (4 tbsp) chopped fresh dill
45 ml (3 tbsp) Dijon mustard
45 ml (3 tbsp) cider vinegar
25-30 ml (1½-2 tbsp) caster sugar
Sea salt and ground black pepper

First prepare the dressing. Place the oil, dill, mustard and vinegar in a bowl. Add 25 ml (1½ tbsp) of the sugar and season generously. Whisk until well combined. Taste and add the extra sugar and more seasoning if necessary: the dressing should be thick, sweet and mustardy. Set aside.

Scrub the potatoes. Place in a saucepan of salted water, bring to the boil, then reduce heat and cook on a medium boil for about 12 minutes or until tender. Drain and refresh in cold water. When the potatoes are cool enough to handle, slice them thickly.

Slice the herrings into 2.5-cm (1-inch) pieces. Peel and thinly slice the shallots. Place the potatoes, herrings and shallots in a bowl, pour over the dressing and toss well.

Separate the lettuce heart into leaves. Wash and dry the lettuce and chicory leaves. Line a serving bowl with the leaves and spoon the salad into the centre. Serve at once. SERVES 4

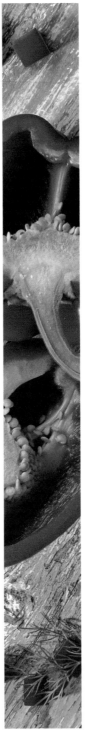

# KARTOFFELSALAT

1 large red pepper
2 spring onions
450 g (1 lb) baby new potatoes
325 g (8 oz) frankfurters (about 8 small frankfurters)

### MUSTARD MAYONNAISE

120 ml (8 tbsp) mayonnaise
20 ml (4 tsp) German mustard
30 ml (2 tbsp) chopped fresh dill
30 ml (2 tbsp) milk
Pinch of sugar
Salt and ground black pepper

Place all the mayonnaise ingredients in a bowl and whisk to combine. Set the mayonnaise dressing aside, but do not refrigerate it.

Halve the pepper, remove the core and seeds and dice the flesh. Slice the spring onions thinly on the diagonal. Place the prepared peppers and spring onions in a serving bowl.

Scrub the potatoes and halve them. Place them in a saucepan of salted water, bring to the boil, then reduce heat and cook on a medium boil for 10-12 minutes until tender. Drain the potatoes and add to the serving bowl.

While the potatoes are cooking, cook the frankfurters according to the instructions on the packet. Drain and slice thickly on the diagonal. Add to the serving bowl.

Pour the dressing over the warm potatoes, frankfurters and prepared peppers and spring onions. Toss to combine and serve at once while the salad is warm. SERVES 4-6

**RIGHT:** Kartoffelsalat

# BRITISH BEEF SALAD

550-g (1¼-lb) piece beef fillet
Ground black pepper
15 ml (1 tbsp) vegetable oil
700 g (1½ lb) baby new potatoes
225 g (8 oz) shelled baby broad beans
12 cherry tomatoes
175 g (6 oz) soft lettuce heart leaves
Horseradish Dressing (see page 78)
Curly parsley sprigs, to garnish

Preheat the oven to 110°C (225°F, Gas mark ¼). Cut the beef fillet in half and coat each piece generously with pepper. Heat the oil in a heavy-based frying pan and sear the pieces of beef over a high heat, turning so they brown all over, for 6-8 minutes. Transfer the beef to a roasting tin and bake for 1 hour and 10 minutes. This method will produce very tender, medium-rare meat. Allow beef to cool.

Scrub the potatoes and place in a saucepan of salted water. Bring to the boil, then reduce to a medium heat and simmer for 10-12 minutes until tender. Drain and refresh in cold water. Slice the cooled potatoes in half.

Cook the broad beans in boiling, salted water for about 5 minutes until tender. Drain and refresh in cold water. Halve the cherry tomatoes. Slice the cooled beef into strips and place the meat in a bowl with the potatoes, broad beans and tomatoes. Pour over the dressing and toss well.

Wash the lettuce leaves and divide the lettuce between four plates. Spoon one-quarter of the beef salad on to each plate. Garnish with parsley sprigs and serve at once.        SERVES 4 AS A MAIN COURSE

# GRILLED GOAT'S CHEESE SALAD

75 g (3 oz) mixed salad leaves, to include oak leaf, baby spinach and lollo rosso
½ small ripe pear, cored and sliced
4 slices ciabatta bread
175 g (6 oz) goat's cheese
15 ml (1 tbsp) walnut oil

**DRESSING**
30 ml (2 tbsp) walnut oil
15 ml (1 tbsp) vegetable oil
15 ml (1 tbsp) white wine vinegar
2.5 ml (½ tsp) Dijon mustard
Pinch of sugar
Salt and ground black pepper

Place the dressing ingredients in a screw-topped jar and shake well to combine. Set aside.

Wash and dry the lettuce and tear large leaves into bite-sized pieces. Place in a bowl with the sliced pears and pour over the dressing. Toss gently to coat and divide between two plates.

Place the bread under a preheated hot grill and toast on one side until lightly golden. Remove and turn the bread over.

Slice the cheese into four pieces and place a piece of cheese on the untoasted side of each bread slice. Drizzle with walnut oil and add some black pepper. Return to the grill and grill for about 2 minutes or until cheese begins to melt. Place two slices of bread and cheese on each plate of salad and serve at once.        SERVES 2

**TOP:** British Beef Salad
**BOTTOM:** Grilled Goat's Cheese Salad

# EXOTIC & ORIENTAL SALADS

*The recipes in this chapter are inspired by the cuisines of South-east Asia and the Far East, as well as the Caribbean and Mexico. For a delicious and substantial main course, try Salmon Teriyaki Salad or, if you like spicy food, experience the robust flavours of Thai Beef Salad. There are also recipes for the vegetarian, such as Mexican Bean Salad and Tofu & Oriental Mushroom Salad.*

## MEXICAN BEAN SALAD

432-g (15-oz) can red kidney beans
432-g (15-oz) can black-eyed beans
Heart of 1 Cos lettuce
2 small avocados

### LIME AND CORIANDER DRESSING
Juice of 1½ limes
Grated zest of ½ lime
90 ml (6 tbsp) sunolive or light olive oil
45 ml (3 tbsp) chopped fresh coriander
5 ml (1 tsp) crushed pink and black peppercorns
Sea salt and pinch of sugar

Place all the dressing ingredients in a screw-topped jar and shake well to combine. Chill until required.

Drain the canned beans and rinse well. Separate the Cos lettuce leaves and wash and dry them.

Line a flat bowl with the lettuce leaves. Peel, stone and slice the avocados, and mix in a large bowl with the beans and dressing. Spoon the salad on to the bed of lettuce and serve at once.          SERVES 4-6

## MEXICAN FISH SALAD

225 g (8 oz) red snapper fillets
Fish stock for poaching
1 small ripe mango
1 green pepper
1 fresh red chilli
2 sticks celery
75 g (3 oz) crisp lettuce leaves
15 ml (1 tbsp) coriander leaves, to garnish

### DRESSING
60 ml (4 tbsp) mayonnaise
15 ml (1 tbsp) vegetable oil
15 ml (1 tbsp) chopped fresh coriander
5 ml (1 tsp) cayenne
½ red chilli, seeded and finely chopped
Juice of 1 lime
Hot chilli sauce, to taste

Poach the snapper fillets in lightly simmering fish stock for 5-6 minutes until cooked. Remove, discard the stock and allow to cool. When cool, flake the fish.

Cut the mango flesh from the stone and slice thinly. Halve, core and seed the pepper and slice the flesh. Slice the chilli into rings. Slice the celery on the diagonal. Wash and dry the lettuce and tear the leaves into bite-sized pieces.

Place the dressing ingredients in a bowl and whisk together until combined. Set aside.

To serve, arrange the lettuce, mango, pepper, chilli and celery on two plates. Pour the dressing over the fish and toss lightly to combine. Spoon half the fish on to each bed of salad, garnish with coriander and serve at once.          SERVES 2 AS A MAIN COURSE

**TOP:** Mexican Bean Salad
**BOTTOM:** Mexican Fish Salad

## CAJUN CHICKEN SALAD

4 skinless, boneless chicken breasts
25 g (1 oz) unsalted butter, melted
2 corn on the cob, each cut into 6 pieces
2 large red peppers
175 g (6 oz) iceberg lettuce, coarsely shredded
Oregano sprigs, to garnish

### SEASONING MIX

7.5 ml (1½ tsp) salt
15 ml (1 tbsp) paprika
5 ml (1 tsp) dried onion granules
5 ml (1 tsp) dried garlic granules
5 ml (1 tsp) dried thyme
5 ml (1 tsp) cayenne
2.5 ml (½ tsp) cracked black pepper
2.5 ml (½ tsp) dried oregano

### SPICY DRESSING

90 ml (6 tbsp) corn oil
30 ml (2 tbsp) lemon juice
1 shallot, finely chopped
1.25 ml (¼ tsp) cayenne
5 ml (1 tsp) Dijon mustard
5 ml (1 tsp) chopped fresh thyme
Pinch of sugar
Salt and ground black pepper

Place all the dressing ingredients in a screw-topped jar and shake to combine. Chill until required.

Mix together all the seasoning mix ingredients. Flatten each chicken breast with a mallet, between sheets of cling film, until about 1.5-cm (½-inch) thick. Brush each chicken breast with some melted butter and press one-quarter of the seasoning mix over each breast to coat completely. Set aside.

Cook the corn in boiling, salted water for 20-25 minutes until tender. Divide each pepper in half lengthways, core and seed, and brush with a little olive oil. Grill the peppers for 10-15 minutes, turning occasionally until slightly charred. Keep warm.

Heat a heavy cast-iron frying pan over a high heat until the pan is smoking and very hot. Add the chicken and cook for 8-10 minutes, turning occasionally, until the outside is blackened and chicken is cooked.

Toss the iceberg lettuce in the dressing. Cut the red pepper into thick strips. Divide the lettuce between four plates. Slice the chicken breasts and divide between the plates. Place three pieces of corn and some red pepper strips on each plate. Serve at once.

SERVES 4 AS A MAIN COURSE

## TABBOULEH

225 g (8 oz) bulghur wheat
50 g (2 oz) flat-leaved parsley, finely chopped
25 g (1 oz) mint leaves, finely chopped
6 spring onions, sliced
2 beef tomatoes, skinned, seeded and chopped
100 g (4 oz) cucumber, very finely chopped

### DRESSING

3 cloves garlic, crushed
Juice of 2 lemons
90 ml (6 tbsp) extra virgin olive oil
Salt and ground black pepper

Place the bulghur wheat in a bowl and just cover with boiling water. Set aside for 30 minutes to allow the water to absorb. Drain thoroughly, place in a clean linen towel and squeeze to remove excess moisture. Place the bulghur wheat in a large bowl and stir in the remaining ingredients.

Place the dressing ingredients in a screw-topped jar and shake well to combine. Pour over the salad, toss gently and set aside for 30 minutes to allow the flavours to develop.

SERVES 6

**RIGHT:** Cajun Chicken Salad

# BALINESE DUCK SALAD

2 × 225 g (8 oz) duck breasts
Groundnut oil for frying
50 g (2 oz) Cos lettuce
50 g (2 oz) Chinese pak choy
100 g (4 oz) beansprouts, washed
4 spring onions, sliced on the diagonal
75 g (3 oz) cucumber, cut into matchsticks

### MARINADE
4 shallots, chopped
4 cloves garlic, chopped
4 green chillies, seeded and chopped
5-cm (2-inch) piece root ginger, peeled and chopped
2.5 ml (½ tsp) turmeric
10 ml (2 tsp) galangal powder
Salt and ground black pepper

### DRESSING
15 ml (1 tbsp) groundnut oil
Juice of 1 lime
3 Kaffir lime leaves, finely chopped
1 stalk lemon grass, finely chopped
10 ml (2 tsp) clear honey
Salt and ground black pepper

Place the marinade ingredients in a blender and process to produce a smooth paste. Slash each duck breast and spread the marinade all over. Refrigerate for at least 1 hour. Place the dressing ingredients in a bowl and whisk to combine. Set aside.

Lightly oil a heavy-based frying pan and cook the duck over a high heat for about 6 minutes on each side. Remove from heat. Slice the duck diagonally.

Wash and dry the Cos and pak choy and tear the leaves into bite-sized pieces. Place in a bowl with the beansprouts, spring onions and cucumber. Pour over the dressing and toss well. Divide the salad and duck between four plates and serve at once.     SERVES 4

# CARIBBEAN PORK SALAD

450 g (1 lb) pork tenderloin, cut into long strips
225 g (8 oz) cubed pumpkin
30 ml (2 tbsp) vegetable oil
1 onion, sliced
1 green pepper, sliced into rings
100 g (4 oz) mixed salad leaves

### SEASONING MIXTURE
10 ml (2 tsp) allspice berries, crushed
2 hot Jamaican peppers, seeded and finely chopped
10 ml (2 tsp) chopped fresh thyme
10 ml (2 tsp) cayenne
2 spring onions, finely chopped
2 cloves garlic, crushed
2.5 ml (½ tsp) salt

### DRESSING
60 ml (4 tbsp) vegetable oil
30 ml (2 tbsp) white wine vinegar
10 ml (2 tsp) chopped fresh thyme
5 ml (1 tsp) Dijon mustard
Salt and ground black pepper

Mix the seasoning ingredients together in a bowl. Add the pork strips and toss. Refrigerate for 1 hour.

Boil the cubed pumpkin for about 7 minutes until tender. Drain and refresh in cold water. Place the dressing ingredients in a screw-topped jar and shake.

Cook the pork in four batches, using one-quarter of the oil for each batch of meat. Cook over a high heat, stirring frequently, for about 2 minutes. Set aside.

Place the sliced onion, green pepper, pumpkin and salad leaves in a bowl. Pour over the dressing and toss gently. Divide the salad between four plates and top each with one-quarter of the pork. Serve at once.

SERVES 4 AS A MAIN COURSE

**RIGHT:** Caribbean Pork Salad

## ASIAN SQUID & SCALLOP SALAD

Vegetable oil for frying
8 large scallops
12 cleaned baby squid, about 275 g (10 oz) in weight
2 spring onions
I starfruit
175 g (6 oz) Chinese cabbage
60 ml (4 tbsp) torn coriander leaves
Coriander sprigs, to garnish

### LEMON GRASS DRESSING

I small stalk lemon grass, very finely chopped
45 ml (3 tbsp) groundnut oil
25 ml (1½ tbsp) soy sauce
25 ml (1½ tbsp) lemon juice
10 ml (2 tsp) sesame oil
7.5 ml (1½ tsp) clear honey
I large clove garlic, crushed

Place all the dressing ingredients in a screw-topped jar and shake well to combine. Set aside.

Lightly oil and preheat a griddle pan or heavy-based frying pan and cook the scallops over a high heat, for about 5 minutes on each side. Remove and set aside. Cook the squid in the frying pan for about I minute on each side.

Slice the spring onions on the diagonal and cut the starfruit into thin slices. Wash the Chinese cabbage and shred coarsely. Toss the coriander leaves with the cabbage and divide between four plates. Arrange the seafood on the plates with the spring onions and star-fruit. Spoon dressing over each salad and serve at once.

SERVES 4 AS A MAIN COURSE

## EXOTIC PRAWN & PINEAPPLE SALAD

175-g (6-oz) piece fresh pineapple
75 g (3 oz) cucumber
2 spring onions
75 g (3 oz) white cabbage
50 g (2 oz) Chinese cabbage
10 cooked king prawns, peeled but with tails intact
2 cooked king prawns, in the shell, to garnish
2 wedges fresh pineapple, to garnish
2.5 ml (½ tsp) sesame seeds, toasted, to garnish

### DRESSING

25 ml (1½ tbsp) groundnut oil
25 ml (1½ tbsp) sesame oil
15 ml (1 tbsp) white wine vinegar
7.5 ml (1½ tsp) soy sauce
7.5 ml (1½ tsp) sesame seeds, toasted
5 ml (1 tsp) tamarind concentrate
5 ml (1 tsp) caster sugar

Place the dressing ingredients in a screw-topped jar and shake well to combine. Set aside.

Cut the piece of pineapple flesh into slim wedges. Peel and dice the cucumber and slice the spring onions on the diagonal.

Wash the two types of cabbage leaves and shred finely. Toss the shredded cabbage with half the dressing and divide between two plates. Arrange the pineapple, prawns, cucumber and spring onions on top and spoon over the remaining dressing.

Garnish each salad with a whole prawn and a wedge of pineapple. Sprinkle over the sesame seeds and serve at once.　　SERVES 2 AS A MAIN COURSE

**TOP:** Exotic Prawn & Pineapple Salad
**BOTTOM:** Asian Squid & Scallop Salad

## THAI BEEF SALAD

450 g (1 lb) beef fillet
275 g (10 oz) Chinese cabbage
175 g (6 oz) cucumber
175 g (6 oz) water chesnuts
1 fresh red chilli
1 small carrot
25 g (1 oz) coriander leaves
30 ml (2 tbsp) groundnut oil

### MARINADE

2 stalks fresh lemon grass, finely chopped
5-cm (2-inch) piece root ginger, peeled and finely chopped
6 Kaffir lime leaves, finely chopped
2 shallots, finely chopped
4 cloves garlic, crushed
Juice of 2 limes
60 ml (4 tbsp) soft brown sugar
20 ml (4 tsp) tarmarind concentrate
10 ml (2 tsp) fish sauce (nam pla)
30 ml (2 tbsp) chilli oil

### DRESSING

30 ml (2 tbsp) fish sauce (nam pla)
30 ml (2 tbsp) rice wine vinegar
30 ml (2 tbsp) groundnut oil
60 ml (4 tbsp) chopped fresh coriander
Pinch of sugar

Place the marinade ingredients in a large bowl and mix together. Slice the beef into long, thin strips and add to the marinade. Toss well and refrigerate for 1 hour.

Place the dressing ingredients in a screw-topped jar and shake well to combine. Set aside.

Shred the Chinese cabbage and cut the cucumber into long strips. Slice the water chestnuts and cut the chilli into rings. Peel the carrot and, using a canelle knife, make ridges along the length of the carrot; then slice the carrot thinly to produce 'flowers'. Place vegetables in a large bowl with the coriander.

Heat a little of the oil in a heavy-based frying pan and fry the beef strips in batches over a high heat, stirring frequently until cooked – about 2 minutes.

To serve, pour the dressing over the raw salad and toss well. Divide between four plates and spoon one-quarter of the beef on each. Serve at once.

SERVES 4 AS A MAIN COURSE

## THAI-STYLE PRAWN & PAWPAW SALAD

1 ripe pawpaw
450 g (1 lb) cooked, peeled prawns
100 g (4 oz) cucumber, cut into matchsticks
75 g (3 oz) beansprouts, washed
4 radishes, thinly sliced
175 g (6 oz) Webb's lettuce, washed and dried
Halved salted peanuts, to garnish

### DRESSING

60 ml (4 tbsp) groundnut oil
30 ml (2 tbsp) sweet chilli sauce
10 ml (2 tsp) Thai fish sauce (nam pla)
2 small cloves garlic, crushed
1 small green chilli, seeded and finely chopped
Grated zest and juice of 1 lime
50 g (2 oz) salted peanuts, coarsely ground

Mix the dressing ingredients in a bowl and set aside.

Peel the pawpaw. Cut the fruit into quarters, re-move seeds and slice the flesh thickly. Place the prawns, cucumber, beansprouts, radishes and pawpaw in a bowl. Pour over the dressing and toss gently.

Divide the lettuce and prawn salad between four plates, garnish with peanuts and serve at once.

SERVES 4 AS A MAIN COURSE

**RIGHT:** Thai Beef Salad

## MUNG BEAN & BASMATI RICE SALAD

2.5 ml (½ tsp) saffron strands
360 ml (12 fl oz) boiling water
100 g (4 oz) mung beans
100 g (4 oz) Basmati rice
30 ml (2 tbsp) vegetable oil
3 shallots, peeled and diced
100 g (4 oz) young leaf spinach, washed
2 large plum tomatoes, peeled, seeded and sliced
50 g (2 oz) raw cashew nuts
5 ml (1 tsp) sea salt

### DRESSING

15 ml (1 tbsp) vegetable oil
15 ml (1 tbsp) lime juice
15 ml (1 tbsp) natural yoghurt
1 clove garlic, crushed
Sea salt and pinch of sugar

Place the safffron strands in a bowl with the boiling water and infuse for 30 minutes. Remove 15 ml (1 tbsp) of saffron liquid and add to the dressing ingredients in a large bowl. Whisk to combine and set aside.

Boil the mung beans for 30-35 minutes until they have begun to split. Drain and add to the dressing.

Place the infused saffron and its water in a saucepan with a little salt. Bring to the boil, add the rice and simmer for about 10 minutes until tender. Drain and add to the mung beans.

Heat 15 ml (1 tbsp) of the oil in a frying pan and sauté the shallots for 2 minutes over a medium-high heat. Add the spinach and sauté for a further minute. Transfer to the bowl of ingredients with the tomatoes.

Heat the remaining oil in a frying pan and fry the cashew nuts over a medium-low heat for 5 minutes, turning constantly until golden. Remove, drain on kitchen paper and sprinkle with sea salt. Add to the bowl. Toss well and serve at once.        SERVES 4

## ORIENTAL CRAB SALAD

225 g (8 oz) mangetout
225 g (8 oz) baby sweetcorn
100 g (4 oz) beansprouts
450 g (1 lb) fresh crabmeat, flaked
100 g (4 oz) young spinach leaves
Sliced fresh red chilli, to garnish

### ROASTED CHILLI DRESSING

4 fresh chillies
15 ml (1 tbsp) grated fresh root ginger
120 ml (8 tbsp) sunflower oil
60 ml (4 tbsp) white wine vinegar
30 ml (2 tbsp) soy sauce
10 ml (2 tsp) soft brown sugar

Prepare the dressing. Place the chillies under a preheated hot grill and grill, turning once, for 3-4 minutes until skins are charred. Remove and allow to cool; then peel off skins, seed and chop the flesh. Place the grilled chilli flesh in a food processor with the remaining dressing ingredients and blend to produce a smooth dressing. Set aside.

Cut the mangetout in half and blanch in boiling, salted water for 30 seconds. Drain and refresh in cold water. Halve the sweetcorn lengthways and blanch in boiling, salted water for 1 minute. Drain and refresh in cold water. Wash the beansprouts. Place the crabmeat, mangetout, sweetcorn and beansprouts in a bowl. Pour over the dressing and toss gently.

Wash and dry the spinach and place in a shallow serving bowl. Spoon the crab salad into the centre, garnish with chilli and serve at once.        SERVES 4

**TOP:** Mung Bean & Basmati Rice Salad
**BOTTOM:** Oriental Crab Salad

## SALMON TERIYAKI SALAD

350 g (12 oz) salmon fillet, sliced into strips
15-cm × 2.5-cm (6-inch × 1-inch) piece kombu
seaweed, soaked in cold water for 2 hours
45 ml (3 tbsp) sesame oil
50 g (2 oz) mooli, peeled and cut into thin strips
50 g (2 oz) carrot, peeled and cut into thin strips
1 stick celery, sliced diagonally
2 spring onions, sliced diagonally
4 radishes, thinly sliced
50 g (2 oz) radicchio leaves

### TERIYAKI MARINADE

45 ml (3 tbsp) shoyu soy sauce
45 ml (3 tbsp) mirin
15 ml (1 tbsp) caster sugar
15 ml (1 tbsp) sesame oil

### DRESSING

30 ml (2 tbsp) sesame oil
30 ml (2 tbsp) rice wine vinegar
15 ml (1 tbsp) shoyu soy sauce
15 ml (1 tbsp) mirin
Pinch of caster sugar

Mix together the marinade ingredients. Add the salmon. Refrigerate for at least 1 hour. Place the dressing ingredients in a screw-topped jar and shake. Set aside.

Drain the soaked seaweed and cut into long strips. Heat 15 ml (1 tbsp) of the sesame oil in a frying pan and add the seaweed. Fry for 1 minute. Remove and cool. Transfer all the prepared vegetables to a bowl.

Heat half the remaining sesame oil in a frying pan and add half the marinated salmon. Cook over a high heat for 2 minutes. Remove and repeat.

Wash and dry the radicchio and divide between four plates. Pour the dressing over the prepared vegetables, toss and divide between the plates with the salmon strips. Serve at once.          SERVES 4

## TOFU & ORIENTAL MUSHROOM SALAD

25 g (1 oz) dried shiitake mushrooms, soaked in
boiling water for 1 hour
50 g (2 oz) oyster mushrooms
40 g (1½ oz) flat field mushrooms
40 g (1½ oz) button mushrooms
25-g (1-oz) piece root ginger, peeled and shredded
30 ml (2 tbsp) vegetable oil
25 g (1 oz) butter
5 g (¼ oz) arame seaweed, soaked in cold water
for 2 hours
1 spring onion, cut into julienne strips
75 g (3 oz) Chinese cabbage, shredded
25 g (1 oz) carrot, peeled and sliced
15 g (½ oz) alfalfa sprouts
15 ml (1 tbsp) sesame seeds, toasted

### DRESSING

100 g (4 oz) silken tofu
15 ml (1 tbsp) shoyu soy sauce
15 ml (1 tbsp) mirin
15 ml (1 tbsp) cider vinegar
10 ml (2 tsp) sesame oil
5 ml (½ tsp) soft dark brown sugar

Whisk the dressing ingredients and set aside.

Drain the soaked, dried mushrooms and cut in half. Slice the other mushrooms thickly. Place in a bowl and toss with the shredded ginger. Heat half the oil and butter in a frying pan and sauté half the mushrooms over a high heat for 2 minutes. Remove and repeat.

Drain the soaked seaweed and place in a large bowl with the cooked mushrooms, spring onion, Chinese cabbage, carrot, alfalfa sprouts and sesame seeds. Toss gently. Serve the salad at once with the dressing passed separately.   SERVES 2 AS A MAIN COURSE

**RIGHT:** Salmon Teriyaki Salad

## GADOH GADOH

350 g (12 oz) potato, peeled and diced
100 g (4 oz) fine green beans, cut into
2.5-cm (1-inch) lengths
175 g (6 oz) fresh pineapple, cut into small chunks
100 g (4 oz) cucumber, diced
175 g (6 oz) mooli (white radish), peeled and cut
into thin matchsticks
100 g (4 oz) fresh beansprouts
100 g (4 oz) Chinese cabbage, finely shredded
50 g (2 oz) white cabbage, finely shredded
3 hard-boiled eggs, shelled and sliced
Prawn crackers
Coriander sprigs, to garnish

### PEANUT SAUCE

1 stalk lemon grass, finely chopped
1 large clove garlic, chopped
2 shallots, chopped
1 large red chilli, seeded and chopped
1.25 ml (¼ tsp) shrimp paste
30 ml (2 tbsp) groundnut oil
100 g (4 oz) crunchy peanut butter
150 ml (¼ pint) coconut milk
Juice of 1 lime
10 ml (2 tsp) soft brown sugar
5 ml (1 tsp) dark soy sauce

Place the first five ingredients for the peanut sauce in a food processor and blend to a smooth paste. Heat the oil in a saucepan, add the paste and cook over a medium heat for about 5 minutes, stirring occasionally. Add the remaining sauce ingredients and cook, stirring, for a further 2-3 minutes. Set aside.

Boil the diced potato for about 8 minutes until tender. Drain and refresh in cold water. Blanch the green beans for 1 minute, drain and refresh in cold water. Place the potatoes, beans, pineapple, cucumber, mooli and beansprouts in a bowl and toss well.

Line a shallow serving dish with the shredded cabbages. Pile the tossed vegetables into the centre and spoon over the peanut sauce. Arrange the sliced egg and prawn crackers on top and garnish with coriander. Serve at once. SERVES 4-6

## INDIAN SALAD

450 g (1 lb) potatoes, peeled and diced
100 g (4 oz) frozen peas
2 tomatoes
75 g (3 oz) onion, thinly sliced
432-g (15-oz) can chick-peas, drained

### DRESSING

15 ml (1 tbsp) vegetable oil
5 ml (1 tsp) ground cumin
5 ml (1 tsp) chilli powder
10 ml (2 tsp) garam masala
60 ml (4 tbsp) mayonnaise
60 ml (4 tbsp) natural yoghurt
5 ml (1 tsp) lemon juice
60 ml (4 tbsp) mango chutney
Salt and ground black pepper

Prepare the dressing. Place the oil in a saucepan with the cumin, chilli and garam masala, and cook over a gentle heat for 1 minute. Allow to cool slightly, then mix in a bowl with the remaining dressing ingredients.

Boil the potatoes for about 8 minutes or until tender. Drain and refresh in cold water. Cook the peas according to the instructions on the packet. Plunge the tomatoes into boiling water to loosen their skins; when cooled, peel skins, seed and dice the flesh.

Place the vegetables and chick-peas in a bowl. Pour over the dressing and toss well. Allow to stand for 1 hour before serving. SERVES 4

**RIGHT:** Gadoh Gadoh

## MOROCCAN LAMB & COUS-COUS SALAD

175 g (6 oz) cous-cous
30 ml (2 tbsp) olive oil
Salt and ground black pepper
150 g (5 oz) boneless, lean lamb, cubed
5 ml (1 tsp) ground cumin
2.5 ml (½ tsp) ground coriander
1.25 ml (¼ tsp) ground cinnamon
15 ml (1 tbsp) chopped fresh mint
50 g (2 oz) whole blanched almonds, toasted
50 g (2 oz) dried apricots, diced
½ red pepper, cored, seeded and diced
12 small black olives
30 ml (2 tbsp) snipped fresh chives
100 g (4 oz) Cos lettuce leaves, washed and dried
4 artichokes in oil, halved, to garnish

### DRESSING

30 ml (2 tbsp) Greek-style yoghurt
45 ml (3 tbsp) olive oil
15 ml (1 tbsp) lemon juice
30 ml (2 tbsp) chopped fresh mint
1.25 ml (¼ tsp) ground cumin
Salt and ground black pepper

Place the cous-cous in a bowl and pour over boiling water to just cover. Set aside for 15 minutes. Fork the grains and stir in half the olive oil. Season well.

Place the lamb in a bowl and add the cumin, coriander, cinnamon and mint. Mix well to combine. Heat the remaining olive oil in a frying pan and cook the spiced lamb over a high heat for about 5 minutes, stirring until cooked through. Remove and add to the cous-cous along with the almonds, apricots, red pepper, olives, chives and seasoning.

Whisk the dressing ingredients in a bowl, pour over the salad and toss gently. Serve the salad on a bed of lettuce, garnished with artichokes.     SERVES 4-6

## CURRIED TURKEY & BULGHUR WHEAT SALAD

225 g (8 oz) bulghur wheat
30 ml (2 tbsp) corn oil
2 small shallots, sliced
2 cloves garlic, crushed
30 ml (2 tbsp) mild curry paste
450 g (1 lb) turkey breast, sliced into strips
50 g (2 oz) raisins
100 g (4 oz) cucumber, peeled and diced
50 g (2 oz) Brazil nuts, roughly chopped
30 ml (2 tbsp) chopped fresh mint
30 ml (2 tbsp) chopped fresh flat-leaved parsley
30 ml (2 tbsp) lime juice
Salt and ground black pepper
Parsley and mint sprigs, to garnish

### DRESSING

60 ml (4 tbsp) corn oil
30 ml (2 tbsp) white wine vinegar
10 ml (2 tsp) mild curry paste
Pinch of sugar
Salt and ground black pepper

Place the bulghur in a bowl and pour over boiling water to cover. Leave for 40 minutes until water is absorbed. Transfer to a clean linen and squeeze to remove excess moisture; place in a large bowl.

Heat the oil in a frying pan, add the shallots, garlic and curry paste and cook for 2 minutes. Stir in the turkey and cook for a further 5-6 minutes. Add to the bulghur wheat along with the raisins, cucumber, Brazil nuts, chopped herbs, lime juice and seasoning.

Shake the dressing ingredients in a screw-topped jar. Pour over the salad. Toss well to coat and serve at once, garnished with herb sprigs.     SERVES 4-6

**TOP:** Curried Turkey & Bulghur Wheat Salad
**BOTTOM:** Moroccan Lamb & Cous-cous Salad

# FRUIT SALADS

*Fruit salads make delicious desserts that are healthy and light, but you could also serve some of the recipes in this chapter for a brunch or breakfast. Included here are salad recipes appropriate for each season of the year, from the light and fruity Red Summer Berry Salad to the stronger flavours of Winter Fruit Salad, made with dried fruit, brandy and cinnamon.*

## STRAWBERRY SALAD WITH PEPPERCORN & ORANGE SYRUP

225 g (8 oz) caster sugar
360 ml (12 fl oz) fresh orange juice
Grated zest of 1 orange
10 ml (2 tsp) crushed pink peppercorns
5 ml (1 tsp) crushed black peppercorns
450 g (1 lb) strawberries

Place the sugar in a saucepan, add the orange juice and heat gently to dissolve the sugar. Bring the mixture to the boil and boil rapidly for 1-2 minutes until slightly syrupy. Remove from the heat and stir in the grated zest and crushed peppercorns.

Hull and halve the strawberries. Place the strawberries in a serving bowl and pour over the peppercorn syrup. Stir gently to mix, cover and chill for several hours before serving. SERVES 4

## RED SUMMER BERRY SALAD

1 vanilla pod
700 g (1½ lb) red summer berries, such as strawberries, raspberries, redcurrants and tayberries
Strawberry leaves and flowers, to decorate
Macaroon biscuits and whipped cream, to serve

### SUGAR SYRUP

100 g (4 oz) granulated sugar
300 ml (½ pint) water

Make the sugar syrup by placing the sugar and water in a saucepan and heating gently to dissolve the sugar. Then increase the heat and boil the syrup for 5-6 minutes. Cool and set aside.

Split the vanilla pod in half lengthways. Scrape out the soft centre and stir it into the sugar syrup. Discard the pod. Allow to infuse for 2 hours.

Prepare the berries, removing stalks and hulling as necessary, and place in a serving bowl. Strain the vanilla sugar syrup over the berries and stir in gently. Cover and chill in the refrigerator.

To serve, decorate the chilled salad with strawberry leaves and flowers, and serve with macaroons and cream. SERVES 4-6

**TOP:** Strawberry Salad
**BOTTOM:** Red Summer Berry Salad

## PEACH, BLUEBERRY & CHERRY FRUIT SALAD WITH KIRSCH

2 ripe peaches
100 g (4 oz) cherries
175 g (6 oz) blueberries
Juice of 1 lemon
90 ml (6 tbsp) kirsch
25 g (1 oz) flaked almonds, toasted
Borage flowers, to decorate (optional)
Vanilla ice cream, to serve (optional)

### SUGAR SYRUP

50 g (2 oz) granulated sugar
150 ml (¼ pint) water

Prepare the sugar syrup as instructed on page 64. Allow to cool.

Wash all the fruit. Halve and stone the peaches and slice them thickly. Halve the cherries and remove the stones. Place the peaches, cherries and blueberries in a serving bowl.

Stir the lemon juice and kirsch into the sugar syrup and pour over the prepared fruit. Stir gently, cover and chill thoroughly. Just before serving, sprinkle the toasted almonds over the fruit salad and decorate with borage flowers. Serve at once with vanilla ice cream, if desired. SERVES 4

## THREE-MELON SALAD WITH MUSCAT WINE & HONEY

*Use a variety of melons of your choice for this fruit salad. The types suggested below make a colourful and delectable combination.*

700 g (1½ lb) watermelon
450 g (1 lb) Charentais melon
450 g (1 lb) Galia melon
300 ml (½ pint) muscat wine
30 ml (2 tbsp) clear honey
Grated zest of 1 lemon
Fresh marigold petals, to decorate (optional)

Using a melon baller, make melon balls with the three different melons. Place the prepared melon balls in a large serving bowl.

Mix together the wine, honey and lemon zest and pour over the melon balls. Stir gently to mix, cover and chill the salad for several hours. Just before serving, scatter a few marigold petals over the salad. SERVES 6

**RIGHT:** Peach, Blueberry & Cherry Fruit Salad

## CARIBBEAN FRUIT SALAD

I large mango
½ medium pineapple
3 large oranges
2 large bananas
4 passion fruit
Grated zest and juice of 2 limes
90 ml (6 tbsp) coconut rum
Prepared Sugar Syrup (see page 64)
60 ml (4 tbsp) coconut flakes, lightly toasted

Peel the mango and cut the flesh from the stone. Slice the flesh and place in a serving bowl.

Peel the pineapple, remove the core and cut the fruit into chunks. Peel the oranges with a sharp knife, removing all the white pith, and cut between the membranes to produce segments. Add the pineapple and orange to the sliced mango.

Peel and slice the bananas and halve the passion fruit. Add the bananas to the bowl of fruit along with the pulp from the passion fruit.

Stir the lime juice and zest, and the rum, into the sugar syrup. Pour the syrup over the fruit, stir gently to mix and chill. Just before serving, sprinkle the coconut flakes over the fruit salad. SERVES 6

## TROPICAL FRUIT SALAD WITH LIME SYRUP

Prepared Sugar Syrup (see page 64)
Grated zest of 2 limes
Freshly squeezed juice of 3 limes
I small mango
I pawpaw
¼ medium pineapple
12 fresh rambutans or lychees
I starfruit
2 bananas
450 g (I lb) watermelon

Place the sugar syrup in a large serving bowl and stir in the lime zest and juice.

Peel the mango and cut the flesh into chunks. Peel and halve the pawpaw, remove seeds and slice the flesh. Peel and core the pineapple and slice the flesh. Peel the rambutans or lychees. Slice the starfruit and bananas and cut the watermelon into small chunks.

Add the prepared fruit to the lime syrup and stir gently to mix. Chill thoroughly before serving.
SERVES 6

**TOP:** Caribbean Fruit Salad
**BOTTOM:** Tropical Fruit Salad

## RHUBARB, BANANA & APRICOT SALAD

450 g (1 lb) rhubarb
100 g (4 oz) caster sugar
150 ml (¼ pint) ginger wine
6 large, firm, ripe apricots, halved and stoned
30 ml (2 tbsp) finely chopped stem ginger in syrup
2 small bananas, sliced
Greek yoghurt or mascarpone cheese, to serve

Preheat the oven to 180°C (350°F, Gas mark 4). Wash the rhubarb and cut it diagonally into 2.5-cm (1-inch) lengths. Place in a shallow ovenproof dish and stir in the sugar and ginger wine. Cover the dish and bake the rhubarb for 20 minutes.

Remove the rhubarb from the oven, add the apricots to the dish and return to the oven for a further 15 minutes, until the rhubarb is soft but still holds its shape and the apricots are tender.

Using a slotted spoon, gently transfer the rhubarb and apricots to a serving dish and stir in the sliced bananas. Strain the syrup from the ovenproof dish into a jug, stir in the chopped stem ginger and pour over the fruit salad. Allow the salad to cool, then chill thoroughly before serving with yoghurt or mascarpone cheese. SERVES 4

## LOW-CALORIE CITRUS FRUIT SALAD

3 pink grapefruit
2 yellow grapefruit
6 tangerines
6 kumquats
Honey or maple syrup
Fresh lemon balm, to decorate

Using a sharp knife, peel a grapefruit, removing all the white pith. Holding the grapefruit over a bowl, to catch the juices, cut between the membranes of the fruit to produce segments. Squeeze any excess juice from the fruit membranes into the bowl. Discard membranes and repeat with all the grapefruit.

Peel the tangerines with a sharp knife, removing all the white pith, and slice the fruit thickly. Wash and thinly slice the kumquats.

Place the grapefruit segments, tangerine and kumquat slices in a serving bowl. Strain the reserved fruit juice and sweeten with a little honey or maple syrup to taste. Pour the juice over the fruit and chill the salad. Serve decorated with fresh lemon balm.

SERVES 4-6

**RIGHT:** Rhubarb, Banana & Apricot Salad

## GREEN FRUIT SALAD WITH MINT

15 g (½ oz) or a generous handful fresh mint leaves
Prepared Sugar Syrup (see page 64),
warmed slightly
30 ml (2 tbsp) freshly squeezed lemon juice
1 large green apple
225 g (8 oz) green-fleshed melon, such as Galia
4 kiwi fruit
100 g (4 oz) seedless green grapes
Mint sprigs, to decorate

Wash the mint and chop coarsely. Add to the warmed sugar syrup, stir well and leave to infuse for at least 2 hours. Then strain the syrup, discard the mint and stir in the lemon juice. Pour the syrup into a serving bowl.

Wash the apple, remove the core and slice thinly. Add the apple slices to the serving bowl with the mint sugar syrup.

Peel the melon and cut the flesh into small chunks. Peel and slice the kiwi fruit and wash the grapes. Add the prepared fruit to the serving bowl. Stir gently to mix, cover and chill the salad thoroughly. Just before serving, decorate the salad with fresh mint sprigs.

SERVES 4

## WINTER FRUIT SALAD

350 g (12 oz) mixed dried fruit, such as prunes, apple rings, peaches, pears and apricots
50 g (2 oz) soft brown sugar
450 ml (¾ pint) milkless Earl Grey tea
1 long strip orange zest
1 cinnamon stick, broken in half
5 cloves
45 ml (3 tbsp) brandy
Mascarpone cheese or crème fraîche, to serve

Place all the ingredients for the fruit salad, except the brandy, in a saucepan. Bring to the boil, stirring occasionally. Reduce the heat, cover the pan and simmer the fruit gently for 20-25 minutes until tender. Stir the brandy into the salad. Serve the salad warm or chilled with mascarpone cheese or crème fraîche.

SERVES 4

**TOP:** Green Fruit Salad with Mint
**BOTTOM:** Winter Fruit Salad

# SALAD DRESSINGS

Along with classic oil-and-vinegar-based dressings, such as the Italian Balsamic Dressing, this chapter features the creamy Blue Cheese Dressing and Guacamole Dressing, as well as unusual varieties, such as Watercress and Horseradish dressings. Use the lighter dressings for delicate leafy salads and the creamier alternatives for more hearty combination salads.

## ITALIAN BALSAMIC DRESSING

90 ml (6 tbsp) extra virgin olive oil
30 ml (2 tbsp) balsamic vinegar
I clove garlic, crushed
I small shallot, finely chopped
Sea salt and ground black pepper

Place all the dressing ingredients in a screw-topped jar and shake to mix thoroughly. Taste and adjust seasoning, if necessary, and store in the refrigerator until required. The dressing will keep well for several days and can be made in larger quantities for convenience.
SERVES 4

*Variation: For a lighter dressing, use 45 ml (3 tbsp) olive oil and 45 ml (3 tbsp) sunflower or corn oil.*

## CLASSIC FRENCH DRESSING

90 ml (6 tbsp) extra virgin olive oil, preferably French
30 ml (2 tbsp) white wine vinegar
I0 ml (2 tsp) Dijon mustard
2.5 ml (½ tsp) caster sugar
2 small cloves garlic, crushed
Sea salt and ground black pepper

Place all the dressing ingredients in a screw-topped jar and shake to mix thoroughly. Taste and adjust seasoning, if necessary, and store in the refrigerator until required. The dressing will keep well for several days.
SERVES 4

## CHIFFONADE DRESSING

90 ml (6 tbsp) extra virgin olive oil
30 ml (2 tbsp) red wine vinegar
5 ml (I tsp) French dark mustard
2.5 ml (½ tsp) caster sugar
15 ml (I tbsp) chopped fresh parsley
15 ml (I tbsp) snipped fresh chives
30 ml (2 tbsp) finely chopped red pepper
I hard-boiled egg, shelled and finely chopped
Salt and ground black pepper

Place the oil, vinegar, mustard and sugar in a bowl and whisk well to combine. Stir in the chopped herbs, red pepper and hard-boiled egg. Season the dressing to taste and use as required. The dressing is best used as soon as it is made.
SERVES 6

**TOP TO BOTTOM:** Italian Balsamic Dressing, Chiffonade Dressing, Classic French Dressing

# THOUSAND ISLAND DRESSING

60 ml (4 tbsp) vegetable oil
60 ml (4 tbsp) olive oil
60 ml (4 tbsp) mayonnaise
30 ml (2 tbsp) tomato ketchup
Juice of 1 orange
20 ml (4 tsp) lemon juice
20 ml (4 tsp) Worcestershire sauce
5 ml (1 tsp) mustard powder
5 ml (1 tsp) paprika
1 small shallot, finely chopped
1 large dill gherkin, finely chopped
30 ml (2 tbsp) chopped fresh parsley
Salt and ground black pepper

Place the first nine ingredients in a bowl and whisk well until thoroughly combined and smooth. Stir in the remaining ingredients. Taste and adjust seasoning, if necessary, and refrigerate until required.

SERVES 4-6

*Variation: Substitute the tomato ketchup for 45 ml (3 tbsp) sun-dried tomato paste.*

# BLUE CHEESE DRESSING

175 g (6 oz) soft blue cheese, such as Fourme d'Ambert or blue Brie, stored at room temperature
45 ml (3 tbsp) soured cream
30 ml (2 tbsp) red wine vinegar
75 ml (5 tbsp) sunflower oil
30 ml (2 tbsp) water
25 ml (1½ tbsp) chopped fresh thyme
Pinch of sugar
Salt and ground black pepper

Place the blue cheese in a bowl and mash to a paste. Place all the remaining ingredients in a separate bowl

and whisk together well, until thoroughly combined. Gradually add the blue cheese to this mixture, beating well after each addition, until the cheese is incorporated and the dressing is smooth and creamy. Taste and adjust seasoning, if necessary. Cover and refrigerate until required. SERVES 4-6

# GUACAMOLE DRESSING

*This dressing is excellent served with a simple crisp salad, as part of a Mexican meal.*

1 large, ripe avocado
Juice of 2 limes
60 ml (4 tbsp) olive oil
30 ml (2 tbsp) finely chopped red onion
½ large fresh red chilli, seeded and finely chopped
30 ml (2 tbsp) chopped fresh coriander
Salt and ground black pepper

Peel and stone the avocado and roughly chop the flesh. Place the avocado flesh in a food processor, add the lime juice and olive oil, and blend to produce a smooth paste. Season well and process again briefly.

Transfer the avocado mixture to a bowl and stir in the chopped onion, chilli and coriander. If the dressing is too thick, add a little water. Taste and adjust seasoning, if necessary. Cover and refrigerate the dressing until required. SERVES 4

**TOP TO BOTTOM:** Thousand Island Dressing, Guacamole Dressing, Blue Cheese Dressing

## PEAR & WALNUT VINAIGRETTE

*This dressing is well-suited to salads that have blue or goat's cheese as one of their ingredients.*

½ ripe pear
75 ml (5 tbsp) walnut oil
30 ml (2 tbsp) raspberry vinegar
Salt and ground black pepper
15 ml (1 tbsp) finely chopped walnuts

Peel and core the pear and roughly chop the flesh. Place in a food processor with the oil and vinegar. Process briefly to produce a smooth dressing.

Transfer to a bowl and season to taste with salt and ground black pepper. Stir in the chopped walnuts and use as required. SERVES 6

## HORSERADISH DRESSING

*This dressing is ideal for beef salads and salads containing an oily fish, such as mackerel.*

60 ml (4 tbsp) sunflower oil
60 ml (4 tbsp) cider vinegar
60 ml (4 tbsp) horseradish sauce
Salt and ground black pepper

Place the dressing ingredients in a bowl and whisk to combine. Taste and adjust seasoning, if necessary, and refrigerate until required. SERVES 4

*Variation: Add 15 ml (1 tbsp) very lightly whipped cream to produce a milder, creamy dressing.*

## WATERCRESS VINAIGRETTE

*This vinaigrette combines well with fish salads and it is also excellent when used to dress a new potato salad.*

50 g (2 oz) fresh watercress
2.5 ml (½ tsp) Dijon mustard
Salt and ground black pepper
150 ml (5 fl oz) extra virgin olive oil
45 ml (3 tbsp) balsamic vinegar

Wash and dry the watercress. Remove any large, tough stalks and place the watercress in a food processor with the mustard and seasoning. Process briefly to chop up the watercress.

Pour the olive oil in a thin steady stream into the food processor with the motor running to produce a thick, smooth dressing. Add the vinegar and process again briefly. Taste and adjust seasoning, if necessary, and refrigerate until required. This dressing will keep well for 2 days in the refrigerator. SERVES 8

**TOP TO BOTTOM:** Watercress Vinaigrette, Horseradish Dressing, Pear & Walnut Vinaigrette

# SANDWICHES

This section offers an enticing selection of sandwich recipes ranging from simple snacks to hearty feasts and will inspire you to create your own unique versions.

The Earl of Sandwich, John Montague, would be amazed to see the kinds of sandwiches we eat today; with exotic ingredients available from all over the world, we have come a long way since 1762 when he invented the sandwich, made up of meat between slices of bread. With the ever-increasing choices of interesting breads, and by using imagination with tasty fillings, sandwiches can be as innovative as you choose.

### BREADS

Today it is possible to buy a wide range of bread with different textures, colours and shapes. Pre-sliced forms of white, wholemeal, multi-grain, rye and granary are all convenient to use, especially if you need very thin slices for delicate sandwiches. Whole loaves keep fresh longer and can be cut to the thickness appropriate for the sandwich filling, which is ideal for open sandwiches that need a substantial base for hearty toppings. Many unusual breads with distinctive flavours, such a ciabatta, focaccia, sourdough and those made with sun-dried tomatoes, olives, nuts and seeds, can now be found in supermarkets as well as from specialist bakers.

Where a recipe specifies crusty white bread, look for whole loaves that may be called farmhouse, bloomer, pain de campagne or pugliese.

In many of the recipes in this section, rolls or baps have been used. They are available in

all shapes and sizes and can be soft or crusty. The choice suggested will be appropriate to the filling. For example, a soft filling needs a soft roll, otherwise the filling with squelch out with the first bite. Crusty rolls are more suitable for sliced, cold meat and cheese fillings. French baguettes are excellent, but must be eaten the same day as purchased, because they quickly become stale.

Pittas, bagels, muffins and tortillas can also be used to make sandwiches. Pittas and bagels in particular are available in many different flavours, such as wholemeal, sesame seed, garlic and onion.

There may be times when there is no bread readily available in your kitchen, so there are a few recipes for quick breads included in the book. With the use of easy-blend dried yeast, a conventional-style loaf is easy to make. Loaves raised with baking powder tend to have a crumbly texture, so they are best eaten with a soft spreadable filling.

### SPREADS AND CONDIMENTS

Butter or polyunsaturated margarine are most often used to spread on bread. They will act as a waterproof coating and prevent the filling from making bread slices soggy. Always spread right over the bread to prevent the edges drying. Butter can be made more interesting with the addition of pesto, herbs, garlic, horseradish, mustard and pastes, such as sun-dried

**RIGHT:** A vast selection of sandwich ingredients can be found in supermarkets, delicatessens and speciality shops. Choose interesting combinations to create your own unique sandwiches.

tomato paste. Mayonnaise has been used in some of the recipes to add moisture to the sandwich and to complement the flavours of the ingredients. Mayonnaise can also have herbs or mustard added for extra flavour. It is also worth looking for a commercial brand of reduced-calorie mayonnaise for a lower-fat spread.

Mustard is an excellent accompaniment to cold meats and there are different strengths, from the milder American and German types to the distinctive Dijon and the grainy varieties which, in particular, complement red meats.

As many of the sandwich recipes use Mediterranean-style breads, the spreads suggested are often based on olives or olive-oil. Ready-made tapenades and olive pastes can be bought, but with a food processor it is really easy to make your own. A vast choice of relishes and chutneys are also available from delis and shops, and they add interest and taste to sandwiches. For a different spread, try a thin layer of tahini or hummus, which can be topped with cheese, cold meats or fresh salad ingredients.

### SANDWICH FILLINGS

There are so many types of sliced meats to use in sandwiches, from simple roasted or poached chicken, cooked beef and boiled ham to cured, smoked and pickled meats, that the choices give plenty of scope for variety. Delicatessens are an excellent source for salamis, pâtés and terrines, as well as cheeses.

Canned fish, such as tuna, salmon and crabmeat, are delicious when mixed with mayonnaise or soft cheese and herbs. Cheeses of all strengths of flavours and texture can be used in sandwiches. Hard cheese can be thinly sliced or grated, some cheese can be crumbled and soft creamy cheese can be spread.

Combine any meats, fish or cheeses with crisp vegetables, such as shredded carrot, celery or iceberg lettuce, and add extra flavour with spreads and condiments.

Remember to keep any prepared sandwiches containing cooked meats, fish, seafood, eggs or cheese in the refrigerator until ready to serve, and consider a chilled method of transporting meat sandwiches if they are not eaten immediately after assembling.

### SANDWICHES FOR ALL OCCASIONS

Sandwiches can be eaten at any time of the day as a snack, main meal or for an afternoon tea break. Some of the recipes in this section are substantial enough for lunch or supper, whereas others are best suited for light luncheons or for hors-d'oeuvres.

The picnic ideas in this section also offer a further choice of sandwiches which could provide the main part of an 'al fresco' meal. Virtually anything sweet or savoury can be transported safely between two slices of bread or in a roll. If you are transporting sandwiches, wrap them well in clingfilm or greaseproof paper to prevent the bread from becoming stale and pack the sandwiches in rigid containers to avoid squashing them. An insulated cooler is best for picnics, but look for slim-line ice packs if packing sandwiches in lunch-boxes.

For a finishing touch to your packed meal, accompany sandwiches with cherry tomatoes, celery and carrot sticks, or pickles and gherkins to provide a contrast in flavour and texture to the sandwich.

**RIGHT:** Colourful and tasty sandwiches really make a memorable picnic, and fresh fruits and vegetables make wonderful accompaniments.

# BREADS & CONDIMENTS

*Sandwiches can be made more exciting by using interesting breads, and this chapter includes a varied selection of quick and easy bread recipes. The Cornmeal Bread and Quick Carrot Bread are made without yeast and are more crumbly in texture than conventional breads. Home-made relishes, salsas and pastes are sure to add flavour to your sandwiches, and a few recipes are featured here. Most will keep for 3-4 days in the refrigerator, but uncooked herb-based salsas or any made with raw tomatoes, such as Tomato & Herb Salsa, are best used the same day they are prepared.*

## CORNMEAL BREAD

100 g (4 oz) plain flour
100 g (4 oz) cornmeal
2.5 ml (½ tsp) salt
5 ml (1 tsp) sugar
10 ml (2 tsp) baking powder
2 eggs
240 ml (8 fl oz) milk
30 ml (2 tbsp) soured cream
50 g (2 oz) butter, melted

Preheat the oven to 200°C (400°F, Gas mark 6). Mix all the dry ingredients together in a large mixing bowl. Set aside.

In a separate bowl, beat together the eggs, milk, soured cream and butter. Add to the dry cornmeal mixture and stir until just combined. Turn into a shallow, well-greased, 20-cm (8-inch) square baking tin and bake for 18-20 minutes, until the sides pull away from the edge of the tin. Cool in the tin for 5 minutes. Cut the Cornmeal Bread into four squares.

MAKES 4 SQUARES

## WALNUT BREAD

350 g (12 oz) plain wholemeal flour
100 g (4 oz) porridge oats
5 ml (1 tsp) salt
7-g (¼-oz) sachet easy-blend dried yeast
15 ml (1 tbsp) dried mixed herbs
75 g (3 oz) walnut pieces, chopped
300 ml (½ pint) warm water
30 ml (2 tbsp) walnut or olive oil
Cracked wheat, to finish

Place all the dry ingredients, except the cracked wheat, into a large bowl and mix together. Add the warm water and oil, and mix to form a soft dough. Knead the dough on a lightly floured surface for about 5 minutes.

Shape the dough into a smooth ball. Place on a greased baking sheet and flatten slightly. Leave in a warm place to rise for 30 minutes. Preheat the oven to 220°C (425°F, Gas mark 7).

Brush the top of the loaf with water, sprinkle over the cracked wheat and bake for 20-25 minutes, or until the loaf sounds hollow when tapped on the bottom. Allow to cool on a wire rack. MAKES 1 LOAF

**TOP:** Walnut Bread
**BOTTOM:** Cornmeal Bread

## QUICK CARROT BREAD

225 g (8 oz) carrot, finely grated
300 g (10 oz) plain flour
30 ml (2 tbsp) baking powder
15 ml (1 tbsp) sugar
5 ml (1 tsp) salt
1 large egg
60 ml (4 tbsp) olive oil
180 ml (6 fl oz) milk

Preheat the oven to 180°C (350°F, Gas mark 4). Place the grated carrot on layers of kitchen paper to absorb excess liquid.

Sift the flour with the baking powder in a large bowl. Stir in the sugar and salt. Fold in the carrots and set aside.

In a separate bowl, beat the egg with the oil and milk. Add the egg mixture to the flour mixture and stir to form a batter. Turn into a greased 21 × 11-cm (8½ × 4½-inch) loaf tin and bake for about 1 hour, or until a skewer inserted into the middle of the loaf comes out clean. Transfer to a wire rack to cool.

MAKES 1 LOAF

### ONION AND ROSEMARY BREAD

Follow the above recipe, omitting the carrot and substituting 225 g (8 oz) chopped onion, sautéed in 25 g (1 oz) butter until soft, and 5 ml (1 tsp) chopped fresh rosemary.

## SUN-DRIED TOMATO ROLLS

450 g (1 lb) strong white flour
5 ml (1 tsp) salt
7-g (¼-oz) sachet easy-blend dried yeast
30 ml (2 tbsp) finely chopped sun-dried tomatoes
50 g (2 oz) mature Cheddar cheese, finely grated
300 ml (½ pint) warm water
30 ml (2 tbsp) olive oil

Mix the first five ingredients in a large bowl. Add the water and olive oil and mix to form a soft dough. Knead the dough for about 5 minutes on a lightly floured surface. Shape into four rolls, place on a greased baking sheet and flatten the dough rolls to about 2 cm (¾ inch) in thickness. Leave in a warm place until doubled in size.

Preheat the oven to 220°C (425°F, Gas mark 7). When the rolls have risen, bake them for about 12 minutes until golden. Cool on a wire rack.

MAKES 4-6 ROLLS

**TOP:** Quick Carrot Bread
**BOTTOM:** Sun-dried Tomato Rolls

## RED PEPPER RELISH

30 ml (2 tbsp) olive oil
I small onion, finely chopped
2 cloves garlic, finely chopped
350 g (12 oz) red peppers, cored, seeded
and chopped
150 ml (¼ pint) vegetable stock
150 ml (¼ pint) dry white wine
5 ml (I tsp) tomato purée
I bay leaf
10 ml (2 tsp) sugar
Salt and ground black pepper

Heat the olive oil in a saucepan. Add the onion and cook gently for about 8 minutes until golden. Add the chopped garlic and red pepper and cook for about 5 minutes, stirring constantly. Add the stock, white wine, tomato purée, bay leaf and sugar. Simmer un-covered for 20-25 minutes until thick and chunky. Sea-son with salt and pepper and allow to cool.

SERVES 4-6

## SWEETCORN RELISH

325-g (11-oz) can sweetcorn kernels
½ red onion, finely chopped
2 sticks celery, finely chopped
I red pepper, cored, seeded and finely diced
I fresh green chilli, seeded and finely chopped
2 cloves garlic, finely chopped
15 ml (I tbsp) white wine vinegar
15 ml (I tbsp) olive oil

Place the sweetcorn kernels in a bowl. Add the re-maining ingredients and mix well. Set aside for about I hour and stir again to mix before serving.

SERVES 4-6

## TOMATO & HERB SALSA

4 plum tomatoes
30 ml (2 tbsp) finely chopped red onion
I clove garlic, finely chopped
45 ml (3 tbsp) finely chopped green pepper
30 ml (2 tbsp) olive oil
30 ml (2 tbsp) chopped fresh coriander
15 ml (I tbsp) chopped fresh parsley
Salt and ground black pepper

Skin the tomatoes by pouring boiling water over them and leaving for about 30 seconds before draining. Allow to cool slightly and peel the skins. Scoop out the seeds, cut the tomatoes into small dice and place in a bowl. Add the remaining ingredients, seasoning with salt and pepper. Mix well, cover and refrigerate until required.

SERVES 4

*Variation: Add 1-2 fresh green chillies, seeded and finely chopped, for a spicy salsa.*

## BLACK OLIVE PASTE

175 g (6 oz) stoned black olives
15 ml (I tbsp) capers
2 canned anchovy fillets
45 ml (3 tbsp) virgin olive oil
I small clove garlic, crushed
Pinch of thyme
Pinch of ground bay leaves

If the olives are packed in brine, rinse them in cold water. Rinse the capers in water and drain. Place all the ingredients in a food processor and blend until very finely chopped and almost a paste in consistency. Use instead of butter in sandwiches.

SERVES 4-6

**CLOCKWISE:** Sweetcorn Relish, Tomato & Herb Salsa, Black Olive Paste, Red Pepper Relish

# LIGHT SELECTIONS

The sandwich recipes in this chapter are suitable for all occasions when light but tasty snacks are required. Along with Mediterranean-style open-faced bruschettas and lightly filled sandwiches for snacks or lunch-time meals, there are delicate egg and cucumber sandwiches for afternoon teas and novel hors-d'oeuvres and starters, such as Nutty Cheese Puffs and Crab Melts. Some, like the Roquefort & Ham Ribbon Sandwiches, are ideal for serving at drinks parties. In addition, many of the sandwich recipes include flavoured butters which can be used in your own inspired creations.

## HAM SALAD SANDWICHES

8 slices wholemeal bread
225 g (8 oz) thinly sliced ham
100 g (4 oz) Cheddar or Double Gloucester cheese, grated
2 tomatoes, sliced
1 punnet mustard and cress, trimmed and washed

### TOMATO BUTTER
75 g (3 oz) butter, softened
10 ml (2 tsp) tomato purée
Squeeze lemon juice
Salt and ground black pepper

Prepare the Tomato Butter. Mix the butter, tomato purée, lemon juice and salt and pepper in a bowl until well blended. Spread over all the slices of bread.

Divide the ham between four slices of bread, and add a layer of cheese and a layer of tomato. Top each sandwich with mustard and cress. Cover with the remaining bread, butter sides down. Cut each sandwich into quarters and serve. SERVES 4

## HERBY EGG SALAD SANDWICHES

6 hard-boiled eggs, shelled
45 ml (3 tbsp) mayonnaise
30 ml (2 tbsp) chopped fresh dill
30 ml (2 tbsp) chopped fresh chives
8 slices white sandwich bread
Salt and ground black pepper

### WATERCRESS BUTTER
50 g (2 oz) butter, softened
45 ml (3 tbsp) finely chopped watercress
15 ml (1 tbsp) chopped fresh parsley

Finely chop the eggs. Place the egg in a bowl, with the mayonnaise, dill and chives. Season with salt and pepper and fold the mixture together to combine. Refrigerate until required.

Prepare the Watercress Butter. Mix the butter, watercress and parsley together in a bowl until well blended. Spread the butter over all the slices of bread.

Top four slices of the buttered bread with the reserved egg mixture. Cover with the remaining bread, butter sides down. Cut the sandwiches into triangles and serve. SERVES 4

**RIGHT:** Ham Salad Sandwiches, Herby Egg Salad Sandwiches

## PROSCIUTTO & TALEGGIO BRUSCHETTA

8 slices Italian bread, such as ciabatta
Extra virgin olive oil
2 cloves garlic, halved
225 g (8 oz) Taleggio or Fontina cheese, rind removed
8 slices prosciutto
2 tomatoes, sliced
Fresh basil sprigs, to garnish

Preheat a grill to hot. Brush the bread with the olive oil and toast under the grill until golden on both sides.

Rub the cut sides of the garlic over the toasted bread. Slice the cheese and divide between the toasted bread. Top each bruschetta with a slice of prosciutto, arranging it in folds. Halve the tomato slices and place in the folds of the prosciutto. Garnish with basil sprigs and serve at once, serving two slices to each person. SERVES 4

## MUSHROOM BRUSCHETTA

12 slices French bread, each about 5 mm (¼ inch) thick
25 g (1 oz) butter
30 ml (2 tbsp) olive oil
2 cloves garlic, thinly sliced
225 g (8 oz) cultivated mushrooms, sliced
225 g (8 oz) wild mushrooms, such as chanterelles or girolles
30 ml (2 tbsp) chopped fresh parsley
Salt and ground black pepper

Preheat a grill to hot and toast the bread slices under the grill until golden on both sides.

Meanwhile, melt the butter in a frying pan and add the oil and garlic. After 30 seconds, stir in the cultivated mushrooms. Cook over a high heat for 3

minutes, tossing them in the pan all the time. Add the wild mushrooms and cook for a further 2 minutes. Stir in the parsley and season with salt and pepper. Spoon on to the toasted bread and serve three bruschetta to each person while still hot. SERVES 4

## TUSCAN-STYLE TOASTS

8 slices sciocco or Italian flat bread
2 tomatoes, cut into small wedges

### ROCKET PESTO
About 30 g (1 oz) rocket leaves
1 clove garlic, crushed
45 ml (3 tbsp) pine nuts, lightly toasted
30 ml (2 tbsp) grated Parmesan cheese
30 ml (2 tbsp) virgin olive oil
Salt and ground black pepper

Preheat a grill to hot. Prepare the pesto. Place the rocket and garlic in a food processor and chop finely. Add 30 ml (2 tbsp) of the pine nuts and blend again until very finely chopped. Add the Parmesan and, with the processor running, add the oil gradually until the mixture becomes smooth. Season with salt and pepper. Set aside.

Toast the bread under the grill until golden on both sides. Spread the Rocket Pesto over the toasted bread. Arrange wedges of tomato on top of each, then scatter over the remaining pine nuts. Serve two toasts to each person. SERVES 4

**TOP TO BOTTOM:** Prosciutto & Taleggio Bruschetta, Mushroom Bruschetta, Tuscan-Style Toasts

## CROQUE MONSIEUR

8 slices white bread
100 g (4 oz) butter
8 thin slices Gruyère or Cheddar cheese
4 slices ham
Ground black pepper
90 ml (6 tbsp) sunflower oil

Butter all the bread slices. Place a slice of cheese on each of four buttered slices. Top each with a slice of ham, season with black pepper and top with another slice of cheese. Finish with the remaining bread slices, butter sides down, to make four sandwiches. Press down firmly.

Melt half the remaining butter in a large frying pan with half the sunflower oil. Fry two sandwiches until golden brown and crisp, turning once. Cook the other two sandwiches in the same way, using the remaining butter and oil. Serve while still hot.        SERVES 4

## PEPPERONI CROQUE MONSIEUR

8 slices white bread
100 g (4 oz) butter
250 g (9 oz) mozzarella cheese, thinly sliced
100 g (4 oz) sliced pepperoni sausage
2 tomatoes, thinly sliced
Ground black pepper
90 ml (6 tbsp) sunflower oil

Butter all the bread slices. Arrange half the cheese over four slices of bread and divide the pepperoni slices between them. Add the tomato slices, season with black pepper and finish each with the remaining cheese. Cover with the remaining bread slices and press down firmly. Follow the instructions for Croque Monsieur, above, to cook the sandwiches. SERVES 4

## NUTTY CHEESE PUFFS

4 thick slices white bread
50 g (2 oz) Cheddar cheese, finely grated
15 ml (1 tbsp) finely chopped onion
30 ml (2 tbsp) mayonnaise
15 ml (1 tbsp) chopped fresh parsley
25 g (1 oz) pecan nuts, chopped
1 egg, separated
Mixed lettuce leaves, to serve (optional)

Preheat a grill to hot. Using a 5-cm (2-inch) round pastry cutter, cut three circles from each slice of bread. Place under the grill and toast until golden on both sides. Set aside. Preheat the oven to 180°C (350°F, Gas mark 4).

Place the cheese, onion, mayonnaise, parsley, nuts and egg yolk into a bowl and mix until combined. In a separate bowl, whisk the egg white until stiff. Fold the egg white into the cheese mixture. Divide between the rounds of toast and place on a baking sheet. Bake for 8-10 minutes.

Serve three rounds to each person while still hot, along with a few lettuce leaves if desired.  SERVES 4

**RIGHT:** Nutty Cheese Puffs

## ROQUEFORT & HAM RIBBON SANDWICHES

100 g (4 oz) Roquefort cheese, rind removed
30 ml (2 tbsp) crème fraîche
100 g (4 oz) ham, finely chopped
6 slices thinly-cut wholemeal or brown bread

Place the Roquefort in a bowl and break into small pieces. Add the crème fraîche and beat together to mix well. Fold in the chopped ham. Spread the mixture on three slices of bread, cover with the remaining bread and trim off the crusts.

Cut each sandwich in half lengthways, then across four times to make each into eight small sandwiches. Serve as an hors-d'oeuvre or for tea.     SERVES 4

## CUCUMBER SANDWICHES

½ cucumber, peeled and thinly sliced
2.5 ml (½ tsp) salt
50 g (2 oz) butter, softened
30 ml (2 tbsp) chopped fresh herbs, such as
parsley, chervil and dill
1.25 ml (¼ tsp) Dijon mustard
8 thin slices white bread
30 ml (2 tbsp) chopped fresh mint

Place the cucumber in a colander and sprinkle with salt. Leave for 30 minutes to draw excess moisture from the cucumber. Pat dry with kitchen paper.

Beat the butter with the herbs and mustard and use it to butter all the bread slices.

Arrange the cucumber slices over four slices of buttered bread. Scatter over the mint and cover with the remaining bread. Press the sandwiches together.

Carefully trim the crusts and cut each sandwich into four squares. Cut each square in half diagonally to make two dainty triangles. Serve for an afternoon tea or light snack.     SERVES 4

## CREAM CHEESE PINWHEELS

3 large slices white bread
3 large slices brown bread
225 g (8 oz) soft cream cheese
30 ml (2 tbsp) soured cream or crème fraîche
100 g (4 oz) smoked salmon, finely chopped
30 ml (2 tbsp) chopped fresh dill
Squeeze lemon juice
Ground black pepper
Fresh dill sprigs, to garnish

Remove the crusts from the bread. Place each on a work surface and flatten with a rolling pin.

Beat the cream cheese and soured cream together in a bowl. Stir in the smoked salmon, dill, lemon juice and a little black pepper. Spread the mixture over all the bread slices. Roll up each slice from the short end to enclose the filling. Wrap each roll in cling film and refrigerate for at least 1 hour.

To serve, remove the cling film and cut each roll into 2-cm (¾-inch) wide slices. Arrange on a serving platter, garnish with dill sprigs and serve as an hors-d'oeuvre or a tea-time treat.     SERVES 4

*Variation: Omit the smoked salmon for a simple herby version, or substitute 50 g (2 oz) chopped ham for the smoked salmon.*

**RIGHT:** Cucumber Sandwiches, Roquefort
& Ham Ribbon Sandwiches,
Cream Cheese Pinwheels

## CRAB MELTS

175 g (6 oz) fresh or canned crabmeat
30 ml (2 tbsp) fromage fraise or crème fraîche
10 ml (2 tsp) lemon juice
10 ml (2 tsp) tomato ketchup
10 ml (2 tsp) chopped fresh parsley
Salt and ground black pepper
2 muffins
10 ml (2 tsp) grated Parmesan cheese
Lemon twists, to garnish (optional)

If using canned crabmeat, drain any excess water in which it is packed. Place the crabmeat in a bowl and break up any large pieces with a fork. In a separate bowl, mix together the fromage fraise, lemon juice, ketchup and parsley. Season with a little salt and pepper and fold the mixture into the crabmeat. Preheat a grill to hot.

Split the muffins and toast them under the grill. Divide the crab mixture between each muffin half and scatter the Parmesan on top. Return the muffins to the grill and cook until the top is golden and the crab is heated through. Cut each muffin half into four and serve four pieces to each person while still hot. Garnish with lemon twists, if desired. SERVES 4

*Variation: Substitute drained canned tuna for the crabmeat in the recipe to make Tuna Melts, and serve the muffin halves either whole for a lunch-time meal or cut into pieces for an hors-d'oeuvre.*

## LEMON PRAWN ROLLS

8 miniature bread rolls, assorted flavours
45 ml (3 tbsp) thick mayonnaise
5 ml (1 tsp) grated lemon zest
10 ml (2 tsp) lemon juice
Ground black pepper
15 ml (1 tbsp) chopped fresh chives
175 g (6 oz) peeled, cooked prawns

Cut the tops off the bread rolls and hollow out the middle of the bottom halves. Place the mayonnaise in a bowl and mix in the lemon zest, lemon juice, a little black pepper and the chopped chives. Set aside.

Reserve eight whole prawns for a garnish. Chop the remaining prawns and fold them into the prepared mayonnaise. Spoon some of the prawn mixture into each bread roll. Replace the bread lids and secure with cocktail sticks. Garnish each sandwich with a whole prawn and serve two sandwiches to each person.

SERVES 4

**RIGHT:** Crab Melts, Lemon Prawn Rolls

# HEALTHY SANDWICHES

Fresh vegetables, fruits, beans and cheeses are ingredients that feature predominantly in the recipes in this chapter. Although the emphasis is on vegetarian-style sandwiches, the Niçoise Rolls include tuna and the Chicken, Celery & Grape Sandwiches are made with gently poached chicken breast. Many of the recipes use raw vegetables and nutty breads, but for a completely fruit-based sandwich try the Tropical Salad Bowl Sandwich made with mango, kiwi, pineapple and muesli bread.

## TOMATO & BROCCOLI PANINI

45 ml (3 tbsp) olive oil
3 cloves garlic, finely chopped
225 g (8 oz) broccoli florets, sliced
Salt and ground black pepper
300 g (10 oz) Italian-style basil bread loaf or ciabatta loaf
2 plum tomatoes, sliced
Fresh basil sprigs, to garnish

Preheat the oven to 180°C (350°F, Gas mark 4). Heat the oil in a frying pan and add the garlic. After 30 seconds add the broccoli and stir-fry for 2 minutes. Add 75 ml (5 tbsp) water, cover and cook for 4-5 minutes until the broccoli is just tender. Drain any excess water, then set aside to cool. When cool, season with salt and pepper to taste.

Place the bread in the oven to warm as directed on the wrapper, or for 5 minutes.

Cut the loaf lengthways and arrange the tomatoes on the base. Season and place the broccoli on top. Cut the loaf into four portions, garnish with basil and serve while the bread is still warm. SERVES 4

## MUSHROOM & PEPPER PANINI

30 ml (2 tbsp) olive oil
225 g (8 oz) chestnut mushrooms, roughly chopped
1 clove garlic
1 red pepper, cored, seeded and roughly chopped
2.5 ml (½ tsp) dried thyme
25 ml (¼ tsp) cayenne
1.25 g (1 oz) sunflower seeds
Salt and ground black pepper
8 slices Spanish-style seeded bread
Crisp lettuce leaves

Heat the olive oil in a frying pan. Add the mushrooms, garlic, red pepper, thyme and cayenne. Cook over a high heat for 5 minutes until the mushrooms soften. Allow to cool.

Transfer the mixture to a food processor. Add the sunflower seeds and blend until the ingredients are finely chopped. Season with salt and pepper.

Spread the mushroom mixture over four bread slices. Place a layer of crisp lettuce leaves on top of each sandwich. Cover with the remaining bread slices and serve. SERVES 4

**TOP:** Tomato & Broccoli Panino
**BOTTOM:** Mushroom & Pepper Panino

## CHEESE & TOMATO PESTO SANDWICHES

8 large slices or 16 small slices multi-grain bread
175 g (6 oz) Edam cheese, sliced
2 beefsteak tomatoes, sliced
Salt and ground black pepper

### TOMATO PESTO
8 oil-packed sun-dried tomatoes
60 ml (4 tbsp) fresh parsley sprigs
2 shallots, coarsely chopped
1 clove garlic
5 ml (1 tsp) balsamic vinegar
30 ml (2 tbsp) oil from the sun-dried tomatoes

Prepare the pesto. Place all the pesto ingredients into a food processor and blend until very finely chopped.

Spread the Tomato Pesto on four large slices of bread or eight small slices. Arrange cheese slices on top of each sandwich. Top each with tomato slices and season with salt and pepper. Cover with the remaining bread. Serve one large sandwich or two small sandwiches to each person. SERVES 4

## AVOCADO & ONION SANDWICHES

1 large avocado
75 g (3 oz) low-fat soft cheese with herbs
Ground black pepper
Quick Carrot Bread (see page 86)
1 small Spanish onion, sliced
30 ml (2 tbsp) chopped fresh parsley or chervil
A little polyunsaturated margarine, softened

Halve the avocado, discard the stone and scoop the flesh into a bowl. Mash with a fork to break it up, but leave small pieces. Mix in the soft cheese and season with pepper.

Cut 12 slices from the carrot loaf. Spread the avocado mixture over six slices and top with a layer of onion. Scatter over the parsley or chervil.

Spread the remaining slices of carrot bread with margarine, place on top of the sandwiches, margarine sides down, and cut each in half. Serve three halves to each person. SERVES 4

**TOP:** Avocado & Onion Sandwich
**BOTTOM:** Cheese & Tomato Pesto Sandwich

## VEGETARIAN CLUB SANDWICHES

100 g (4 oz) young spinach leaves, washed
225 g (8 oz) cashew nuts
75 ml (5 tbsp) Greek yoghurt or crème fraîche
Salt and ground black pepper
2 large carrots, peeled
6 spring onions, thinly sliced
10 ml (2 tsp) poppyseeds
15 ml (1 tbsp) extra virgin olive oil
10 ml (2 tsp) lemon juice
A little butter or polyunsaturated margarine, softened
12 slices multi-grain bread

Roughly shred the spinach leaves. Place the spinach in a saucepan with just the water that clings to the leaves and cook over a medium heat, stirring for 2 minutes or until wilted. Drain any excess water and allow to cool. Preheat a grill to hot.

Place the cashew nuts on a baking sheet and toast under the hot grill until golden. Allow to cool. Transfer the nuts to a food processor and blend until finely chopped. Mix the nuts, spinach and yoghurt together in a bowl. Season with salt and pepper and set aside.

With a vegetable peeler, shave thin ribbons of carrot down the length of each carrot, discarding the inner core of each carrot. Place in a bowl and add the spring onions and poppyseeds. Sprinkle over the olive oil and lemon juice and toss to mix well. Set aside.

Butter four slices of bread. Top each with one-quarter of the spinach and nut mixture. Spread another four slices of bread with butter and place over the sandwiches, butter sides up. Divide the carrot mixture between the portions and cover with the remaining bread. Cut each sandwich into four triangles and serve at once.   SERVES 4

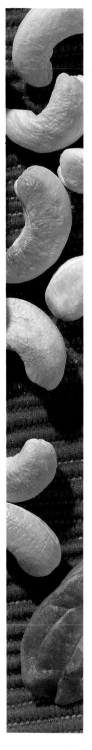

## COTTAGE CHEESE MOSAIC SANDWICHES

*The white, green and orange colours of the ingredients make beautifully coloured sandwiches that are healthy and tasty, too.*

Walnut Bread (see page 10)
225 g (8 oz) cottage cheese
1 bunch watercress or rocket, trimmed and chopped
2 clementines or satsumas
Ground black pepper

Place the cottage cheese and watercress or rocket in a large mixing bowl. Peel the clementines or satsumas, removing all the white pith, and cut in between the membranes to produce segments. Chop the fruit segments into small pieces and add to the cottage cheese. Mix all the ingredients together to combine well.

Cut eight slices of bread from the loaf. Divide the filling between four of the slices and top with the remaining bread. Cut each sandwich in half to serve.

SERVES 4

**RIGHT:** Vegetarian Club Sandwich

## ZESTY BEAN PITTAS

30 ml (2 tbsp) olive oil
I small onion, finely chopped
225 g (8 oz) parsnips, finely diced
I fresh green chilli, seeded and finely chopped
2 cloves garlic, finely chopped
5 ml (I tsp) garam masala
2.5 ml (½ tsp) ground cumin
5 ml (I tsp) lemon juice
430-g (15-oz) can butter beans, drained
Salt and ground black pepper
30 ml (2 tbsp) chopped fresh coriander
3 tomatoes, sliced
4 pitta breads, split lengthways
Extra olive oil (optional)

Heat the oil in a frying pan. Add the onion and parsnips and cook gently for 8-10 minutes until the parsnips begin to soften. Add the chilli, garlic and spices and cook for a further 2 minutes. Cool slightly.

Transfer the mixture to a food processor, along with the lemon juice and butter beans. Process until the ingredients are finely chopped and soft, but before the mixture becomes a paste. Season with salt and pepper and stir in the coriander.

To serve, layer the tomato slices in each pitta and top with the bean spread. Drizzle in a little extra olive oil, if desired, and serve.          SERVES 4

*Variation: Substitute eight slices of country-style bread for the pittas and layer the bean spread on four slices. Top with the tomatoes, a little olive oil and the remaining bread slices.*

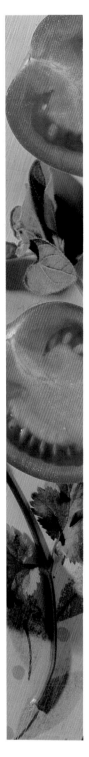

## FETA & TOMATO PITTAS

4 radicchio leaves, shredded
6 Cos lettuce leaves, shredded
175 g (6 oz) feta cheese, cut into small pieces
10-cm (4-inch) piece cucumber, diced
4 plum tomatoes, diced
12 radishes, sliced
8 black olives, stoned and chopped
4 individual pitta breads
Small onion rings, to garnish (optional)

### DRESSING
30 ml (2 tbsp) olive oil
15 ml (I tbsp) lemon juice
5 ml (I tsp) dried oregano
I clove garlic, finely chopped
Salt and ground black pepper

Place the prepared radicchio, lettuce, feta, cucumber, tomato, radish and olives in a large bowl.

Whisk all the dressing ingredients together in a small bowl until thoroughly combined. Stir into the prepared salad ingredients and toss gently together.

Cut open the pitta breads to make pockets and spoon one-quarter of the filling into each one. Serve garnished with onion rings, if desired.          SERVES 4

**TOP:** Feta & Tomato Pittas
**BOTTOM:** Zesty Bean Pitta

## CHICKEN, CELERY & GRAPE SANDWICHES

3 skinless, boneless chicken breasts
150 ml (¼ pint) chicken stock
60 ml (4 tbsp) dry white wine
30 ml (2 tbsp) Greek yoghurt
30 ml (2 tbsp) reduced-calorie mayonnaise
30 ml (2 tbsp) chopped fresh mint
100 g (4 oz) green or red seedless grapes, halved
3 sticks celery, sliced
A little butter, softened
8 slices French or Italian country bread
Lollo rosso or oak leaf lettuce

Place the chicken breasts in a large frying pan, pour over the stock and wine and slowly bring to a simmer. Cover and poach the chicken for about 15 minutes until the chicken is tender. Allow to cool in the liquid, then lift the chicken from the pan and set aside.

Bring the remaining liquid to the boil and boil rapidly until reduced to 45 ml (3 tbsp). Pour the liquid into a bowl and allow to cool. When cool, whisk in the yoghurt, mayonnaise and mint. Place the grapes and celery in a separate bowl and fold in the yoghurt mixture. Set aside.

Lightly butter four of the bread slices and arrange a layer of lettuce leaves on top of each. Slice the reserved chicken and place over the lettuce. Top with the celery and grape mixture. Cover with the remaining bread slices, cut each sandwich in half and serve.

SERVES 4

## TROPICAL SALAD BOWL SANDWICHES

*The meusli bread combines well with the fruit in this recipe, but for a lower-calorie sandwich you may like to substitute a light slimming bread.*

1 mango
2 kiwis
2 rings canned pineapple
45 ml (3 tbsp) Greek yoghurt
5-cm (2-inch) piece fresh root ginger, peeled
A little butter or polyunsaturated margarine, softened
8 slices meusli bread with fruit and nuts
Shredded lettuce
Tropical dried fruit and nut mix,
to serve (optional)

Peel the mango and kiwis and cut into thin slices. Chop the pineapple into chunks. Set aside.

Place the yoghurt in a bowl. Cut the root ginger into manageable pieces and squeeze through a garlic press into the bowl. Allow the juice and purée from the ginger to mix into the yoghurt and stir well to combine. Set aside.

Lightly butter the slices of bread and top four slices with some shredded lettuce. Arrange the mango and kiwi slices on top of each and scatter over the pineapple. Spoon on the gingered yoghurt and top with the remaining bread. Serve with the tropical fruit and nut mix, if desired.

SERVES 4

**RIGHT:** Tropical Salad Bowl Sandwich

## NICOISE ROLLS

200-g (7-oz) can tuna in brine, drained

100 g (4 oz) cooked new potatoes, diced

50 g (2 oz) cooked French green beans, cut into short lengths

4 spring onions, chopped

45 ml (3 tbsp) reduced-calorie mayonnaise

15 ml (1 tbsp) lemon juice

4 olive rolls or individual French baguettes

45 ml (3 tbsp) Black Olive Paste (see page 88) or sun-dried tomato paste

4 hard-boiled eggs, shelled and sliced

½ bunch watercress, washed and trimmed

2 tomatoes, sliced

Salt and ground black pepper

30 ml (2 tbsp) extra virgin olive oil

Flake the tuna in a bowl and add the potato, green beans and spring onion. In a separate bowl, mix the mayonnaise and lemon juice together. Stir the mayonnaise into the tuna mixture and set aside.

Cut the rolls or baguettes in half lengthways and remove some of the soft bread for the inside base to make a hollow in each half. Spread each base with olive or sun-dried tomato paste and arrange sliced egg along the length, followed by sprigs of watercress. Top with the tuna mixture and slices of tomato.

Season with salt and pepper and drizzle a little olive oil over each sandwich. Cover with the bread lids and serve at once.                                              SERVES 4

## ROCKET & PARMESAN ROLLS

50 g (2 oz) rocket leaves, washed and dried

75 g (3 oz) closed-cup mushrooms, sliced

50 g (2 oz) Parmesan cheese

4 Sun-dried Tomato Rolls (see page 86)

### DRESSING

45 ml (3 tbsp) extra virgin olive oil

10 ml (2 tsp) balsamic vinegar

1 clove garlic, finely chopped

2.5 ml (1/2 tsp) Dijon mustard

Salt and ground black pepper

Place the rocket leaves and mushrooms in a bowl. Whisk all the dressing ingredients together in a separate bowl, seasoning with salt and pepper to taste. Stir the dressing into the rocket salad and toss together well to coat the leaves and mushrooms.

Using a vegetable peeler, shave the Parmesan cheese into flakes.

Cut the rolls horizontally and divide the dressed rocket salad between them. Top each sandwich with the Parmesan flakes and serve.            SERVES 4

**TOP:** Rocket & Parmesan Rolls

**BOTTOM:** Niçoise Roll

# ROAST VEGETABLE SANDWICHES

2 whole bulbs garlic
Olive oil
3 small beetroot
2 medium carrots, peeled
2 medium courgettes
2 small red onions, thickly sliced
8 slices sunflower or multi-grain bread
Salt and ground black pepper

Preheat the oven to 200°C (400°F, Gas mark 6). Remove the papery skin from the garlic bulbs. Cut off 5 mm (¼ inch) from the stem ends. Place in an earthenware garlic baker or on a piece of foil. Drizzle with 5 ml (1 tsp) olive oil. If using foil, wrap loosely around the garlic. Bake for 30-40 minutes until the garlic cloves are soft. Remove from the oven and set aside.

While the garlic is baking, place the beetroot in a saucepan, cover with water and bring to the boil. Boil for about 30 minutes until the beetroot is tender. Drain and cut into 5-mm (¼-inch) thick slices. Toss in a little oil and place at one end of a large baking tin.

Slice the carrots and courgettes on the diagonal to make large slices, about 5 mm (¼ inch) thick. Transfer to the baking tin with the onion slices. Brush the vegetables with a little oil.

Roast the vegetables in the oven for about 10 minutes. Remove the courgettes if they are tender and golden. Continue to roast the remaining vegetables for 10-15 minutes more, until they are tender and golden. Roast a little longer if a charring effect is preferred. Remove from the oven and set aside.

Lightly toast all the bread slices. Squeeze the garlic cloves and spread the purée over four of the toasted slices. Arrange the roast vegetables over the four slices and top with the remaining toast. Serve at once while still warm. SERVES 4

# CREAMY GOAT'S CHEESE SANDWICHES

Onion and Rosemary Bread (see page 86)
150 g (5 oz) mild, soft French goat's cheese
3 plum tomatoes, sliced
Black Olive Paste (see page 88) or a commercial variety
Salad leaves, to garnish

Cut 12 slices from the bread loaf. Spread the slices with the goat's cheese and top with slices of tomato.

Spread the remaining slices of bread with the Black Olive paste and place on top of the tomatoes, paste sides down. Cut each sandwich in half. Serve three halves to each person, garnished with some green salad leaves. SERVES 4

**RIGHT:** Roast Vegetable Sandwich

# HEARTY OPTIONS

*The recipes in this chapter cater for those with hearty appetites, and many are influenced by the substantial sandwiches so popular in America. Along with some variations on classic favourites from the deli, you will find more exotic alternatives, such as the hoisin-flavoured Chinese Pork Rolls and the garlicky Greek Lamb Sandwiches. Some of the sandwiches can be a little messy to eat and are best served with a knife and fork, such as the Silver Dollars and the Spicy Mexican Sandwiches. Also featured are selections that make hearty breakfast sandwiches, such as Smoked Salmon & Egg Bagels.*

## SMOKED SALMON & EGG BAGELS

25 g (I oz) butter
9 eggs
60 ml (4 tbsp) milk
Salt and ground black pepper
100 g (4 oz) smoked salmon, roughly chopped
15 ml (I tbsp) chopped fresh parsley
4 bagels, split, lightly toasted and buttered
2 spring onions, thinly sliced

Melt the butter in a non-stick frying pan. Beat the eggs and milk together in a bowl and season with salt and pepper. Pour the egg mixture into the pan and cook over a medium heat, stirring to scramble the eggs.

When the eggs are almost set, stir in the smoked salmon and parsley. Cook for about 30 seconds more, until the eggs are cooked but still have a creamy appearance. Divide the scrambled eggs between the four bottom halves of the toasted bagels, garnish with the spring onion and cover with the tops of the bagels. Serve at once while still hot.                    SERVES 4

## FRITTATA SANDWICHES

40 g (I½ oz) butter
I small onion, finely chopped
450 g (I lb) fresh spinach, washed and roughly chopped, or 175 g (6 oz) frozen leaf spinach, thawed
Large pinch nutmeg
6 large eggs
Salt and ground black pepper
75 g (3 oz) Cheddar cheese, grated
2 slices wholemeal or soft-grain bread
Tomato wedges, to serve

Heat the butter in a 23-cm (9-inch) diameter non-stick frying pan. Add the onion and cook for 4-5 minutes until golden. If using fresh spinach, place in a large saucepan with the water that remains on the leaves, and cook for 3-4 minutes until wilted, stirring all the time. Drain the excess liquid from the spinach. If using frozen spinach, press out excess water through a sieve. Stir the spinach into the onion and season with the nutmeg. Cook for 3-4 minutes to heat the spinach.

Beat the eggs and season with salt and pepper. Pour the eggs on to the spinach and scatter over the cheese. Reduce the heat to very low and cook for 8-10 minutes until almost set. Preheat a grill to hot.

Place the frying pan under the grill and cook until the top of the frittata is set and golden.

To serve, cut the frittata into four wedges and place each portion between two slices of bread. Cut each sandwich in half and serve while still hot, accompanied by tomato wedges.                    SERVES 4

**RIGHT:** Frittata Sandwich

## PASTRAMI SANDWICHES WITH CARMELIZED ONIONS

8 slices Polish-style rye bread, buttered
Mild mustard
8 deli-style dill cucumbers, sliced
225 g (8 oz) sliced pastrami
Extra dill cucumbers, to serve (optional)

### CARMELIZED ONIONS
450 g (1 lb) onions, thinly sliced
45 ml (3 tbsp) olive oil
15 ml (1 tbsp) brown sugar
15 ml (1 tbsp) white wine vinegar
15 ml (1 tbsp) Worcestershire sauce

Prepare the Carmelized Onions. Place the onions and olive oil in a frying pan and cook over a moderate heat for about 5 minutes until the onions begin to soften. Stir in the brown sugar and continue to cook until the onions are soft and golden.

Add the vinegar, Worcestershire sauce and 45 ml (3 tbsp) water. Simmer until all the liquid has evaporated. Transfer to a bowl and set aside to cool.

Spread four of the slices of bread with mustard and divide the sliced dill cucumbers between them. Arrange the pastrami slices on top of each sandwich. Spoon one-quarter of the Carmelized Onions on top of each and cover with the remaining bread. Serve with extra dill cucumbers, if desired.     SERVES 4

## REUBEN SANDWICHES

225 g (8 oz) sliced salt beef
8 slices light rye bread with caraway seeds, lightly buttered
225 g (8 oz) sauerkraut
60 ml (4 tbsp) Thousand Island or Russian dressing
8 slices Swiss cheese
50 g (2 oz) butter
30 ml (3 tbsp) olive oil
French fries, to serve (optional)

Arrange half the salt beef on four slices of the bread. Top each with one-quarter of the sauerkraut and 15 ml (1 tbsp) Thousand Island or Russian dressing. Place two slices of Swiss cheese on each sandwich and finish with the remaining salt beef. Cover with the remaining slices of bread.

Heat half the butter with half the oil in a large frying pan. Transfer two of the assembled sandwiches to the frying pan. Place a plate or small chopping board on top of the sandwiches to press them down while they are cooking. Cook over a medium heat until golden and crisp. Turn over and cook the other side (by which time the cheese should have melted).

Repeat the cooking process for the two remaining sandwiches. Serve the reubens while still hot with French fries, if desired.     SERVES 4

**TOP:** Reuben Sandwich
**BOTTOM:** Pastrami Sandwich with Carmelized Onions

## SILVER DOLLARS

4 small turkey breast fillets, about 450 g (1 lb)
in total weight
15 ml (1 tbsp) barbecue seasoning
30 ml (2 tbsp) olive oil
4 large thick slices sourdough bread
12 rashers streaky bacon
225 g (8 oz) courgettes, cut into julienne strips
20 ml (4 tsp) sesame seeds
Boiled baby new potatoes, to serve (optional)

### WELSH RAREBIT

20 g (¾ oz) butter
15 ml (1 tbsp) flour
45 ml (3 tbsp) milk
30 ml (2 tbsp) beer
100 g (4 oz) Cheddar cheese, grated
5 ml (1 tsp) Dijon mustard
5 ml (1 tsp) Worcestershire sauce

Preheat a grill to hot. Place the turkey fillets between cling film and pound with a wooden mallet until no more than 1 cm (½ inch) thick. Sprinkle over the barbecue seasoning and brush with a little of the olive oil.

Place the turkey fillets on a grill pan and cook under the grill for about 15 minutes until tender, turning once. Toast the bread under the grill during this time.

Meanwhile, heat the remaining oil in a large frying pan. Add the bacon and fry on both sides until crisp and golden. While the bacon is cooking, prepare the Welsh Rarebit.

Melt the butter in a saucepan. Add the flour and cook over a low heat for 2 minutes, stirring constantly. Add the milk and beer and stir until the mixture is smooth and thick. Add the cheese, mustard and Worcestershire sauce and stir until the cheese has melted. Remove from the heat and set aside.

Lift the bacon from the frying pan and drain on kitchen paper.

Place the courgette strips in the pan and sauté until golden and tender. Set aside.

Remove the turkey from the grill. Spread the Welsh Rarebit over the four slices of toast and place under the grill until bubbling.

To assemble, arrange three slices of bacon on top of each sandwich and top each with a turkey breast. Pile one-quarter of the courgettes on top of each and sprinkle 5 ml (1 tsp) of sesame seeds over each sandwich. Serve at once while still hot, accompanied by the new potatoes if desired.          SERVES 4

## BACON, LETTUCE & TOMATO SANDWICHES

8 rashers back bacon, rinds removed
8 thick slices white bread
Mayonnaise
4 tomatoes, sliced
Lettuce leaves

Preheat a grill to hot. Place the bacon on a grill pan and cook under the grill until crisp and golden. Meanwhile toast the bread and spread each slice with a generous helping of mayonnaise. Arrange tomato slices on four slices of toast. Top each with some lettuce leaves and two slices of bacon. Cover each sandwich with the remaining toast, cut in half and serve at once.

SERVES 4

*Variation: Spread the top slices of toast with crunchy peanut butter for an interesting alternative.*

**RIGHT:** Silver Dollar

## MEDITERRANEAN CHICKEN SANDWICHES

*These sandwiches can be served either hot or cold,
depending on your preference.*

4 small, skinless, boneless chicken breasts
2 cloves garlic, crushed
30 ml (2 tbsp) olive oil
5 ml (1 tsp) dried Mediterranean herbs
Salt and ground black pepper
45 ml (3 tbsp) plain or garlic mayonnaise
8 slices sun-dried tomato bread
2 large plum tomatoes, sliced
Handful of fresh basil leaves
Red and yellow cherry tomato salad, to serve
(optional)

Carefully cut the chicken breasts in half horizontally to make eight thin slices. Transfer to a shallow glass or ceramic dish.

Mix the garlic, olive oil, herbs and salt and pepper together in a small bowl. Pour over the chicken, tossing to coat well. Cover with cling film and leave to marinate for 1 hour.

Heat a non-stick frying pan or ridged griddle pan. Lift the chicken slices from the dish and cook over a moderately high heat for 2-3 minutes on each side until golden. Remove from the heat. If serving the sandwiches cold, transfer the chicken to a plate and set aside to cool.

Spread the mayonnaise on four slices of bread. Arrange tomato slices on the bread and top each slice with two pieces of chicken. Season with salt and pepper and scatter a few basil leaves on top. Cover with the remaining bread and serve hot or cold, accompanied by the tomato salad if desired.     SERVES 4

## STEAK SANDWICHES WITH RED ONION RELISH

4 very thin American-style sandwich steaks
Steak seasoning
30 ml (2 tbsp) olive oil
8 slices white bloomer loaf, lightly toasted
French fries, to serve (optional)

### RED ONION RELISH
30 ml (2 tbsp) olive oil
225 g (8 oz) red onions, sliced
15 ml (1 tbsp) brown sugar
30 ml (2 tbsp) red wine vinegar
Small knob of butter

Prepare the relish. Heat the olive oil in a frying pan. Add the onions and cook gently for 15-20 minutes until the onions are tender. Pour in 150 ml (¼ pint) water, add the brown sugar and vinegar, and simmer until almost all the liquid has evaporated and the onions are tender. Stir in the butter and set aside (this relish is best served warm).

Season the steaks with a little steak seasoning. Heat a ridged griddle pan or large frying pan and pour in the olive oil. Cook the steaks over a high heat for 2-3 minutes on each side. Place a cooked steak on each of four toasted bread slices. Top with the relish and cover with the remaining toasted bread. Serve at once while still hot, accompanied by French fries if desired.
SERVES 4

*Variation: To make a Cheese Steak Sandwich, top each steak with a thin slice of cheese and melt the cheese under a hot grill before topping the sandwich with the relish. You may like to use an individual baguette or roll in place of the white bread.*

**TOP:** Steak Sandwich with Red Onion Relish
**BOTTOM:** Mediterranean Chicken Sandwich

# HOT ITALIAN HOAGIES WITH POTATO WEDGES

4 wholemeal hoagie rolls (large finger rolls)
3 tomatoes, skinned and sliced (see Tomato and Herb
Salsa on page 88 for skinning tomatoes)
Salt and ground black pepper
100 g (4 oz) sliced cold meats, such as ham, salami or
mortadella
175 g (6 oz) Dolcelatte cheese

## POTATO WEDGES
2 large baking potatoes
45 ml (3 tbsp) olive oil
Salt

Preheat the oven to 200°C (400°F, Gas mark 6). Prepare the potatoes. Scrub the potatoes and cut into 12 thin wedges. Place in a roasting tin, pour over the olive oil and toss until the wedges are well coated with oil. Season with a little salt. Bake for 40 minutes, turning once during cooking, until the potato wedges are crisp and golden.

Meanwhile split the hoagie rolls in half lengthways. Place a layer of tomatoes on the bottom of each roll and season with salt and pepper.

Cut the sliced meats in half and divide them between the rolls, arranging them in overlapping folds.

Cut the cheese into rough slices (the cheese is soft so the slices will be irregular shapes) and add to the sandwiches. Place the bread lids on top and wrap each sandwich in foil. Place in the oven during the last 15 minutes of the cooking time for the Potato Wedges. Unwrap the hoagies and serve hot, accompanied by the crisp Potato Wedges.  SERVES 4

# HOT SALAMI BAGUETTES

1 medium baguette, about 40 cm (16 inches) long
30 ml (2 tbsp) olive oil
2 medium onions, thinly sliced
4 cloves garlic, thinly sliced
2 red peppers, cored, seeded and thinly sliced
6 tomatoes, skinned and chopped (see Tomato and
Herb Salsa on page 88 for skinning tomatoes)
Pinch of hot chilli flakes
Salt and ground black pepper
225 g (8 oz) Milano salami
150 g (5 oz) mozzarella cheese, roughly chopped
5 ml (1 tsp) dried oregano
Crisp green salad, to serve (optional)

Cut the baguette in half and then each piece in half lengthways to produce four portions.

Heat the olive oil in a frying pan. Add the onions and cook for 4-5 minutes until lightly browned. Add the garlic and peppers and cook for about 2 minutes. Stir in the tomatoes and chilli flakes and cook for about 3 minutes more until the tomatoes begin to soften. Season the mixture with salt and pepper. Preheat a grill to hot.

Spoon one-quarter of the tomato mixture on to each portion of baguette. Divide the salami between each, folding over the slices so they fit on to the bread. Scatter over the chopped mozzarella cheese and sprinkle on the oregano.

Place the open-face baguettes under the grill and cook until the cheese melts. Serve while still hot, accompanied by a crisp green salad if desired.
SERVES 4

**TOP:** Hot Salami Baguette
**BOTTOM:** Hot Italian Hoagie with Potato Wedges

# MEATBALL SANDWICHES

45 ml (3 tbsp) olive oil
240 ml (8 fl oz) beef stock
25 g (1 oz) butter
1 large onion, sliced into rings
4 thick slices country-style white bread, toasted

### MEATBALLS

450 g (1 lb) lean minced beef
50 g (2 oz) finely chopped onion
50 g (2 oz) wholemeal breadcrumbs
2.5 ml (½ tsp) paprika
1.25 ml (¼ tsp) allspice
1.25 ml (¼ tsp) grated nutmeg
1 egg, beaten
Salt and ground black pepper

### THREE-MUSTARD MAYONNAISE

60 ml (4 tbsp) mayonnaise
15 ml (1 tbsp) wholegrain mustard
5 ml (1 tsp) English mustard
5 ml (1 tsp) Dijon mustard
5 ml (1 tsp) honey

Place all the ingredients for the meatballs into a food processor. Mix together by operating the processor in short bursts. Form into about 36 small balls.

Mix all the ingredients for the Three-Mustard Mayonnaise together in a bowl. Set aside.

Heat 30 ml (2 tbsp) of the olive oil in a large frying pan. Add the meatballs and fry until they are browned all over. Pour in the stock and simmer for 15 minutes, or until three-quarters of the liquid has evaporated.

Meanwhile, heat the remaining oil and butter in a separate frying pan and cook the onions until crispy.

To serve, spread all the toasted bread with the mustard mayonnaise. Pile one quarter of the meatballs on each slice and top each with one-quarter of the crispy onions. Serve hot.                    SERVES 4

# AMERICAN MEATLOAF SANDWICHES

*Meatloaf sandwiches are delicious when served hot, but can also be eaten cold if you prefer.*

30 ml (2 tbsp) olive oil
1 medium onion, chopped
1 clove garlic
175 g (6 oz) mushrooms, chopped
450 g (1 lb) lean minced beef
75 g (3 oz) fresh breadcrumbs
30 ml (2 tbsp) chopped fresh parsley
15 ml (1 tbsp) Worcestershire sauce
1 egg, beaten
2.5 ml (½ tsp) dried thyme
Few drops Tabasco
Pinch of allspice
Salt and ground black pepper
8-12 slices chollah or country-style white bread, lightly buttered
Mustard or ketchup (optional)
Sweetcorn Relish, to serve (see page 88)

Preheat the oven to 180°C (350°F, Gas mark 4). Heat the olive oil in a frying pan. Add the onion and cook gently until soft. Add the garlic and mushrooms and cook until the mushrooms are just tender. Transfer to a large mixing bowl.

Add the minced beef, breadcrumbs, parsley, Worcestershire sauce, egg, thyme, Tabasco and all-spice to the mixture. Season and mix together well. Transfer to a 900-g (2-lb) loaf tin. Cover with foil and bake for about 1 hour. Allow to cool slightly in the tin.

To serve, turn the meatloaf out of the pan and slice. Place each slice between slices of buttered bread, adding mustard or ketchup if desired. Serve accompanied by the Sweetcorn Relish.                    SERVES 4-6

**RIGHT:** Meatball Sandwich

## CHINESE PORK ROLLS

700 g (1½ lb) pork fillet
1 small red pepper, cored, seeded and thinly sliced
4 spring onions, thinly sliced
12 canned water chestnuts, drained and sliced
100 g (4 oz) Chinese cabbage, shredded
10 ml (2 tsp) sunflower or sesame oil
10 ml (2 tsp) dark soy sauce
4 large, soft white baps, split
Spring onion tassels, to garnish

### MARINADE

30 ml (2 tbsp) dark soy sauce
15 ml (1 tbsp) dry sherry
15 ml (1 tbsp) hoisin sauce
10 ml (2 tsp) sunflower oil
2 cloves garlic, crushed
10 ml (2 tsp) honey
15 ml (1 tbsp) chopped fresh root ginger
2.5 ml (½ tsp) Chinese five-spice powder

Place the pork in a shallow glass or ceramic dish. Mix the marinade ingredients together in a small bowl and pour over the pork. Cover and marinate for at least 2 hours or, preferably, overnight in the refrigerator.

Preheat the oven to 200°C (400°F, Gas mark 6). Lift the pork from the marinade and place on a wire rack in a roasting tin. Cook for about 30 minutes until tender, basting occasionally with the remaining marinade. Set aside to cool.

Mix the red pepper, spring onion, water chestnuts and Chinese cabbage together in a bowl. Pour over the oil and soy sauce and toss together to combine.

Slice the pork and divide between the split baps. Top each with one-quarter of the vegetable mixture and serve garnished with spring onion tassels.

SERVES 4

## SPICY MEXICAN SANDWICHES

450 g (1 lb) stir-fry pork or pork fillet, cut into thin strips
10 ml (2 tsp) ground cumin
5 ml (1 tsp) mild chilli powder
2.5 ml (½ tsp) ground coriander
2.5 ml (½ tsp) salt
2.5 ml (½ tsp) ground black pepper
45 ml (3 tbsp) sunflower oil
Cornmeal Bread (see page 84)
1 avocado, peeled, stoned and sliced
Tomato and Herb Salsa (see page 88)
75 g (3 oz) Cheddar cheese, grated
Pickled hot chillies, to garnish
Green salad, to serve

Place the pork in a shallow glass dish. Mix the cumin, chilli, coriander, salt and pepper together in a small bowl. Scatter the mixed seasoning over the pork, tossing to coat evenly. Set the pork aside for at least 30 minutes.

Heat the sunflower oil in a large frying pan or wok. Add the pork and stir-fry for 8-10 minutes until cooked.

Cut the Cornmeal Bread into four squares and cut each square in half horizontally.

Arrange avocado slices on the base of each cornmeal square. Divide the pork between the portions. Spoon the Tomato and Herb Salsa on the sandwiches and finish with the grated cheese. Place a bread lid on each sandwich. Serve immediately, garnished with pickled chillies and accompanied by a green salad.

SERVES 4

**TOP:** Spicy Mexican Sandwich
**BOTTOM:** Chinese Pork Roll

# TANDOORI CHICKEN PITTAS

4 small, skinless boneless chicken breasts
75 g (3 oz) long-grain or basmati rice
75 g (3 oz) ready-to-eat dried apricots, chopped
10-cm (4-in) piece cucumber, diced
15 ml (1 tbsp) mayonnaise
45 ml (3 tbsp) plain yoghurt
4 individual pitta breads
Green salad, to serve

## TANDOORI MARINADE

150 ml (¼ pint) plain yoghurt
30 ml (2 tbsp) lemon juice
15 ml (1 tbsp) ground coriander
10 ml (2 tsp) mild curry paste
1.25 ml (¼ tsp) chilli powder

Place the chicken in a shallow glass dish. Mix all the Tandoori Marinade ingredients together in a bowl. Spoon the marinade over the chicken to coat well. Cover with cling film and refrigerate for at least 2 hours, but preferably overnight.

Preheat a grill to medium-heat. Place the chickens in a grill pan and cook under the grill for 15-20 minutes, turning once, until the chicken is tender. Remove and set aside to cool. When cooled, dice the chicken.

While the chicken is cooking, boil the rice until tender, according to the instructions on the packet. Drain the rice well, rinse under cold water and drain again.

Place the cooked rice in a bowl with the apricots, cucumber and diced chicken. Mix the mayonnaise with the yoghurt and stir into the chicken mixture.

Split the pittas to make pockets and spoon one-quarter of the tandoori chicken into each one. Serve the pittas with the green salad.          SERVES 4

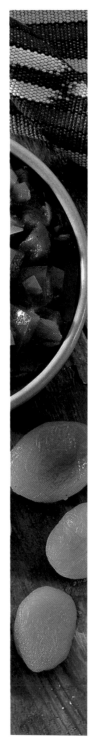

# GREEK LAMB SANDWICHES

700 g (1½ lb) fillet-end leg of lamb
4 Greek bread rolls or pitta breads
Cos lettuce leaves
Handful of fresh mint leaves, shredded
Red Pepper Relish (see page 88)
Black olives, to serve

## MARINADE

45 ml (3 tbsp) olive oil
15 ml (1 tbsp) tomato purée
3 cloves garlic, finely chopped
5 ml (1 tsp) dried Mediterranean herbs
Grated zest and juice of 1 lemon
Salt and ground black pepper

Using a sharp knife, remove the bones from the joint of lamb, but leave the meat in one long piece.

Mix the marinade ingredients together in a bowl. Spread the marinade over the lamb. Coating well. Place the joint in a roasting tin and set aside for about 1 hour. Preheat the oven to 200°C (400°F, Gas mark 6).

Cook the lamb for about 45 minutes until tender and slightly pink in the middle. Transfer to a board, cover with foil and leave for 10 minutes before slicing.

Split the bread rolls. Divide the lettuce leaves and mint between the bottom halves of the bread and top with slices of lamb. Spoon one-quarter of the Red Pepper Relish over each and top with the bread lids. Serve immediately, accompanied by olives.   SERVES 4

*Variation:* Spread the garlic purée from a bulb of roasted garlic (see Roast Vegetable Sandwiches on page 112) on the bottom halves of the sandwiches for an extra garlicky flavour.

**TOP:** Greek Lamb Sandwich
**BOTTOM:** Tandoori Chicken Pittas

## SPICY FISH SANDWICHES

75 g (3 oz) long-grain rice
450 g (1 lb) fresh cod or haddock fillet
4 spring onions, chopped
20 cashew nuts
2 small fresh red chillies, seeded and chopped
10 ml (2 tsp) light soy sauce
1 small egg, beaten
Oil for frying
8 large slices white or brown bread, buttered

### CORIANDER SALSA

40 g (1½ oz) fresh coriander leaves
2 cloves garlic, chopped
1-2 fresh green chillies, seeded and roughly chopped
1 green pepper, cored, seeded and roughly chopped
10 ml (2 tsp) finely chopped fresh root ginger
30 ml (2 tbsp) plain yoghurt

Boil the rice until tender, according to the instructions on the packet. Rinse the rice under cold water and drain well. Set aside.

Skin the fish, remove any bones and chop the flesh roughly. Transfer to a food processor and add the spring onions, cashew nuts and chilli. Blend until all the ingredients are chopped.

Add the soy sauce, egg and rice and blend briefly to mix (do not allow the mixture to become a paste). Transfer to a bowl and refrigerate for about 1 hour.

Meanwhile, make the salsa. Place the coriander, garlic, chillies, pepper and ginger into the clean bowl of the food processor. Blend until finely chopped. Transfer to a mixing bowl and stir in the yoghurt. Refrigerate until required.

Shape the fish mixture into 16 small flat patties. Pour enough oil into a frying pan to cover the bottom. Heat the oil and cook the fish cakes over a medium heat for 3-4 minutes on each side until golden. Drain on kitchen paper.

To serve, place four fish cakes on each of four slices of buttered bread. Place a spoonful of Coriander Salsa on each sandwich and cover with the remaining four slices of bread. Cut each sandwich in half and serve while still warm. SERVES 4

## PRAWN ROLLS WITH AVOCADO SALSA

4 long soft finger rolls
225 g (8 oz) peeled, cooked prawns
5 ml (1 tsp) grated lemon zest
Lettuce leaves and lemon wedges, to garnish

### AVOCADO SALSA

1 medium avocado
30 ml (2 tbsp) lemon or lime juice
2 tomatoes, finely diced
4 spring onions, finely chopped
15 ml (1 tbsp) olive oil
15 ml (1 tbsp) chopped fresh parsley
Salt and ground black pepper

Prepare the salsa. Halve the avocado, remove the stone and peel. Dice the flesh. Place the avocado in a bowl with the lemon or lime juice and gently toss together. Add the remaining salsa ingredients, seasoning with salt and pepper.

Split the rolls lengthways, but keep them intact. Spoon one-quarter of the salsa into each roll. Mix the prawns with the lemon zest and carefully divide between the rolls. Serve garnished with lettuce leaves and lemon wedges. SERVES 4

**RIGHT:** Spicy Fish Sandwich

# PICNIC & LUNCH-BOX SANDWICHES

*Because sandwiches are the most popular food to transport, this chapter is devoted to a range of flavourful filled rolls and sandwiches that are suitable for packed lunches and picnics. There are special stuffed loafs, such as the Mediterranean Picnic Loaf, which are whole loaves of bread filled with layers of ingredients. These giant sandwiches are ideal for picnics because they can be transported whole and cut into thick slices or wedges when required. When packing sandwiches, it is a good idea to refrigerate them before wrapping securely in cling film or greaseproof paper.*

## POPPYSEED KNOTS WITH CELERY & APPLE FILLING

4 poppyseed bread knots
I red apple
15 ml (I tbsp) lemon juice
2 sticks celery, chopped
50 g (2 oz) Lancashire or Cheshire cheese, crumbled
25 g (I oz) walnuts, chopped
30 ml (2 tbsp) soured cream
30 ml (2 tbsp) mayonnaise

Cut the top off each poppyseed knot and reserve for using as a lid. Using a serrated-edged knife, scoop out the soft insides.

Core and chop the apple into small pieces, place in a small bowl and toss with the lemon juice. Add the celery, crumbled cheese and walnuts.

Stir the soured cream and mayonnaise together in a separate bowl, then fold the dressing into the salad ingredients. Spoon the filling into the scooped-out rolls, pressing down firmly. Replace the bread lids. Wrap before packing into a lunch-box.          SERVES 4

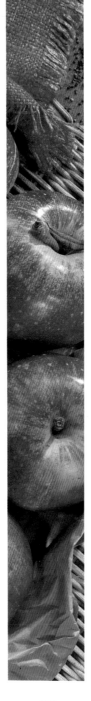

## BRIE & ROAST PEPPER ROLLS

2 red peppers
30 ml (2 tbsp) extra virgin olive oil
2 cloves garlic, thinly sliced
4 rustic bread rolls
8 sun-dried tomatoes in oil
175 g (6 oz) ripe Brie
Fresh basil leaves

Preheat a grill to hot. Place the peppers under the grill and turn until the skin is charred all over. Remove the peppers and place them in a polythene bag. Set aside for 20 minutes. Peel off the skin, discard the seeds and cut the flesh into strips.

Place the strips in a bowl, pour the olive oil over and toss together with the sliced garlic. Set aside.

Cut the rolls in half horizontally, place two sun-dried tomatoes on the bottom half of each with a little drizzle of the oil they are packed in. Slice the Brie and arrange on top of each sandwich.

Spoon over the peppers with the garlic, scatter over a few basil leaves and replace the lids. Wrap and refrigerate until required.          SERVES 4

**LEFT:** Poppyseed Knots with
Celery & Apple Filling
**RIGHT:** Brie & Roast Pepper Roll

## PROVENCAL HAM ROLLS

4 ciabatta rolls
175 g (6 oz) thinly sliced ham
2 large tomatoes, sliced (optional)
Fresh basil leaves (optional)

### AUBERGINE TAPENADE

1 aubergine, about 300 g (10 oz) in weight
Olive oil, to brush
1 red pepper
100 g (4 oz) stoned calmata olives
1 clove garlic, crushed
10 ml (2 tsp) lemon juice
6 fresh basil leaves
15 ml (1 tbsp) olive oil
Salt and ground black pepper

Preheat the oven to 200°C (400°F, Gas mark 6). Make the tapenade. Halve the aubergine and prick the skin all over. Brush the aubergine with the oil and place in a roasting tin, cut sides down.

Halve the red pepper, core and remove the seeds. Brush with oil and place in the roasting tin with the aubergine. Bake the vegetables for about 30 minutes until tender.

Scoop the flesh from the aubergine and squeeze out the excess liquid. Place the flesh in a food processor. Peel the skin from the pepper and roughly chop the flesh. Add to the processor with the olives, garlic, lemon juice, basil and olive oil. Blend until finely chopped. Season to taste with salt and pepper.

Cut the rolls in half horizontally and spread the bottom halves generously with the tapenade. Arrange the ham on top of each sandwich. Divide the tomato between the rolls and add a basil leaf, if desired. Place the bread lids on top. Wrap and refrigerate before packing for a lunch-box or picnic.        SERVES 4

## ITALIAN PICNIC SLICES

1 ciabatta loaf
Extra virgin olive oil
handful of salad leaves, such as radicchio, curly endive and escarole
100 g (4 oz) sliced garlic sausage or Italian salami
Olives, to serve (optional)

### TOMATO SALAD

4 firm ripe tomatoes, chopped
1 small red onion, finely chopped
15 ml (1 tbsp) chopped fresh basil or parsley
5 ml (1 tsp) balsamic vinegar
Salt and ground black pepper

Prepare the Tomato Salad. Place the chopped tomatoes in a bowl with the onion, herbs and vinegar. Season well with salt and pepper and mix together to combine. Set aside.

Cut the bread in half lengthways and moisten the cut surface with olive oil. Place a layer of salad leaves on the base, add the sliced garlic sausage or salami, then carefully spoon over the Tomato Salad.

Cover with the loaf top and gently press the sandwich together. Wrap tightly in cling film and refrigerate before packing for a picnic. To serve, cut the loaf into four portions and serve with the olives, if desired.

SERVES 4

*Variation: Omit the garlic sausage and use 175 g (6 oz) mozzarella cheese (preferably the buffalo variety), sliced. Add some thick slices of roast yellow pepper (see Brie and Roast Pepper Rolls on page 132 for roasting peppers).*

**TOP:** Italian Picnic Slices
**BOTTOM:** Provençal Ham Roll

## ROAST BEEF SANDWICHES WITH GARLIC BUTTER

I large whole bulb garlic
5 ml (I tsp) olive oil
50 g (2 oz) butter, softened
60 ml (4 tbsp) crème fraîche
30 ml (2 tbsp) horseradish sauce
8 slices granary bread
300 g (10 oz) rare roast beef, thinly sliced
½ Spanish onion, thinly sliced

To roast the garlic, preheat the oven to 200°C (400°F, Gas mark 6). Remove the papery skin from the bulb of garlic. Cut off 5 mm (¼ inch) from the stem end. Place in an earthenware garlic baker or on a piece of foil and drizzle over the olive oil. If using foil, wrap loosely. Bake for 40 minutes until the cloves are soft. Allow to cool.

Squeeze the garlic to remove it from the skin and beat into the butter to combine. Mix the crème fraîche and horseradish sauce in a separate mixing bowl. Set aside.

Spread the garlic butter over four slices of bread. Divide the slices of beef between them. Top with onion slices and finish each with a dollop of the horseradish mixture. Cover with the remaining bread and cut each sandwich in half. Wrap for a lunch-box or picnic, if desired. SERVES 4

## TURKEY SANDWICHES WITH CONFETTI SLAW

8 slices light rye bread
A little butter or polyunsaturated margarine, softened
Crisp lettuce leaves
225 g (8 oz) wafer-thin turkey

### CONFETTI SLAW
100 g (4 oz) red cabbage, finely shredded
100 g (4 oz) white cabbage, finely shredded
50 g (2 oz) broccoli stalks, finely shredded
I small carrot, peeled and grated
30 ml (2 tbsp) reduced-calorie mayonnaise
30 ml (2 tbsp) plain yoghurt
Salt and ground black pepper

Begin by making the slaw. Place the prepared vegetables in a bowl. In a separate bowl mix together the mayonnaise and yoghurt and season well. Stir the dressing into the vegetables and toss gently to coat. Set aside.

Lightly butter the slices of bread. Cover four slices with crisp lettuce leaves and divide the turkey between them. Top with the Confetti Slaw, cover with the remaining slices of rye bread and gently press together. Wrap in foil or cling film and refrigerate before packing in a lunch-box or for a picnic. SERVES 4

**RIGHT:** Turkey Sandwiches with Confetti Slaw

## AUBERGINE & ROAST TOMATO SANDWICHES

*The aubergine and roast tomatoes can be prepared the day before and stored in an airtight container in the refrigerator until required.*

2 small aubergines, about 350 g (12 oz) in weight
Salt
45 ml (3 tbsp) olive oil
5 ml (1 tsp) ground cumin
6 large tomatoes, skinned (see Tomato and Herb Salsa on page 88 for skinning tomatoes)
3 cloves garlic, finely chopped
Extra virgin olive oil, to drizzle
Ground black pepper
15 ml (1 tbsp) chopped fresh oregano or 2.5 ml (½ tsp) dried oregano
8 slices country-style white bread
75 ml (5 tbsp) pine nuts, lightly toasted

Cut the aubergine into 5-mm (¼-inch) thick slices. Sprinkle with salt and leave to drain in a colander for 30 minutes. Preheat a grill to hot. Rinse the aubergine slices and pat them dry with kitchen paper. Place in a grill pan.

Mix together the oil and cumin, then brush the aubergine with half the oil. Grill the aubergine until golden, turn the slices over, brush with the remaining oil, and cook again until golden. Transfer to a plate and allow to cool.

Preheat the oven to 200°C (400°F, Gas mark 6). Cut each tomato into three slices, and place in a roasting tin. Scatter over the garlic, drizzle with a little olive oil, season with black pepper and sprinkle with the oregano. Cook for 30 minutes until the tomatoes are slightly charred. Allow to cool.

Arrange the aubergine slices on four slices of bread. Top with the tomatoes, scatter over the pine nuts and finish with the remaining bread.      SERVES 4

## MEDITERRANEAN PICNIC LOAF

1 small farmhouse crusty loaf
45 ml (3 tbsp) pesto sauce
225 g (8 oz) cooking, skinned chicken breast
25 g (1 oz) rocket or young spinach leaves, shredded
3 plum tomatoes, sliced
30 ml (2 tbsp) olive oil
Salt and ground black pepper
150 g (5 oz) mozzarella cheese, sliced
100 g (4 oz) antipasto artichokes in oil, drained
100 g (4 oz) sliced ox tongue
A little butter, softened

Cut off the base of the loaf, about 1.25 cm (½ inch) from the bottom. Scoop out the inside from the top of the loaf so the walls are also 1.25 cm (½ inch) thick.

Spread the pesto around the inside of the hollowed-out loaf. Cut the chicken into thick slices and place half of them inside the loaf. Add a layer of half the rocket or spinach, then a layer of tomatoes using half the amount. Drizzle over half the olive oil.

Season with salt and pepper, then add all of the cheese and the artichokes. Add the remaining tomatoes and season again. Top with all the tongue and the remaining chicken. Finally add the remaining rocket or spinach, drizzle over the remaining oil and season.

Butter the edges of the base and place on the loaf. Wrap tightly in cling film and refrigerate overnight. To serve, unwrap and cut into thick slices.      SERVES 4-6

*Variation: Substitute Black Olive Paste (see page 88) for the pesto in the recipe. Use salami and Fontina cheese in place of the chicken, tongue and mozzarella. A round country loaf can be substituted for the farmhouse loaf, if preferred.*

**Right:** Mediterranean Picnic Loaf

## SALAMI & HERB CHEESE WEDGES

*Any flavour of Italian focaccia bread can be used in this recipe. Onion, cheese, garlic and herb, and sun-dried tomato varieties all make interesting sandwiches.*

30 ml (2 tbsp) extra virgin olive oil
1 small onion, sliced
1 small red pepper, cored, seeded and sliced
1 small yellow pepper, cored, seeded and sliced
1 focaccia bread, about 275 g (10 oz) in weight
75 g (3 oz) soft herb cheese, such as
*Boursin aux fines herbes*
15 slices cucumber
Lettuce leaves
Salt and ground black pepper
100 g (4 oz) thinly sliced salami

Heat the olive oil in a frying pan. Add the onion and cook for 3-4 minutes until the onion begins to soften. Add the sliced peppers and continue to cook until the peppers are tender, stirring constantly. Transfer to a plate and set aside to cool.

Cut the focaccia bread in half horizontally. Spread the soft herb cheese on the base and arrange the cucumber slices on top. Add a few lettuce leaves and season with salt and pepper.

Layer the salami over the lettuce and top with the prepared pepper mixture. Cover with the top of the focaccia. Wrap in foil or cling film and refrigerate until required. To serve, cut the loaf into wedges.

SERVES 4

## CHEESE & HAM MUFFALETTA

1 large, round rustic loaf or flat country-style bread
A little butter, softened
100 g (4 oz) Cheddar or Swiss cheese, thinly sliced
60 ml (4 tbsp) spicy fruit chutney, such as
peach chutney
175 g (6 oz) honey-roast ham
½ bunch watercress, washed and trimmed
Cherry tomatoes, to serve (optional)

Cut the loaf in half horizontally. Remove a little of the crumb from the top half, then spread butter on both sides of the loaf.

Arrange the slices of cheese on the base, and spread the chutney evenly over the cheese. Arrange the ham on top, overlapping each slice. Cover the ham with the watercress and place the bread lid on top. Press the loaf together gently. Wrap in foil or cling film and re-frigerate until required. To serve, cut into wedges and serve with cherry tomatoes, if desired. SERVES 4-6

**TOP LEFT:** Salami & Herb Cheese Wedges
**BOTTOM RIGHT:** Cheese & Ham Muffaletta

# PIZZAS

This section explores pizza-making in its widest sense, with five chapters covering standard thin-crust and deep-pan pizzas through calzoni and sfincioni to speciality pizzas made from unusual bases. Some of the recipes in this section are familiar favourites, while others are exciting new innovations, inspired by international cuisines.

In Italian the word 'pizza' means pie, so the American term 'pizza pie' is really a repetition of the same word. The pizza was first brought from Italy to America in 1905 by Gennaro Lombardi, who opened the first pizzeria in New York. His version of the pizza pie from Naples is now international food and the world would be unhappy without it!

### PIZZA DOUGH

To make your own pizza dough, always use 'strong' flour or bread flour, as this has a high gluten content which allows the yeast to raise the dough to its maximum point. Easy-blend dried yeast is used in all the recipes in this section because it is so simple to handle and can be stored long-term in your cupboard. When making deep-pan pizza dough, the easy-blend dried yeast can be increased to 15 ml (1 tbsp) in any of the four dough recipes on page 146. This will create an even lighter dough.

### KNEADING

To knead by hand, place the prepared dough ball on a lightly floured surface and, with floured hands, press down on the dough with the heel of your hand and push it away from you. Fold the pressed dough back over itself and repeat, turning the dough round a little

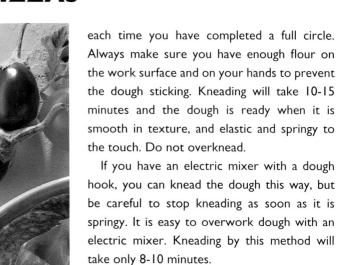

each time you have completed a full circle. Always make sure you have enough flour on the work surface and on your hands to prevent the dough sticking. Kneading will take 10-15 minutes and the dough is ready when it is smooth in texture, and elastic and springy to the touch. Do not overknead.

If you have an electric mixer with a dough hook, you can knead the dough this way, but be careful to stop kneading as soon as it is springy. It is easy to overwork dough with an electric mixer. Kneading by this method will take only 8-10 minutes.

### STORING DOUGH

Pizza dough may be stored in the refrigerator for up to 2 days, sealed in a lightly oiled polythene bag and then used as suggested in the recipes. Alternatively, the dough can be frozen for up to 3 months if wrapped in cling film or in polythene bags and sealed in an airtight box. Thaw the dough for a few hours at room temperature before using.

### PREPARING THIN-CRUST BASES

To shape a thin-crust pizza base by rolling, place a ball of dough on a lightly floured surface and roll it out with a floured rolling pin to produce a flat disk. Continue rolling the dough to produce a thin circle about 5 mm ($\frac{1}{4}$ inch) thick. Place the circle on a baking sheet dusted with cornmeal and continue as described in the recipe. Cornmeal on the baking sheets

**RIGHT:** Choose the freshest ingredients possible from supermarkets and speciality shops for your pizza creations.

produces a crisp base. If you like thin bases, but prefer them to be not too crispy, roll the dough out to about 1.5 cm (½ inch) thick.

Thin-crust bases can also be made by stretching the dough. Place the ball of dough on a lightly floured surface and shape it into a flat disk with floured hands. Then press out from the centre of the dough to produce a circle. Once it has nearly reached its desired thickness, place one hand on the centre of the dough circle and gently stretch it with the other hand to form the finished circle.

## PREPARING DEEP-PAN BASES

Deep-pan pizza cases generally have a rim to contain the filling. To shape the bases, place a ball of dough on a lightly floured surface and roll it out until it is about 1.5-2 cm (½-¾ inch) thick. Roll out so the dough is about 2.5 cm (1 inch) larger all round than the base of the pizza pan. Place the circle of dough in the pan and pull the edges of the dough up around the sides of the pan to create the rim. Smooth out the base with the heel of your hand. Then allow the dough base to rise as described in the individual recipes before continuing. If you prefer a thinner crusted deep-pan pizza, do not allow the prepared base to rise but fill and cook the pizzas as quickly as possible.

## PIZZA SAUCES

Although a tomato-based sauce is the most popular, many other recipes can be used. All sauces, however, need to be fairly thick so they will stay on the base. Sauces can be made in advance and stored in the refrigerator for 4-5 days. The fresh pestos on page 152 will keep for up to 2 weeks in the refrigerator provided they are covered with a layer of oil.

## CHEESE TOPPING

Cheese is very popular on pizzas, but is not essential to produce a wonderful-tasting pizza. If you dislike cheese or are calorie-counting, leave cheese out of the recipe and use more sauce or other toppings.

A good melting cheese is essential for pizza, and cheese should be grated, crumbled or thinly sliced so it melts and spreads evenly. Mozzarella is a classic pizza cheese, and you can also buy hard mozzarella which is easy to grate. Soft cheese make good base cheeses for sauce-less pizzas as they spread easily.

## EQUIPMENT

Good pizzas can be made at home with very simple equipment. Apart from mixing bowls and rolling pins, the only essential equipment are baking sheets and tins.

In this section, all the thin-crust pizzas, calzoni and sfinicioni have been made using heavy baking sheets dusted with cornmeal. If you are a frequent pizza maker, a baking stone would be a useful piece of equipment to own. The stone needs to be thoroughly heated in the oven before the uncooked pizza is placed directly on it and baked. Pizza peels are long-handled paddle-like utensils which are useful for transporting pizzas to the baking stone.

Deep-pan pizzas should be made in pizza pans. A heavy pizza pan made from black steel is an advantage as it will hold heat and withstand high oven temperatures without warping. However, a good-quality, oiled baking pan will also produce successful results.

**RIGHT:** Wonderfully tasty pizzas can be made easily without any special equipment.

# PIZZA BASES & SAUCES

*Homemade dough bases are actually very easy to prepare and will enable you to use unusual bases that cannot be bought. Sauces also play a vital part in good pizzas. Choose from one of the three tomato-based sauces or try Roasted Pepper Sauce for a rich, Mediterranean flavour. Corn Sauce is excellent with chicken and seafood.*

## BASIC PIZZA DOUGH

350 g (12 oz) strong white flour
5 ml (1 tsp) salt
6 g (2¼ tsp) easy-blend dried yeast
15 ml (1 tbsp) olive oil
240 ml (8 fl oz) lukewarm water

Sift the flour, salt and yeast into a large mixing bowl. Make a well in the centre and pour in the oil and water. Stir thoroughly, gradually drawing in all the flour to form a soft dough.

Knead the dough by hand, on a well-floured surface, for 12-15 minutes until it is smooth, elastic and shiny.

Place the kneaded dough in an oiled bowl, turning the dough ball around until it is completely covered in oil. Cover the bowl with cling film and leave to rise in a warm place for 1½-2 hours until it has doubled in size.

Turn the dough on to a floured surface, knock it back and knead again briefly for about 30 seconds. Roll out and use as required.

*Variation: Add 30 ml (2 tbsp) freshly chopped herbs of your choice to the flour, salt and yeast at the beginning of the recipe.*

**CLOCKWISE:** Cornmeal Pizza Dough, Herby Basic Pizza Dough, Wholemeal Pizza Dough

## CORNMEAL PIZZA DOUGH

250 g (8 oz) strong white flour
5 ml (1 tsp) salt
6 g (2¼ tsp) easy-blend dried yeast
100 g (4 oz) coarse cornmeal
15 ml (1 tbsp) olive oil
240 ml (8 fl oz) lukewarm water

Sift the flour, salt and yeast into a large mixing bowl, then stir in the cornmeal. To finish, follow the Basic Pizza Dough recipe.

## WHOLEMEAL PIZZA DOUGH

150 g (5 oz) strong white flour
200 g (7 oz) strong wholemeal flour
5 ml (1 tsp) salt
6 g (2¼ tsp) easy-blend dried yeast
15 ml (1 tbsp) vegetable oil
240 ml (8 fl oz) lukewarm water

Sift the two flours, salt and yeast into a large bowl. To finish, follow the Basic Pizza Dough recipe.

## RICH PIZZA DOUGH

225 g (8 oz) strong white flour
5 ml (1 tsp) salt
6 g (2¼ tsp) easy-blend dried yeast
75 ml (5 tbsp) lukewarm milk
40 g (1½ oz) unsalted butter, melted
1 egg, beaten

Sift the flour, salt and yeast into a large bowl. Make a well and pour in the milk, butter and egg. To finish, follow the Basic Pizza Dough recipe.

## BASIC TOMATO SAUCE

2 x 400-g (14-oz) cans chopped tomatoes
45 ml (3 tbsp) olive oil
2 cloves garlic, crushed
2.5 ml (½ tsp) caster sugar
Grated zest of ½ lemon
Salt and ground black pepper
30 ml (2 tbsp) chopped fresh parsley

Place the chopped tomatoes, olive oil, garlic, sugar, lemon zest and seasoning in a saucepan. Bring to a boil, then reduce the heat and simmer, uncovered, for 40-50 minutes until the sauce is thick and pulpy. Stir in the chopped parsley and taste; adjust seasoning if necessary.

Allow the sauce to cool. If you prefer a smoother sauce, purée the cooled mixture in a food processor. Store the sauce in the refrigerator and use as required. It will keep fresh for 3-4 days.

MAKES ABOUT 600 ML (1 PINT)

## FRESH TOMATO & HERB SAUCE

900 g (2 lb) ripe plum tomatoes
1 medium onion
30 ml (2 tbsp) chopped celery leaves
15 ml (1 tbsp) soft brown sugar
Salt and ground black pepper
150 ml (¼ pint) red wine
30 ml (2 tbsp) chopped fresh herbs of your choice, such as oregano, parsley or basil

Chop the tomatoes roughly and place them in a heavy-based saucepan. Chop the onion finely and add this to the pan, along with the celery leaves, sugar, seasoning and red wine. Cover and simmer the tomato mixture for 15 minutes. Uncover the pan, stir the tomato mixture and simmer for a further 40 minutes. Allow the mixture to cool, then purée it in a blender until the sauce is thick and smooth. Stir in the fresh herbs and taste; adjust seasoning if necessary.

Store the sauce in the refrigerator and use as required to top pizza bases, or to serve with calzone. It will keep fresh for 4-5 days. Alternatively, freeze the sauce in small quantities and defrost when needed.

MAKES ABOUT 850 ML (1½ PINTS)

**TOP:** Basic Tomato Sauce
**BOTTOM:** Fresh Tomato & Herb Sauce

## TOMATO & CHILLI SAUCE

900 g (2 lb) ripe tomatoes
3 cloves garlic, unpeeled
45 ml (3 tbsp) olive oil
3-4 fresh red chillies, seeded and finely chopped
2 shallots, finely chopped
5 ml (1 tsp) caster sugar
Salt and ground black pepper

Preheat the grill to hot. Grill the tomatoes for 12 minutes, turning occasionally, until they soften and the skins begin to become charred. Remove and allow to cool. Grill the garlic cloves for 10 minutes until they are browned and softened. Remove and allow to cool, then peel off skins and mash garlic. Do not peel the tomatoes, just chop them roughly.

Heat the oil in a saucepan and add the chillies and shallots. Cook for 5 minutes, then stir in the tomatoes, garlic, sugar and seasoning. Simmer, uncovered, for 15 minutes until the sauce is thick. Allow the sauce to cool, then purée it in a blender until smooth. Taste and adjust seasoning if necessary.

Store the sauce in the refrigerator and use as required to top pizza bases, or to serve with calzone. It will keep fresh for 4-5 days. Alternatively, freeze the sauce in small quantities and defrost when needed.

MAKES ABOUT 850 ML (1½ PINTS)

## ROASTED PEPPER SAUCE

3 red peppers
3 orange peppers
45 ml (3 tbsp) olive oil
4 shallots, chopped
2 cloves garlic, crushed
300 ml (½ pint) vegetable stock
15 ml (1 tbsp) red wine vinegar
5 ml (1 tsp) caster sugar
Salt and ground black pepper

Halve the peppers lengthways and remove the cores and seeds. Place them skin-side up on a baking tray and cook under a preheated hot grill for 10-12 minutes until the skins begin to blacken and blister. Allow the grilled peppers to cool, then skin them and chop coarsely.

Heat the oil in a pan and sauté the shallots and garlic for 4-5 minutes until softened. Add the skinned, chopped peppers, the stock, vinegar, sugar and seasoning, and cook the mixture, uncovered, for 10-15 minutes until the liquid has reduced slightly.

Allow the mixture to cool and then purée it to produce a smooth, thick sauce. Taste and adjust seasoning if necessary. Store the sauce in the refrigerator and use as required. It will keep fresh for 4-5 days.

MAKES ABOUT 700 ML (1¼ PINTS)

**TOP:** Roasted Pepper Sauce
**BOTTOM:** Tomato & Chilli Sauce

## CORN SAUCE

50 g (2 oz) butter
I onion, chopped
3 cloves garlic, crushed
510-g (1-lb 2-oz) can sweetcorn kernels, drained
300 ml (½ pint) vegetable stock
150 ml (¼ pint) double cream
Salt and ground black pepper
30 ml (2 tbsp) lemon juice
5 ml (1 tsp) caster sugar
30 ml (2 tbsp) chopped fresh parsley

Melt the butter in a pan and sauté the onion and garlic for 5 minutes until soft. Reserve 60 ml (4 tbsp) of the sweetcorn and add the rest to the onion mixture. Stir in the stock and cook the mixture over a high heat for 10 minutes until liquid has reduced slightly. Add the cream and seasoning, and boil the sauce for 10-15 minutes to reduce it further. Once reduced, stir in the lemon juice and sugar.

Allow the sauce to cool, then purée it in a food processor until smooth. Stir in the parsley and reserved sweetcorn; taste and adjust seasoning if necessary.

Store the sauce in the refrigerator and use as required. It will keep well for 4-5 days.

MAKES ABOUT 600 ML (I PINT)

## FRESH PARSLEY PESTO

75 g (3 oz) chopped fresh parsley
2 cloves garlic, crushed
40 g (1½ oz) pine nuts, toasted
40 g (1½ oz) flaked almonds, toasted
65 g (2½ oz) freshly grated Parmesan cheese
Salt and ground black pepper
150 ml (¼ pint) extra virgin olive oil

Place all the ingredients except the olive oil in a food processor and process until well combined and paste-like. Drizzle 120 ml (4 fl oz) of the olive oil into the paste in a thin stream until it is well combined; a smooth, thick pesto sauce should be produced.

Spoon the pesto into a bowl and pour over the remaining olive oil, then cover and store in the refrigerator. The pesto will keep well for up to 2 weeks. Use as required.        MAKES ABOUT 350 G (12 OZ)

## FRESH BASIL PESTO

100 g (4 oz) fresh basil leaves, chopped
3 cloves garlic, crushed
75 g (3 oz) pine nuts, toasted
65 g (2½ oz) freshly grated Parmesan cheese
Salt and ground black pepper
120 ml (4 fl oz) extra virgin olive oil

Prepare basil pesto following the method for Parsley Pesto above. Use 90 ml (6 tbsp) of the olive oil to make the pesto and the remaining 30 ml (2 tbsp) of oil to cover the pesto. Use as required.

MAKES ABOUT 400 G (14 OZ)

**COUNTER CLOCKWISE:** Fresh Basil Pesto,
Fresh Parsley Pesto, Corn Sauce

# THIN-CRUST PIZZAS

This chapter includes thin, crispy pizzas to suit every taste. Most of the recipes make two large pizzas which would serve two people as a main meal or four as a snack. Sun-dried Tomato Pizza and Pesto, Tomato & Garlic Pizza makes four smaller pizzas suitable for light lunches.

## SUN-DRIED TOMATO PIZZA

Basic Pizza dough (see page 146)
Cornmeal for dusting
60 ml (4 tbsp) olive oil
350 g (12 oz) Fresh Tomato & Herb Sauce
(see page 148)
225 g (8 oz) mozzarella cheese
12 halves of sun-dried tomato in oil
16 green olives
20 ml (4 tsp) chopped fresh oregano

Prepare the dough. When it is ready to use, divide it into four equal portions. Roll out or stretch pizza dough as described on page 142. Make four 20-cm (8-inch) thin-crust pizza bases. Place the bases on baking sheets lightly dusted with cornmeal and brush them all over with 30 ml (2 tbsp) of the olive oil.

Spread 90 ml (6 tsp) of the sauce over each pizza base, leaving a 1.5-cm (½-inch) border. Slice the mozzarella and divide between the pizzas. Cut the sun-dried tomatoes into thick slices and scatter over the pizzas along with the green olives. Drizzle over the remaining oil.

Bake the pizzas, in batches, in a preheated oven at 240°C (475°F, Gas mark 9) for 12-15 minutes, until the crusts are golden. Remove, sprinkle with oregano and serve at once.

MAKES FOUR 20-CM (8-INCH) PIZZAS

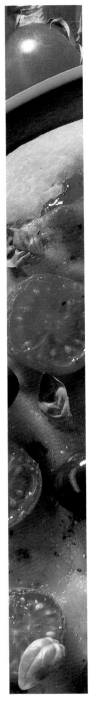

## PIZZA MARGHERITA

Basic Pizza Dough (see page 146)
Cornmeal for dusting
60 ml (4 tbsp) olive oil
180 ml (6 fl oz) Basic Tomato Sauce (see page 148)
100 g (4 oz) hard mozzarella cheese, grated
16 cherry tomatoes, halved
16 small black olives
Salt and ground black pepper
Several fresh basil leaves

Prepare the dough. When it is ready to use, divide it into two equal portions. Roll out or stretch pizza dough as described on page 142. Make two 25-cm (10-inch) thin-crust pizza bases. Place the bases on baking sheets lightly dusted with cornmeal. Prick the centres of each base several times with a fork and brush them all over with half the olive oil.

Spread half the tomato sauce over each base to within 1.5 cm (½ inch) of the edges. Scatter the cheese over each pizza.

Divide the halved tomatoes and the black olives between the two pizzas. Season with salty and ground black pepper, and drizzle the remaining olive oil over each pizza.

Bake the pizzas in a preheated oven at 240°C (475°F, Gas mark 9) for 12-15 minutes, until the crusts are golden and the cheese has melted. Remove from the oven, scatter some fresh basil over each pizza, and serve at once.

MAKES TWO 25-CM (10-INCH) PIZZAS

**RIGHT:** Pizza Margherita

## PIZZA TRE PEPPERONI

Rich Pizza Dough (see page 146)
1 red pepper
1 orange pepper
1 yellow pepper
Cornmeal for dusting
60 ml (4 tbsp) olive oil
2 cloves garlic, crushed
180 ml (6 fl oz) Tomato & Chilli Sauce
(see page 150)
Salt and ground black pepper
10 ml (2 tsp) chopped fresh parsley

Prepare the dough. While waiting for the dough to prove, prepare the grilled peppers. Halve the peppers and remove the core and seeds. Place them, cut-side down, on a baking sheet and grill for about 10 minutes until the skins begin to blacken. Place the peppers in a plastic bag and allow to cool. When cool, remove skins and slice peppers into thick strips.

When the dough is ready to use, divide it into two equal portions. Roll out or stretch the pizza dough as described on page 142. Make two 25-cm (10-inch) thin-crust pizza bases. Place bases on baking sheets lightly dusted with cornmeal, prick the centre of each base with the prongs of a fork, and brush with 45 ml (3 tbsp) of the olive oil mixed with the garlic.

Spread the sauce over the two bases, leaving a 1.5 cm (½-inch) border. Scatter the mixed grilled pepper strips over the pizza and season. Drizzle the remaining olive oil over the pizzas.

Bake the pizzas in a preheated oven at 240°C (475°F, Gas mark 9) for 10-12 minutes. Remove from the oven, scatter with parsley and serve at once.

MAKES TWO 25-CM (10-INCH) PIZZAS

## ROASTED GARLIC & AUBERGINE PIZZA

Basic Pizza Dough (see page 146)
100 g (4 oz) aubergine, sliced into 10 circles
4 cloves garlic, peeled and thickly sliced
Olive oil for brushing
Cornmeal for dusting
75 g (3 oz) soft, creamy goat's cheese
30 ml (2 tbsp) sun-dried tomato paste
100 g (4 oz) goat's cheese with rind
Salt and ground black pepper
10 ml (2 tsp) torn flat-leaf parsley

Prepare the dough. While waiting for the dough to prove, place the aubergine and garlic slices on a baking sheet and brush with olive oil. Cook the garlic in a pre-heated oven at 200°C (400°F, Gas mark 6) for 4-5 minutes and the aubergines for 8-9 minutes. Allow them to cool.

When the dough is ready to use, divide it into two equal portions. Roll out or stretch the pizza dough as described on page 142. Make two 25-cm (10-inch) thin-crust pizza bases. Place bases on baking sheets lightly dusted with cornmeal and brush with olive oil.

Mix together the soft, creamy goat's cheese and the sun-dried tomato paste. Spread over the two bases, leaving a 1.5-cm (½-inch) border. Slice the goat's cheese with rind into eight thin circles and place four on each pizza. Divide the aubergine and garlic between the pizzas, season and drizzle with olive oil.

Bake the pizzas in a preheated oven at 240°C (475°F, Gas mark 9) for 12-15 minutes. Sprinkle with parsley and serve at once.

MAKES TWO 25-CM (10-INCH) PIZZAS

**LEFT:** Pizza Tre Pepperoni
**RIGHT:** Roasted Garlic & Aubergine Pizza

## PIZZA FRUTTI DI MARE

2 x 23-cm (9-inch) ready-made thin and crispy pizza
bases
Cornmeal for dusting
60 ml (4 tbsp) olive oil
45 ml (3 tbsp) chopped fresh mixed herbs, such as
parsley, chives and chervil
75 g (3 oz) curd cheese
30 ml (2 tbsp) milk
Salt and ground black pepper
100 g (4 oz) Emmental cheese, grated
350 g (12 oz) frozen fruits de mer (mixed seafood),
defrosted and well drained
45 ml (3 tbsp) grated Parmesan cheese
15 ml (1 tbsp) fresh chervil leaves

Place the pizza bases on baking sheets lightly dusted
with cornmeal. Mix together 45 ml (3 tbsp) of the olive
oil with the chopped mixed herbs and brush over the
pizza bases.

Mix together the curd cheese, milk and seasoning,
and spread this mixture over the two bases, leaving a
1.5-cm (½-inch) border around the edges. Scatter over
the grated Emmental and divide the seafood between
the pizzas. Sprinkle over the Parmesan cheese, grind
some salt and pepper on top and drizzle the remaining
olive oil over the pizzas.

Bake the pizzas in a preheated oven at 220°C
(425°F, Gas mark 7) for 12-14 minutes, until the crusts
are crisp and golden and the cheese has melted.
Remove from the oven, scatter with chervil and serve
immediately.

MAKES TWO 23-CM (9-INCH) PIZZAS

## ANCHOVY, BROCCOLI & PINE NUT PIZZA

Wholemeal Pizza Dough (see page 146)
450 g (1 lb) small broccoli florets
50-g (2-oz) can anchovy fillets, drained
150 ml (¼ pint) extra virgin olive oil
Ground black pepper
Cornmeal for dusting
2 cloves garlic, crushed
50 g (2 oz) Parmesan cheese, grated
30 ml (2 tbsp) pine nuts

Prepare the dough. While waiting for the dough to
prove, cook the broccoli florets in boiling, salted water
for 3 minutes. Drain and reserve a quarter of the
florets.

Reserve four anchovy fillets and chop the rest
finely. Heat 75 ml (5 tbsp) of the olive oil in a pan and
cook the chopped anchovies over a medium heat for
4-5 minutes, mashing them with the back of a spoon.
Add the broccoli and cook, stirring, for 2 minutes.
Season and set aside.

When the dough is ready for use, divide it into two.
Roll out the pizza dough as described on page 142.
Make two 28-cm (11-inch) thin-crust bases. Place
bases on baking sheets lightly dusted with cornmeal.
Mix 60 ml (4 tbsp) of the olive oil with the garlic and
brush over the pizzas. Divide the broccoli topping
between the two pizzas, leaving a 1.5-cm (½-inch)
border. Cut the reserved anchovies into slivers and
scatter over the pizzas, with the Parmesan and the
remaining olive oil.

Bake in the preheated oven at 240°C (475°F, Gas
mark 9) for 7 minutes. Remove and scatter over the
reserved broccoli and the pine nuts. Return to the
oven for 6-7 minutes and serve.

MAKES TWO 28-CM (11-INCH) PIZZAS

**RIGHT:** Pizza Frutti Di Mare

## BLUE CHEESE, BACON & MUSHROOM PIZZA

Rich Pizza Dough (see page 146)
Cornmeal for dusting
30 ml (2 tbsp) olive oil
175 g (6 oz) curd cheese
30 ml (2 tbsp) milk
20 ml (4 tsp) snipped fresh chives
Salt and ground black pepper
175 g (6 oz) Dolcelatte cheese
4 rashers streaky bacon, cooked
50 g (2 oz) brown cap mushrooms

Prepare the dough. When it is ready for use, divide it into two equal portions. Roll out or stretch the pizza dough as described on page 142. Make two 28-cm (11-inch) thin-crust pizza bases. Place the bases on baking sheets lightly dusted with cornmeal, prick the centre of each base several times with a fork and brush them all over with 15 ml (1 tbsp) of the olive oil.

Mix the curd cheese with the milk, chives and seasoning. Spread over the bases, leaving a 15-cm (½ inch) border. Slice the Dolcelatte cheese thinly and arrange it in a spoke-like pattern over each pizza. Cut the bacon into 2.5-cm (1-inch) pieces and scatter these evenly over the pizzas. Slice the mushrooms and divide these between the pizzas. Grind over some black pepper and drizzle the pizzas with the remaining olive oil.

Bake the pizzas in a preheated oven at 240°C (475°F, Gas mark 9) for 12-13 minutes, until the crusts are golden and the cheese has melted. Serve at once.

MAKES TWO 28-CM (11-INCH) PIZZAS

## MIXED MUSHROOM PIZZA

Cornmeal Dough (see page 146)
Cornmeal for dusting
45 ml (3 tbsp) olive oil
2 cloves garlic, crushed
30 ml (2 tbsp) chopped fresh parsley
60 ml (4 tbsp) ricotta cheese
15 ml (1 tbsp) milk
Salt and ground black pepper
75 g (3 oz) butter
350 g (12 oz) mixed mushrooms, such as field, button, chestnut and girolles, sliced
10 ml (2 tsp) lemon juice
30 ml (2 tbsp) snipped fresh chives
45 ml (3 tbsp) grated pecorino cheese

Prepare the dough. When it is ready for use, divide it into two. Roll out the dough as described on page 142. Make two 25-cm (10-inch) thin-crust pizza bases. Place the bases on baking sheets lightly dusted with cornmeal. Mix together 30 ml (2 tbsp) of the oil with the garlic and parsley and brush over the bases.

Mix together the ricotta cheese and milk, season and spread the mixture over the bases, leaving a 5-cm (2-inch) border.

Melt the butter in a large frying pan, add the remaining oil and mushrooms. Sauté over a high heat for 2 minutes. Remove from heat, season well and stir in the lemon juice and chives. Spoon over the bases, leaving a 1.5-cm (½-inch) border. Sprinkle over the pecorino.

Bake in a preheated oven at 240°C (475°F, Gas mark 9) for 12-15 minutes, until the crusts are crisp and the mushrooms cooks. Serve immediately.

MAKES TWO 25-CM (10-INCH) PIZZAS

**TOP:** Blue Cheese, Bacon & Mushroom Pizza
**BOTTOM:** Mixed Mushroom Pizza

## SMOKED CHICKEN & PARSLEY PESTO PIZZA

Basic Pizza Dough, using herby variation with
chopped basil (see page 146)
Cornmeal for dusting
60 ml (4 tbsp) olive oil
120 ml (4 fl oz) Fresh Parsley Pesto (see page 152)
8 halves sun-dried tomatoes in oil
175 g (6 oz) skinned smoked chicken
30 ml (2 tbsp) grated Parmesan cheese
ground black pepper
10 ml (2 tsp) chopped fresh parsley

Prepare the dough. When it is ready for use, divide it
into two equal portions. Roll out or stretch the pizza
dough as described on page 142. Make two 25-cm (10-
inch) thin-crust pizza bases. Place the bases on baking
sheets lightly dusted with cornmeal. Brush all over
with 30 ml (2 tbsp) of the olive oil. Spread the Parsley
Pesto over the bases, leaving a 1.5-cm (½-inch) border
around the edges.

Bake the pizzas in a preheated oven at 240°C
(475°F, Gas mark 9) for 7 minutes and, while the pizzas
are cooking, cut the sun-dried tomatoes into thick
strips and slice the smoked chicken. Remove the pizzas
from the oven and scatter over the tomatoes and
chicken. Sprinkle with Parmesan and pepper. Drizzle
over the remaining olive oil.

Return the pizzas to the oven and bake for a further
7 minutes, until crisp and golden. Remove from the
oven, scatter over the parsley, and serve immediately.

MAKES TWO 25-CM (10-INCH) PIZZAS

## PESTO, TOMATO & GARLIC PIZZA

Cornmeal Pizza Dough (see page 146)
Cornmeal for dusting
80 ml (5 tbsp) extra virgin olive oil
60 ml (4 tbsp) Fresh Basil Pesto (see page 152)
4 plum tomatoes
2 large cloves garlic
Salt and ground black pepper
30 ml (2 tbsp) torn fresh basil leaves

Prepare the cornmeal dough. When it is ready for
use, divide it into four equal portions. Roll out or
stretch the pizza dough as described on page 142.
Make four 18-cm (7-inch) thin-crust pizza bases. Place
the bases on baking sheets lightly dusted with cornmeal and brush them all over with 30 ml (2 tbsp) of the
olive oil. Mix another 30 ml (2 tbsp) of oil with the
pesto sauce and spread this mixture over the four
bases leaving a 1.5-cm (½-inch) border.

Slice the tomatoes thickly. Peel the garlic and slice
the cloves into slivers. Divide the sliced tomatoes and
garlic between the four bases. Season with salt and
black pepper, and drizzle the remaining olive oil over
each pizza.

Bake the pizzas, in batches, in a preheated oven at
240°C (475°F, Gas mark 9) for 10-12 minutes, until
crisp and golden. Remove from the oven, scatter with
the basil leaves and serve at once.

MAKES FOUR 18-CM (7-INCH) PIZZAS

**RIGHT:** Smoked Chicken & Parsley Pesto Pizza

## SPRING VEGETABLE PIZZA

Cornmeal Pizza Dough (see page 146)
Cornmeal for dusting
45 ml (3 tbsp) olive oil
2 cloves garlic, crushed
300 g (10 oz) mozzarella cheese
75 g (3 oz) pecorino cheese
12 stalks asparagus
2 small courgettes
10 yellow cherry tomatoes
4 spring onions
30 ml (2 tbsp) pine nuts
Salt and ground black pepper

Prepare the dough. When dough is ready for use, divide it into two equal portions. Roll out or stretch the pizza dough as described on page 142. Make two 25-cm (10-inch) thin-crust pizza bases. Place the bases on baking sheets lightly dusted with cornmeal. Mix together 30 ml (2 tbsp) of the olive oil and the crushed garlic and brush over the pizza bases.

Slice the mozzarella cheese thinly and grate the pecorino cheese. Divide the two cheeses between the bases, leaving a 1.5-cm (½-inch) border around the edges. Trim and cut the asparagus into 5-cm (2-inch) lengths, blanch briefly and drain. Slice the courgettes, halve the cherry tomatoes and cut the spring onions into thick slices. Divide between the pizzas. Sprinkle over the pine nuts, season well and drizzle over the remaining olive oil.

Bake the pizzas in a preheated oven at 240°C (475°F, Gas mark 9) for 12-14 minutes until crisp and golden. Serve at once.

MAKES TWO 25-CM (10-INCH) PIZZAS

## PIZZA NICOISE

Wholemeal Pizza Dough (see page 146)
Cornmeal for dusting
45 ml (3 tbsp) extra virgin olive oil
225 g (8 oz) Fresh Tomato & Herb Sauce
(see page 148)
198-g (7-oz) can tuna in oil
½ onion, very thinly sliced
12 black olives
Salt and ground black pepper
100 g (4 oz) fine green beans
30 ml (2 tbsp) chopped fresh parsley

Prepare the dough. When it is ready for use, divide it into two equal portions. Roll out or stretch the pizza dough as described on page 142. Make two 28-cm (11-inch) thin-crust pizza bases. Place the bases on baking sheets lightly dusted with cornmeal and brush with half the olive oil.

Spread the Tomato & Herb Sauce over the bases, leaving a 1.5-cm (½-inch) border. Drain and flake the tuna. Divide it between the pizzas with the onion slices and black olives. Season well and drizzle over the remaining olive oil.

Bake the pizzas in a preheated oven at 240°C (475°F, Gas mark 9) for 12 minutes. While they are cooking, top and tail the beans and cut them into 2.5-cm (1-inch) lengths. Cook the beans in boiling salted water for 4 minutes, then drain.

Remove the pizzas, scatter over the beans and return to the oven for a further 3-4 minutes, until the crusts are crisp and golden. Remove from the oven, sprinkle with parsley and serve.

MAKES TWO 28-CM (11-INCH) PIZZAS

**LEFT:** Spring Vegetable Pizza
**RIGHT:** Pizza Niçoise

# PIZZA QUATTRO STAGIONI

Basic Pizza Dough (see page 146)
Cornmeal for dusting
45 ml (3 tbsp) olive oil
180 ml (6 fl oz) Basic Tomato Sauce
(see page 148)

### QUARTER I
30 ml (2 tbsp) grated Parmesan cheese
2 large slices mortadella
2 marinated artichokes in oil, halved

### QUARTER II
50 g (2 oz) butter
15 ml (1 tbsp) oil
2 cloves garlic, finely chopped
100 g (4 oz) mixed mushrooms, sliced
Salt and ground black pepper

### QUARTER III
100 g (4 oz) mozzarella cheese, chopped
2 small plum tomatoes, chopped
Salt and ground black pepper
8 large basil leaves, torn

### QUARTER IV
75 g (3 oz) cooked mussels (shelled weight)
2.5 ml (½ tsp) grated lemon zest
15 ml (1 tbsp) olive oil
15 ml (1 tbsp) chopped fresh oregano

Prepare the dough. When it is ready for use, divide it into two equal portions. Roll out or stretch the pizza dough as described on page 142. Make two 25-cm (10-inch) thin-crust pizza bases. Place the bases on baking sheets lightly dusted with cornmeal and brush with 30 ml (2 tbsp) of the olive oil. Spread the Basic Tomato Sauce over the bases, leaving a 1.5-cm (½-inch) border around the edges.

Mark the four quarters on each pizza. For Quarter I on each pizza, sprinkle the Parmesan over the tomato sauce, slice the mortadella and place this over the cheese and top with two halves of artichoke. For Quarter II, heat the butter and oil in a pan and sauté the garlic and mushrooms for a couple of minutes. Season well and divide this mixture between the second quarters on each pizza. For Quarter III, mix together the ingredients and divide them between the third quarters on each pizza. For Quarter IV, combine the ingredients and divide them between the remaining quarters. Grind some black pepper over the two completed pizzas and drizzle with the remaining olive oil.

Bake the pizzas in a preheated oven at 240°C (475°F, Gas mark 9) for 12-15 minutes until the crusts are crisp and golden and the topping cooked. Serve immediately.

MAKES TWO 25-CM (10-INCH) PIZZAS

**RIGHT:** Pizza Quattro Stagioni

## PISSALADIERE PIZZA

Basic Pizza Dough (see page 146)
90 ml (6 tbsp) olive oil
3 large red onions, very thinly sliced
Salt and ground black pepper
10 ml (2 tsp) caster sugar
15 ml (1 tbsp) chopped fresh oregano
Cornmeal for dusting
2 cloves garlic, crushed
120 ml (4 fl oz) Fresh Tomato & Herb Sauce
(see page 148)
10 anchovy fillets
16 black olives

Prepare the dough. Prepare the onion topping while dough is proving. Heat 45 ml (3 tbsp) of the oil in a heavy-based pan and cook the onions very slowly over a gentle heat for 15-20 minutes until they are soft but not browned. Season and stir in the sugar and oregano. Set aside to cool.

Roll out or stretch pizza dough as described on page 142. Make two 25-cm (10-inch) thin-crust pizza bases. Place the bases on baking sheets lightly dusted with cornmeal. Mix together 30 ml (2 tbsp) of the olive oil and the crushed garlic and brush over the bases.

Divide the tomato sauce between the bases, leaving a 1.5-cm (½-inch) border around the edges. Divide the onions between the pizzas. Rinse the anchovy fillets and dry them on paper towels. Slice them in half lengthways. Use the anchovies to make a lattice pattern over the onion mixture. Stud with the black olives and drizzle the remaining oil over.

Bake the pizzas in a preheated oven at 240°C (475°F, Gas mark 9) for 12-14 minutes until crisp and golden. Serve at once.

MAKES TWO 25-CM (10-INCH) PIZZAS

## PUTTANESCA PIZZA

Cornmeal Pizza Dough or Wholemeal Pizza Dough
(see page 146)
Cornmeal for dusting
45 ml (3 tbsp) olive oil
225 g (8 oz) Tomato & Chilli Sauce
(see page 150)
2 plum tomatoes
1 large red chilli
12 black olives
15 ml (1 tbsp) capers in brine, drained
6 anchovies
30 ml (2 tbsp) chopped fresh parsley
Ground black pepper

Prepare the dough. When it is ready for use, divide it into two. Roll or stretch the pizza dough as described on page 142. Make two 28-cm (11-inch) thin-crust pizza bases. Place the bases on baking sheets lightly dusted with cornmeal and brush with olive oil.

Spread the Tomato & Chilli Sauce over the bases, leaving a 1.5-cm (½-inch) border around the edges. Slice the tomatoes thickly and add them to the pizzas. Slice the chilli and scatter the slices over the pizzas, along with the olives and capers. Rinse the anchovies and dry them on paper towels; cut each in half lengthways. Place three crosses of anchovy on each pizza. Drizzle over the remaining olive oil. Bake the pizzas in a preheated oven at 240°C (475°F, Gas mark 9) for 14-15 minutes, until the crusts are crisp and golden. Remove from the oven and sprinkle with parsley and ground black pepper. Serve immediately.

MAKES TWO 28-CM (11-INCH) PIZZAS

**TOP:** Pissaladière Pizza
**BOTTOM:** Puttanesca Pizza

## PIZZA SALUMERIA

Rich Pizza Dough (see page 146)

Cornmeal for dusting

45 ml (3 tbsp) olive oil

10 ml (2 tsp) chopped fresh thyme

100 g (4 oz) hard mozzarella cheese, grated

25 g (1 oz) Parmesan cheese, freshly grated

8 slices Milano salami

8 slices hot Italian salami

4 slices prosciutto (Parma) ham

4 slices bresaola

Ground black pepper

A few small thyme sprigs, to garnish

Prepare the dough. When it is ready for use, divide it into two. Cut off a small piece of dough from each portion and set aside. Roll out the dough as described on page 142. Make two 23-cm (9-inch) thin-crust pizza bases. Place on baking sheets lightly dusted with cornmeal and prick each base several times with a fork. Mix together 30 ml (2 tbsp) of the oil and the 10 ml thyme and brush over the bases.

Cut each piece of reserved dough into two and, with floured hands, shape each piece into a 'dough rope' that is long enough to stretch across the diameter of the pizza. Place two ropes at right angles across each pizza.

Mix together the two cheeses. Top all the pizza quarters with the cheese mixture, taking care to keep the dough ropes exposed. Spread cheese to 1.5 cm (½ inch) of the edges. Divide the cured meats between the quarters, drizzles over the remaining olive oil and add pepper.

Bake the pizzas in a preheated oven at 240°C (475°F, Gas mark 9) for 12 minutes, until the crusts are crisp and golden. Remove, garnish with the thyme sprigs and serve at once.

MAKES TWO 23-CM (9-INCH) PIZZAS

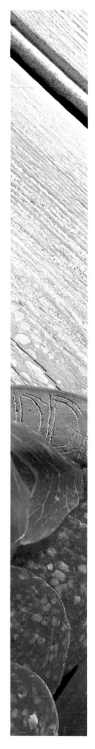

## SICILIAN HOT PIZZA

Rich Pizza Dough (see page 146)

Cornmeal for dusting

45 ml (3 tbsp) olive oil

180 ml (6 fl oz) Tomato & Chilli Sauce (see page 150)

1 green pepper

1 green chilli

½ onion

10 black olives

Ground black pepper

Prepare the dough. When it is ready for use, divide it into two equal portions. Roll out or stretch the pizza dough as described on page 142. Make two 25-cm (10-inch) thin-crust pizza bases. Place on baking sheets lightly dusted with cornmeal, prick each base several times with a fork. And brush them with 30 ml (2 tbsp) of the olive oil.

Spread the Tomato & Chilli Sauce over the bases, leaving a 1.5-cm (½-inch) border. Arrange four slices of salami on each pizza. Slice the pepper into ten thin slices, remove the core and seeds and divide the slices between the pizzas. Slice the chilli and onion, and scatter over the pizza bases. Top each pizza with five olives and drizzle over the remaining olive oil. Grind pepper over the top.

Bake the pizzas in a preheated oven at 240°C (475°F, Gas mark 9) for 13-15 minutes, until crusts are crisp and golden. Remove from the oven serve at once.

MAKES TWO 25-CM (10-INCH) PIZZAS

**RIGHT:** Pizza Salumeria

# DEEP-PAN PIZZAS

*Deep-pan pizzas have thick bases and sides that form a shallow casing. They hold more topping than thin-crust pizzas, which makes them robust and satisfying. Deep-pan pizzas are either served whole as a main meal for those with good appetites or cut into wedges or slices. Spicy Chorizo & Chick-pea Pizza and Chinese Chicken Pizza are made as square pizzas, but can be cooked in the traditional round shape if preferred. Pizza Pasticcio uses pasta in a pizza case to create an unusual combination, while Chicago-style Stuffed Pizza Pie is based on the classic stuffed pizza developed by Italian immigrants to Chicago and combines salami, broccoli and two cheeses in a cornmeal crust.*

## CHICAGO-STYLE STUFFED PIZZA PIE

Cornmeal Pizza Dough (see page 146) made with 15 ml (1 tbsp) easy-blend yeast as suggested on page 142)
Olive oil for brushing
Fresh Tomato & Herb Sauce (see page 148), to serve

### STUFFING
175 g (6 oz) small broccoli florets
100 g (4 oz) salami, diced into small cubes
100 g (4 oz) fontina cheese, diced
40 g (1½ oz) Parmesan cheese, grated
Salt and ground black pepper
90 ml (6 tbsp) Fresh Tomato & Herb Sauce (see page 148)

Prepare the dough. When it is ready for use, divide it into one-third and two-third portions. Roll out and pull the two-thirds portion of dough to form a 33-cm (13-inch) circle. Oil a 28-cm (11-inch) deep-pan pizza tin and press the prepared dough circle into the tin. Trim the top edge of the dough evenly. Prick the base of the dough several times with the prongs of a fork.

Prepare the stuffing. Blanch the broccoli in boiling, salted water for 3 minutes. Drain and refresh it, and place in a bowl. Add the salami, fontina cheese, 25 g (1 oz) of the Parmesan and season the mixture. Mix gently. Spread the tomato sauce over the pizza base. Top with the broccoli and cheese filling and press down gently to produce an even layer.

Roll out the one-third portion of dough to make a 28-cm (11-inch) circle. Place this dough circle over the stuffed pizza and press down gently on to the filling. Seal the two edges of dough together and crimp the edges. Cut a small cross on top of the pizza lid to allow steam to escape. Brush the lid of the pizza with some olive oil.

Bake the pizza pie in the bottom of a preheated oven at 240°C (475°F, Gas mark 9) for 10 minutes. Remove the pie from the oven and sprinkle the remaining Parmesan cheese over the top. Return the pie to the top part of the oven and bake for a further 20 minutes, until the crust is golden. Serve the pizza pie, but into thick slices, with extra sauce.

MAKES ONE 28-CM (11-INCH) PIZZA PIE

**RIGHT:** Chicago-style Stuffed Pizza Pie

## AMERICAN HOT PIZZA

2 x 23-cm (9-inch) ready-made deep-pan pizza bases
45 ml (3 tbsp) olive oil
Cornmeal for dusting
180 ml (6 fl oz) Roasted Pepper Sauce
(see page 150)
75 g (3 oz) hard mozzarella cheese, grated
2 x 100 g (4 oz) raw Italian sausages, skins removed
and crumbled
10 thick slices hot pepperoni salami
½ green pepper, cut into rings
½ yellow pepper, cut into rings
½ red onion, sliced
5-10 ml (1-2 tsp) dried chilli flakes
1 fresh green chilli, seeded and finely sliced
30 ml (2 tbsp) grated pecorino cheese

Brush the two pizza bases all over with half the oil and place them on baking sheets lightly dusted with cornmeal. Spread the pepper sauce over the two bases leaving a 1.5-cm (½-inch) border around the edges. Scatter the mozzarella cheese over the sauce, along with the crumbled Italian sausage. Arrange the slices of pepperoni, pepper rings, and onion slices over the bases. Sprinkle over the dried chilli flakes and top with the fresh green chilli and grated pecorino cheese. Drizzle the remaining olive oil over the pizzas.

Bake the pizzas in a preheated oven at 220°C (425°F, Gas mark 7) for 15-18 minutes, until the bases are crisp and the topping cooked. Remove from the oven and serve immediately.

MAKES TWO 23-CM (9-INCH) PIZZAS

## PIZZA PARMA

Basic Pizza Dough (see page 146)
60 ml (4 tbsp) olive oil
2 cloves garlic, crushed
270 ml (9 fl oz) Basic Tomato Sauce
(see page 148)
225 g (8 oz) mozzarella cheese
8 thin slices prosciutto (Parma ham)
10 small black olives
Ground black pepper

Prepare the dough. When it is ready for use, divide it into two equal portions and shape it to fit two 23-cm (9-inch) oiled deep-dish pizza pans as described on page 144. Cover the pans with cling film and allow the dough to rise in a warm place for 30 minutes. Prick the dough with a fork at 1.5-cm (½-inch) intervals and bake in a preheated oven at 240°C (475°F, Gas mark 9) for 10 minutes.

Remove the bases from the oven. Mix together 45 ml (3 tbsp) of the olive oil and the crushed garlic, and brush this lightly over the pizza crusts. Spread the tomato sauce over the bases. Slice the mozzarella cheese into eight thick slices and arrange these on top of the pizzas, along with the slices of prosciutto. Scatter over the black olives and top each pizza with freshly ground black pepper. Drizzle over the remaining olive oil.

Return the pizzas to the oven for a further 15 minutes, or until the crusts are golden and the topping cooked. Remove from the oven and serve at once.

MAKES TWO 23-CM (9-INCH) PIZZAS

**TOP:** Pizza Parma
**BOTTOM:** American Hot Pizza

## PIZZA FLORENTINE

Basic Pizza Dough (see page 146)
Cornmeal for dusting
45 ml (3 tbsp) olive oil
350 g (12 oz) young leaf spinach
225 g (8 oz) cream cheese
A little grated nutmeg
Salt and ground black pepper
4 small shallots, chopped
3 cloves garlic, crushed
2 large plum tomatoes, sliced
2 eggs

Prepare the dough. When it is ready for use, divide it into two equal portions and shape it to fit two 23-cm (9-inch) oiled deep-dish pizza pans as described on page 144. Cover the pans with cling film and allow the dough to rise in a warm place for 30 minutes. Prick the dough with a fork at 1.5-cm (½-inch) intervals and bake in a preheated oven at 240°C (475°F, Gas mark 9) for 5 minutes.

Remove and brush the crusts with 15 ml (1 tbsp) of the olive oil. Steam the spinach lightly and reserve 100 g (4 oz). Process the rest of the spinach in a food processor with the cream cheese, nutmeg and seasoning. Transfer to a bowl.

Heat 30 ml (2 tbsp) of the oil in a saucepan and sauté the shallots and garlic for 5 minutes until soft; stir into the spinach mixture. Divide the mixture between the bases and arrange the reserved spinach on the top. Arrange the tomato around the edge of each pizza.

Return to the oven for a further 16 minutes, then remove and crack an egg on to the centre of each pizza. Return to the oven for a further 7-8 minutes, until the eggs are just set. Remove the pizzas and serve immediately.

MAKES TWO 23-CM (9-INCH) PIZZAS

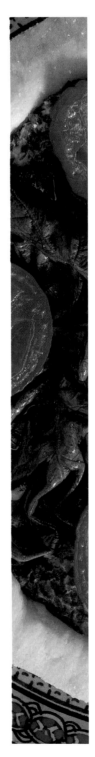

## PIZZA NAPOLETANA

2 x 23-cm (9-inch) ready-made deep-pan pizza bases
30 ml (2 tbsp) olive oil
Cornmeal for dusting
180 ml (6 fl oz) Basic Tomato Sauce
(see page 148)
2 small courgettes
1 small red onion
8 anchovies
20 ml (4 tsp) capers in brine, drained
10 calamata olives
15 ml (1 tbsp) fresh thyme leaves
Ground black pepper

Brush the pizza bases all over with half the oil. Place them on baking sheets lightly dusted with cornmeal and spread them with the tomato sauce, leaving a 1.5-cm (½-inch) border around the edges.

Slice the courgettes thinly, and peel and slice the onion. Divide the courgettes and onion rings between the pizzas. Rinse the anchovy fillets and dry them on paper towels. Halve the anchovies lengthways, quarter them and scatter over the pizza bases, along with the capers, olives and thyme. Top each pizza with ground black pepper and drizzle over the remaining olive oil.

Bake the pizzas in a preheated oven at 220°C (425°F, Gas mark 7) for 16-18 minutes, until the bases are crisp and the topping cooked. Remove from the oven and serve immediately.

MAKES TWO 23-CM (9-INCH) PIZZAS

**RIGHT:** Pizza Florentine

## CHINESE CHICKEN PIZZA

Basic Pizza Dough (see page 146)
60 ml (4 tbsp) groundnut oil
5 ml (1 tsp) sesame oil
350 g (12 oz) skinless, boneless chicken,
cut into chunks
2 cloves garlic, finely chopped
90 ml (6 tbsp) hoisin sauce
2 small red chillies, seeded and sliced
20 ml (4 tsp) sesame seeds
10 ml (2 tsp) soy sauce
6 spring onions
1 small red pepper, seeded and cored and cut into
small diamond shapes

Prepare the dough. When it is ready for use, divide it into two equal portions and shape to fit two 23-cm (9-inch) oiled square deep-dish pizza pans as described on page 144. Cover with cling film and allow to rise in a warm place for 30 minutes. Prick the bases with a fork and bake in a preheated oven at 240°C (475°F, Gas mark 9) for 5 minutes.

Remove the bases from the oven. Mix together 30 ml (2 tbsp) of the groundnut oil and the sesame oil, and brush the pizza crusts lightly. Heat the remaining groundnut oil in a pan, add the chicken and garlic, and cook over a high heat for 1-2 minutes. Remove and stir in the hoisin sauce, red chillies, 10 ml (2 tsp) of the sesame seeds and the soy sauce. Slice the spring onions thinly on the diagonal, reserve 45 ml (3 tbsp) of the green tops, and stir the rest into the chicken mixture. Spoon over the pizza bases. Scatter over the pepper diamonds and sesame seeds.

Return the pizzas to the oven for a further 16-18 minutes. Remove, sprinkle with the reserved spring onion tops and serve at once.

MAKES TWO 23-CM (9-INCH) PIZZAS

## CHORIZO & CHICK-PEA PIZZA

Basic Pizza Dough (see page 146)
75 ml (5 tbsp) olive oil
1 onion, sliced
5 ml (1 tsp) ground cumin
200g cooked chick-peas
180 ml (6 fl oz) Tomato & Chilli Sauce
(see page 150)
50 g (2 oz) mature Gouda cheese, grated
50 g (2 oz) provolone cheese, grated
20-24 thick slices chorizo sausage
6 rings each red and green peppers
2 pickled jalapeño chillies, sliced

Prepare the dough. When it is ready for use, divide it into two and shape it to fit two 23-cm (9-inch) oiled square deep-dish pizza pans as described on page 144. Cover with cling film and allow to rise in a warm place for 30 minutes. Prick the bases with a fork and bake in a preheated oven at 240°C (475°F, Gas mark 9) for 5 minutes.

Remove and lightly brush 30 ml (2 tbsp) of the olive oil over the crusts. Heat 30 ml (2 tbsp) of the oil in a pan and sauté the onion for 2 minutes; stir in the cumin and chick-peas and cook for the further 2 minutes. Stir into the Tomato & Chilli Sauce. Divide the sauce between the bases. Mix together the two cheeses and sprinkle over the pizzas, along with the sliced chorizo. Drizzle over the remaining olive oil.

Return to the oven for a further 10 minutes. Remove and divide the pepper and chillies between them, bake for a further 10 minutes. Serve at once.

MAKES TWO 23-CM (9-INCH) PIZZAS

**LEFT:** Chinese Chicken Pizza
**RIGHT:** Chorizo & Chick-pea Pizza

## PIZZA PASTICCIO

Cornmeal Pizza Dough (see page 146)

90 ml (6 tbsp) olive oil

270 ml (9 fl oz) Fresh Tomato & Herb Sauce
(see page 148)

450 g (1 lb) young leaf spinach, steamed and squeezed
dry of excess moisture

1 large onion, chopped

2 cloves garlic, crushed

Salt and ground black pepper

30 ml (2 tbsp) chopped fresh parsley

50 g (2 oz) spaghetti, cooked 'al dente'

150 ml (¼ pint) soured cream

50 g (2 oz) hard mozzarella cheese, grated

100 g (4 oz) smoked chicken, in thin strips

30 ml (2 tbsp) grated Parmesan cheese

Prepare the dough. When it is ready for use, divide it into two equal portions and shape to fit two 23-cm (9-inch) oiled deep-dish pizza pans as described on page 144. Cover with cling film and allow to rise in a warm place for 30 minutes. Prick the bases with a fork and bake in a preheated oven at 240°C (475°F, Gas mark 9) for 5 minutes.

Remove and brush with 15 ml (1 tbsp) of the olive oil. Spread the sauce over the bases, then a layer of spinach. (Use half the spinach).

Heat 45 ml (3 tbsp) of the oil in a pan and cook the onion and garlic for 3 minutes; season well and stir in the parsley, spaghetti, soured cream and mozzarella. Fold in the reserved spinach. Spoon over the bases and drizzle over the remaining olive oil.

Return the pizzas to the oven and cook for 15 minutes. Remove and scatter the chicken and Parmesan over the top, pressing down lightly. Bake for a further 5 minutes and serve immediately.

MAKES TWO 23-CM (9-INCH) PIZZAS

## HAM, PINEAPPLE & CORN PIZZA

Basic Pizza Dough (see page 146)

Olive oil for brushing

225 g (8 oz) Corn Sauce (see page 152)

100 g (4 oz) mozzarella cheese, grated

40 g (1½ oz) Parmesan cheese, grated

60 ml (4 tbsp) snipped fresh chives

Salt and ground black pepper

6 slices honey-roast ham

4 slices fresh pineapple, cores removed

Prepare the dough. When it is ready for use, divide it into two equal portions and roll and shape it to fit two 23-cm (9-inch) oiled deep-dish pizza pans as described on page 144. Cover with cling film and allow the dough to rise in a warm place for 30 minutes. Prick the bases of the dough with a fork and bake in a preheated oven at 240°C (475°F, Gas mark 9) for 5 minutes.

Remove the bases from the oven and brush the crusts lightly with olive oil. Spread the Corn Sauce over the bases. Mix the mozzarella with most of the Parmesan (reserving 30 ml (2 tbsp) of the Parmesan for sprinkling) and the snipped chives. Season the mixture well and spoon over the Corn Sauce. Cut the ham into thick strips and the pineapple into chunks; divide between the pizzas. Top with pepper and the reserved Parmesan. Drizzle a little olive oil over the pizzas.

Return the pizzas to the oven and cook for 15-20 minutes until the crusts are golden and the topping cooked. Remove and serve at once.

MAKES TWO 23-CM (9-INCH) PIZZAS

**RIGHT:** Pizza Pasticcio

## PIZZA PESCATORE

Rich Pizza Dough (see page 146)

45 ml (3 tbsp) olive oil

30 ml (2 tbsp) chopped fresh parsley

360 ml (12 fl oz) Corn Sauce (see page 152)

175 g (6 oz) mixed seafood preserved in oil, such as
mussels, octopus and baby squid

150 g (5 oz) fresh or canned salmon

75 g (3 oz) Parmesan cheese, grated

Ground black pepper

30 ml (2 tbsp) snipped fresh chervil

Prepare the dough. When it is ready for use, divide it into two equal portions and roll and shape it to fit two 23-cm (9-inch) oiled deep-dish pizza pans as described on page 144. Cover with cling film and allow the dough to rise in a warm place for 30 minutes. Prick the bases of the dough with a fork at 1.5-cm (½-inch) intervals and bake in a preheated oven at 240°C (475°F, Gas mark 9) for 10 minutes.

Remove the bases from the oven. Mix together olive oil and parsley, and brush this mixture lightly over the pizza bases. Spread the Corn Sauce over the bases. Divide the mixed seafood between the two pizzas. Break the salmon into large flakes and divide between the pizzas. Sprinkle over the Parmesan and top with some ground black pepper.

Return the pizzas to the oven and bake for a further 12-15 minutes, until the seafood and sauce are warmed through and the salmon is cooked. Remove from the oven, sprinkle with the chervil and serve at once.           MAKES TWO 23-CM (9-INCH) PIZZAS

## GREEK-STYLE PIZZA

Basic Pizza Dough (see page 146)

60 ml (4 tbsp) olive oil

1 small onion, chopped

2 cloves garlic, crushed

225 g (8 oz) minced lamb

30 ml (2 tbsp) tomato purée

20 ml (4 tsp) chopped fresh parsley

Salt and ground black pepper

120 ml (4 fl oz) Basic Tomato Sauce
(see page 148)

12 thin slices aubergine

100 g (4 oz) feta cheese, crumbled

10 ml (2 tsp) chopped fresh oregano

Prepare the dough. When it is ready for use, divide into two and shape to fit two 23-cm (9-inch) oiled deep-dish pizza pans as described on page 144. Cover with cling film and allow the dough to rise in a warm place for 30 minutes.

Heat 15 ml (1 tbsp) of the oil in a pan and sauté the onion and garlic for 3-4 minutes. Add the lamb and cook for 5 minutes. Stir in the tomato purée, parsley and seasoning and cook for a further 10 minutes.

Prick the bases of the dough with a fork and bake in a preheated oven at 240°C (475°F, Gas mark 9) for 5 minutes. Remove and brush the crusts with 15 ml (1 tbsp) of the olive oil. Spread the sauce over the bases and divide the filling between the pizzas. Brush the aubergine with the remaining olive oil and season. Scatter over the feta cheese and aubergine.

Return the pizzas to the oven and cook for 15-20 minutes, until the crusts and feta are golden. Remove, sprinkle with oregano and serve at once.

MAKES TWO 23-CM (9-INCH) PIZZAS

**TOP:** Pizza Pescatore
**BOTTOM:** Greek-style Pizza

## CHILLI CON CARNE PIZZA

Cornmeal Pizza Dough (see page 146)
60 ml (4 tbsp) olive oil
1 onion, chopped
2 cloves garlic, crushed
5 ml (1 tsp) ground cumin
5 ml (1 tsp) chilli powder
225 g (8 oz) minced beef
400-g (14-oz) can chopped tomatoes
5 ml (1 tsp) dried oregano
15 ml (1 tbsp) black treacle
15 ml (1 tbsp) tomato purée
435-g (15-oz) can red kidney beans, drained
Salt and ground black pepper
75 g (3 oz) Cheddar cheese, grated
60 ml (4 tbsp) soured cream
20 ml (4 tsp) chopped coriander

Prepare the dough. When it is ready, divide it into two and shape to fit two 23-cm (9-inch) oiled deep-dish pizza pans as described on page 144. Cover with cling film and leave in a warm place for 30 minutes.

Heat 30 ml (2 tbsp) of the oil in a pan and sauté the onion and garlic for 2 minutes. Stir in the cumin and chilli powder, and cook for a further minute. Add the beef and cook, stirring, for 3-4 minutes. Stir in the tomatoes and oregano, and simmer for 30 minutes. Add the treacle, tomato purée, kidney beans and seasoning, and cook for 15 minutes.

Prick the bases of the dough with a fork and bake in a preheated oven at 240°C (475°F, Gas mark 9) for 10 minutes. Remove and brush with the remaining oil. Divide the chilli con carne between the pizzas and sprinkle over the cheese.

Return the pizzas to the oven and cook for 15-20 minutes. Remove and drizzle each pizza with soured cream. Sprinkle over the coriander and serve.

MAKES TWO 23-CM (9-INCH) PIZZAS

## ENGLISH CHEESE PIZZA

Basic Pizza Dough (see page 146)
olive oil for brushing
90 ml (6 tbsp) Basic Tomato Sauce (see page 148)
100 g (4 oz) red Leicester cheese, grated
30 ml (2 tbsp) chopped walnut pieces
75 g (3 oz) cream cheese
Salt and ground black pepper
100 g (4 oz) Stilton cheese, crumbled
100 g (4 oz) Cheddar cheese, grated
30 ml (2 tbsp) snipped fresh chives

Prepare the dough. When it is ready for use, divide it into two and roll and shape to fit two 23-cm (9-inch) oiled deep-dish pizza pans as described on page 144. Cover with cling film and leave in a warm place for 30 minutes. Prick the bases of the dough with a fork and bake in a preheated oven at 240°C (475°F, Gas mark 9) for 10 minutes.

Remove the bases from the oven and brush lightly with olive oil. Spread the tomato sauce over the bases. Mix together the red Leicester cheese and walnuts, and divide over a third of each pizza base. Mix the cream cheese with some salt and pepper and spoon over the second third of each pizza base. Scatter the crumbled Stilton over the cream cheese. Mix together the Cheddar and chives, and divide mixture over the last third of each pizza base. Top with black pepper.

Return the pizzas to the oven and cook for 15 minutes, or until the cheese topping has melted. Remove and serve at once.

MAKES TWO 23-CM (9-INCH) PIZZAS

**RIGHT:** Chilli Con Carne Pizza

# CALZONI & SFINCIONI

*This chapter includes two often-neglected types of pizza which deserve greater recognition. A calzone is a folded pizza, encasing a filling. Calzoni can be either deep-fried or oven-baked, producing different textures in the cooked dough. A sfincione is a stuffed flat pie originally from Sicily. It should be served cut into thick wedges.*

## CHICKEN & CORN CALZONE

Basic Pizza Dough (see page 146)
1 egg white, lightly beaten
Oil for deep-frying

### FILLING

4 rashers streaky bacon, rinds removed
275 g (10 oz) smoked chicken, skinned and diced
240 ml (8 fl oz) Corn Sauce, (see page 152)
1 spring onion, chopped
Salt and ground black pepper

Prepare the dough. While the dough is proving, make the filling.

Grill the bacon rashers for 3 minutes on each side until crisp. Allow to cool, then snip into bite-sized pieces. Place in a bowl with the rest of the filling ingredients and mix well.

When the dough is ready for use, divide it into five equal portions. Roll out each portion to produce an 18-cm (7-inch) circle. Place one-fifth of the filling on one half of each dough circle. Brush the edges of each circle with a little egg white and fold the circle over. Seal the edges.

Heat the oil for deep-frying and fry the calzoni for 5 minutes until golden. Remove with a slotted spoon and drain on paper towels. Serve at once.

MAKES FIVE 18-CM (7-INCH) CALZONI

## CALZONE CAPONATA

Basic Pizza Dough (see page 146)
Olive oil for brushing
Roasted Pepper Sauce (see page 150), to serve

### FILLING

30 ml (2 tbsp) olive oil
1 medium onion, chopped
2 cloves garlic, crushed
100 g (4 oz) aubergine, diced
100 g (4 oz) courgettes, diced
½ red pepper and ½ green pepper, diced
1 stick celery, chopped
4 anchovies, chopped
15 ml (1 tbsp) capers
30 ml (2 tbsp) chopped fresh basil
100 g (4 oz) mozzarella cheese, diced
Salt and ground black pepper

Prepare the dough. While the dough is proving, heat the oil in a saucepan, and cook the onion and garlic for 2 minutes. Add the aubergine and courgette, and cook for 4 minutes. Add the peppers, celery and anchovies for a further 2 minutes. Remove and stir in the capers, basil, mozzarella and seasoning.

When the dough is ready for use, divide it into five. Roll out each portion to produce an 18-cm (7-inch) circle. Place one-fifth of the filling on one half of each dough circle. Brush the edges of each circle with a little water and fold the circle over. Seal the edges.

Place the calzoni on baking sheets. Brush with olive oil. Bake in a preheated oven at 240°C (475°F, Gas mark 9) for 15-20 minutes. Serve with the sauce.

MAKES FIVE 18-CM (7-INCH) CALZONI

**TOP:** Chicken & Corn Calzone
**BOTTOM:** Calzone Caponata

## COURGETTE & SMOKED HAM CALZONE

Basic Pizza Dough (see page 146)
1 egg white, lightly beaten
Oil for deep-frying

### FILLING
30 ml (2 tbsp) olive oil
5 small shallots, peeled and chopped
2 cloves garlic, crushed
150 g (5 oz) courgettes
Salt and ground black pepper
150 g (5 oz) smoked ham
150 g (5 oz) Cheddar cheese

Prepare the dough. While the dough is proving, make the filling.

Heat the oil in a saucepan. Add the shallots and garlic, and sauté for 4-5 minutes. Cut the courgettes into julienne strips, add them to the pan, and cook for a further 2 minutes. Season the mixture well, then transfer it to a bowl and leave to cool. Slice the ham into thin strips and grate the cheese. Stir these into the cooled onion and courgettes mixture.

When the dough is ready for use, divide it into five equal portions. Roll out each portion to produce an 18-cm (7-inch) circle. Place one-fifth of the filling on one half of each dough circle. Brush the edges of each circle with a little egg white and fold the circles over to produce five semi-circles. Seal the edges of each Calzone well.

Heat the oil for deep-frying. When it is hot enough, fry the calzoni for 5 minutes at a time until crisp and golden. Remove from the oil with a slotted spoon and drain on paper towels. Serve at once.

MAKES FIVE 18-CM (7-INCH) CALZONI

## CALZONE CARBONARA

Basic Pizza Dough (see page 146)
Cornmeal for dusting
Olive oil for brushing
25ml freshly grated Parmesan cheese

### FILLING
60 ml (4 tbsp) olive oil
20 rashers bacon, rinds removed, chopped
3 cloves garlic, crushed
400 g (14 oz) cream cheese
1 egg yolk
Salt and ground black pepper

Prepare the dough. While the dough is proving, make the filling.

Heat the oil in a frying pan. Add the bacon and garlic, and cook for 6 minutes until golden. Drain on paper towels and allow to cool. Mix together the cream cheese and egg yolk, and season. Stir the bacon and garlic into the cream cheese mixture.

When the dough is ready for use, divide it into five equal portions. Roll out each portion to produce an 18-cm (7-inch) circle. Place one-fifth of the filling on one half of each dough circle. Brush the edges of each circle with a little water and fold the circles over to produce five semi-circles. Seal the edges well.

Place the calzoni on baking sheets lightly dusted with cornmeal. Brush with olive oil and sprinkle with Parmesan cheese. Bake in a preheated oven at 240°C (475°F, Gas mark 9) for 15 minutes until crisp and golden. Remove from the oven and serve at once.

MAKES FIVE 18-CM (7-INCH) CALZONI

**RIGHT:** Courgette & Smoked Ham Calzone

## AVOCADO, SCAMORZA & TOMATO CALZONE

Basic Pizza Dough (see page 146)
Cornmeal for dusting
Olive oil for brushing
25ml freshly grated Parmesan cheese

### FILLING

150 g (5 oz) scamorza cheese (smoked mozzarella)
1 large avocado
2 small tomatoes
20 ml (4 tsp) snipped fresh chives
20 ml (4 tsp) chopped fresh parsley
Salt and ground black pepper

Prepare the dough. While the dough is proving, make the filling.

Dice the scamorza and place it in a bowl. Peel the avocado and remove the stone; dice the flesh and add it to the cheese. Dice the tomato and add it to the bowl, along with the herbs and seasoning. Mix well to combine.

When the dough is ready for use, divide it into five equal portions. Roll out each portion to produce an 18-cm (7-inch) circle. Place one-fifth of the filling on one half of each dough circle. Brush the edges of each circle with a little water and fold the circles over to produce five semi-circles. Seal the edges of each Calzone well.

Place the calzoni on baking sheets lightly dusted with cornmeal. Brush with olive oil and sprinkle with Parmesan cheese. Bake in a preheated oven at 240°C (475°F, Gas mark 9) for 15 minutes until crisp and golden. Remove from the oven and serve at once.

MAKES FIVE 18-CM (7-INCH) CALZONI

## SPICY BEEF CALZONE

Basic Pizza Dough (see page 146)
1 egg white, lightly beaten
Oil for deep-frying

### FILLING

45 ml (3 tbsp) vegetable oil
2 small onions, peeled and chopped
3 cloves garlic, crushed
2 green chilli, seeded and sliced
275 g (10 oz) lean minced beef
25ml tomato purée
5-7.5 ml (1-1½ tsp) paprika
1 large tomato, chopped
Salt and ground black pepper
150 g (5 oz) fontina cheese, diced

Prepare the dough. While the dough is proving, make the filling.

Heat the oil in a pan and sauté the onion and garlic for 3 minutes. Add the chilli and cook for a further minute. Stir in the beef and cook, stirring constantly, for 4 minutes. Add the tomato purée, paprika, tomato and seasoning, and cook for a further 4 minutes. Leave to cook. Stir in the diced cheese.

When the dough is ready for use, divide it into five. Roll out each portion to produce an 18-cm (7-inch) circle. Place one-fifth of the filling on one half of each dough circle. Brush the edges of each circle with a little beaten egg white and fold the circles over. Seal the edges.

Heat the oil for deep-frying and fry the calzoni in batches for 5 minutes at a time until golden. Remove from the oil with a slotted spoon and drain on paper towels. Serve immediately.

MAKES FIVE 18-CM (7-INCH) CALZONI

**TOP:** Avocado, Scamorza & Tomato Calzone
**BOTTOM:** Spicy Beef Calzone

## SPINACH & PINE NUT CALZONE

Cornmeal Pizza Dough (see page 146)
Cornmeal for dusting
Olive oil for brushing

### FILLING

275 g (10 oz) cooked spinach
275 g (10 oz) ricotta cheese
75 ml (5 tbsp) pine nuts, toasted
75 ml (5 tbsp) grated Parmesan cheese
25ml sun-dried tomato paste
Salt and ground black pepper

Prepare the dough. While the dough is proving, make the filling.

Squeeze any excess moisture from the spinach. Chop the spinach and place it in a mixing bowl. Add the remaining ingredients and mix well until evenly combined.

When the dough is ready for use, divide it into five equal portions. Roll out each portion to produce an 18-cm (7-inch) circle. Place one-fifth of the filling on one half of each dough circle. Brush the edges of each circle with a little water and fold the circles over to produce five semi-circles. Seal the edges of each Calzone well to enclose the filling.

Place the calzoni on baking sheets lightly dusted with cornmeal. Brush with olive oil. Bake in a pre-heated oven at 240°C (475°F, Gas mark 9) for 15 minutes until crisp and golden. Remove from the oven and serve at once.

MAKES FIVE 18-CM (7-INCH) CALZONI

## THREE-CHEESE CALZONE

Basic Pizza Dough (see page 146)
Cornmeal for dusting
Olive oil for brushing
Fresh tomato & Herb Sauce (see page 148)

### FILLING

150 g (5 oz) ricotta cheese
150 g (5 oz) Emmental cheese, grated
150 g (5 oz) Parmesan cheese, grated
5 halves sun-dried tomatoes in oil, chopped
10 black olives, pitted and chopped
25 ml (5 tsp) snipped fresh chives
Salt and ground black pepper

Prepare the dough. While the dough is proving, make the filling.

Place all the ingredients for the filling in a large bowl and mix well. Set aside.

When the dough is ready for use, divide it into five equal portions. Roll out each portion to produce an 18-cm (7-inch) circle. Place one-fifth of the filling on one half of each dough circle. Brush the edges of each circle with a little water and fold the circles over. Seal the edges well.

Place the calzoni on baking sheets lightly dusted with cornmeal. Brush with olive oil. Bake in a pre-heated oven at 240°C (475°F, Gas mark 9) for 15 minutes until golden. Remove and serve with Fresh Tomato & Herb Sauce.

MAKES FIVE 18-CM (7-INCH) CALZONI

**RIGHT:** Spinach & Pine Nut Calzone

## SEAFOOD CALZONE

Basic Pizza Dough (see page 146)
Cornmeal for dusting
Olive oil for brushing
20 ml (4 tsp) freshly grated pecorino cheese

### FILLING

60 ml (4 tbsp) olive oil
4 small shallots, chopped
100 g (4 oz) cooked peeled prawns
225 g (8 oz) scallops, chopped
100 g (4 oz) cooked mussels (shelled weight)
2.5 ml (½ tsp) saffron strands, infused in 30 ml
(2 tbsp) water for 10 minutes
Salt and ground black pepper
100 g (4 oz) mozzarella cheese, diced
20 ml (4 tsp) chopped fresh chervil

Prepare the dough. While the dough is proving, make the filling.

Heat the oil in a large saucepan. Add the shallots and cook for 3 minutes. Add the prepared seafood and cook for 4 minutes. Stir in the saffron strands with the water and season. Allow to cook slightly. Stir in the mozzarella and chervil.

When the dough is ready for use, divide it into four. Roll out each portion to produce an 23-cm (9-inch) circle. Place one-quarter of the filling on one half of each dough circle. Brush the edges of each circle with a little water and fold the circles over. Seal the edges. Place the calzoni on baking sheets lightly dusted with cornmeal. Brush with olive oil and sprinkle with pecorino cheese. Bake in a preheated oven at 240°C (475°F, Gas mark 9) for 15-20 minutes. Remove and serve at once.

MAKES FOUR 23-CM (9-INCH) CALZONI

**TOP:** Salt Cod Calzone
**BOTTOM:** Seafood Calzone

## SALT COD CALZONE

Basic Pizza Dough, using herby variation, coriander as the herb (see page 146)
Olive oil for brushing
60 ml (4 tbsp) grated provolone cheese
Basic Tomato Sauce (see page 148), to serve

### FILLING

175 g (6 oz) salt cod
1 large clove garlic, crushed
75 ml (5 tbsp) each milk and extra virgin olive oil
100 g (4 oz) curd cheese
45 ml (3 tbsp) chopped coriander
8 stuffed olives, sliced
15 ml (1 tbsp) olive oil
75 g (3 oz) leeks, sliced

Soak the salt cod in cold water for 24 hours, changing the water three or four times.

Prepare the dough. While the dough is proving, place the cod in a pan of fresh water. Bring it to the boil, then simmer for 8-10 minutes. Drain and allow to cool. Remove the skin and bones and flake the flesh. Place the flaked fish in a food processor with the garlic. Process briefly. Combine the milk with the extra virgin olive oil and pour into the processor with the motor running. Add the curd cheese and coriander and process briefly. Transfer to a bowl and stir in the olives. Heat the oil in a pan and sauté the leeks for 1 minute. Stir into the cod mixture.

When the dough is ready, divide it into four. Roll out each portion to produce an 23-cm (9-inch) circle. Place one-quarter of the filling on half of each circle. Brush the edges with a water, fold over and seal.

Place the calzoni on baking sheets. Brush with olive oil and sprinkle 15 ml (1 tbsp) of provolone over each. Bake in a preheated oven at 240°C (475°F, Gas mark 9) for 15-20 minutes. Remove and serve with the sauce. MAKES FOUR 23-CM (9-INCH) CALZONI

## ITALIAN SAUSAGE & LEEK SFINCIONE

Basic Pizza Dough (see page 146)
Cornmeal for dusting
Olive oil for brushing
Basic Tomato Sauce (see page 148), to serve

### FILLING

30 ml (2 tbsp) olive oil
½ onion
2 small leeks, chopped
2 Italian sausages, sliced
Salt and ground black pepper
100 g (4 oz) mozzarella cheese, grated

Prepare the dough. While the dough is proving, make the filling.

Heat the oil in a pan and sauté the onion for 4 minutes. Add the leeks for a further minute. Stir in the sliced sausages and cook for 2 more minutes. Remove from the heat, season and leave to cool. Stir in the diced mozzarella.

When the dough is ready for use, divide it into two equal portions. Roll out one portion to produce an 25-cm (10-inch) circle. Place the circle on a baking sheet lightly dusted with cornmeal and spread the filling over the circle, leaving a 5-cm (2-inch) border. Roll out the remaining portion of dough to produce anther 25-cm (10-inch) circle. Dampen the edges of the first circle with water and place the remaining circle on top. Press down gently. Seal the edges and cut a cross in the top.

Brush liberally with olive oil and bake in a preheated oven at 240°C (475°F, Gas mark 9) for 20-25 minutes.

Serve hot, cut into wedges, passing the sauce separately.   MAKES ONE SFINCIONE

**RIGHT:** Italian Sausage & Leek Sfincione

## VEGETABLE SFINCIONE

Basic Pizza Dough (see page 146)
Cornmeal for dusting
Olive oil for brushing
15 ml (1 tbsp) grated Parmesan cheese

### FILLING

1 red pepper, quartered and cored
1 orange pepper, quartered and cored
1 large red onion, thickly sliced lengthways
45 ml (3 tbsp) olive oil
150 g (5 oz) creamy, soft goat's cheese
1 clove garlic, crushed
10 ml (2 tsp) chopped fresh thyme
Salt and ground black pepper

Prepare the dough. While the dough is proving, make the filling.

Place the peppers, skin-side up, on a rack and grill for 12 minutes until the skins are charred. When cool, peel off and discard their skins. Place the onion slices on a rack and brush with half the olive oil. Grill for 3 minutes. Turn them over, brush with oil, and grill for 3 minutes. Allow to cool place the cheese, garlic, thyme and seasoning in a bowl and mix well.

When the dough is ready, divide it into two. Roll out one portion to produce an 25-cm (10-inch) circle. Place on a baking sheet lightly dusted with cornmeal. Place half the red onion and the orange pepper on the circle, leaving a 5-cm (2-inch) border. Top with the cheese mixture, remaining onion and red pepper.

Roll out the remaining dough to produce anther 25-cm (10-inch) circle. Dampen the edges of the first circle and place the remaining circle on top. Press down gently. Seal the edges and cut a cross in the top. Brush with olive oil and sprinkle over the Parmesan.

Bake in a preheated oven at 240°C (475°F, Gas mark 9) for 20-25 minutes. Serve hot, cut into thick wedges.   MAKES ONE SFINCIONE

## FENNEL SFINCIONE

Basic Pizza Dough (see page 146)
Cornmeal for dusting
Walnut oil for brushing

### FILLING

75 g (3 oz) fennel, sliced
45 ml (3 tbsp) olive oil
1 small red pepper, sliced
½ onion, sliced
1 clove garlic, crushed
50 g (2 oz) Bel Paese cheese, cubed
40 g (1½ oz) curd cheese
15 ml (1 tbsp) chopped fresh parsley
25 g (1 oz) pistachio nuts
Salt and ground black pepper

Prepare the dough. While the dough is proving, make the filling.

Blanch the fennel for 1½ minutes; drain and refresh under cold water. Heat the oil in a large pan and sauté the onion and garlic for 2 minutes. Add the fennel and red pepper, and sauté for a further 3 minutes. Transfer to a bowl and allow to cool. Add the two cheeses, parsley, pistachios and seasoning and mix well.

When the dough is ready for use, divide it into two. Roll out one portion to produce an 25-cm (10-inch) circle. Place the circle on a baking sheet lightly dusted with cornmeal. Spread the filling over the circle, leaving a 5-cm (2-inch) border. Roll out the remaining portion of dough to produce anther 25-cm (10-inch) circle. Dampen the edges of the first circle with water and place the remaining circle on top. Press down gently. Seal the edges and cut a cross in the top.

Brush liberally with olive oil.

Bake in a preheated oven at 240°C (475°F, Gas mark 9) for 20-25 minutes. Serve hot, cut into thick wedges.　　MAKES ONE SFINCIONE

## GORGONZOLA, ARTICHOKE & SALAMI SFINCIONE

Cornmeal Pizza Dough (see page 146)
Cornmeal for dusting
30 ml (2 tbsp) Walnut oil
30 ml (2 tbsp) chopped walnuts

### FILLING

75 g (3 oz) Gorgonzola cheese, cubed
50 g (2 oz) Milano salami, cut into thin strips
2 artichoke hearts marinated in oil, cut into bite-sized pieces
50 g (2 oz) ricotta cheese
15 ml (1 tbsp) snipped fresh chives
Ground black pepper

Prepare the dough. While the dough is proving, place all the ingredients for the filling in a large bowl and mix gently. Set aside.

When the dough is ready for use, divide it into two equal portions. Roll out one portion to produce a 25-cm (10-inch) circle. Place the circle on a baking sheet lightly dusted with cornmeal. Spread the filling over the circle, leaving a 5-cm (2-inch) border around the edges. Roll out the remaining portion of dough to produce a 25-cm (10-inch) circle. Dampen the edges of the first circle with water and place the remaining circle on top. Press down gently and seal the edges. Cut a cross in the top. Brush with walnut oil and scatter over the walnuts.

Bake in a preheated oven at 240°C (475°F, Gas mark 9) for 20-25 minutes until golden. Serve hot, cut into thick wedges.　　MAKES ONE SFINCIONE

**TOP:** Fennel Sfincione
**BOTTOM:** Gorgonzola, Artichoke & Salami Sfincione

# SPECIALITY PIZZAS

*This chapter creates pizzas in the broadest sense, using all sorts of bases, from French bread and focaccia to puff pastry and naan bread. These pizzas are small, and suitable for light snacks or party food. Some use very simple basic ingredients, while others are more exotic. Dessert pizzas have also been included. Banana, Rum & Raisin Pizza has a Caribbean flavour while Calzone Sorpresa will appeal to chocoholics.*

## PARMA HAM & FIG PIZZAS

4 x 15-cm (6-inch) ready-made thin-crust
pizza bases
60 ml (4 tbsp) extra virgin olive oil
2 cloves garlic, crushed
8 slices prosciutto (Parma ham)
4 ripe fresh figs
Ground black pepper

Place the pizza bases on two baking sheets. Mix together 30 ml (2 tbsp) of the olive oil and the crushed garlic. Brush all over the bases.

Bake the pizza bases in a preheated oven at 220°C (425°F, Gas mark 7) for 10 minutes. Remove from the oven and top each pizza with two slices of prosciutto. Peel the figs, if desired, and slice each fig into four. Arrange the sliced fig over the prosciutto and top each pizza with a generous grinding of black pepper. Drizzle the remaining olive oil over the pizzas.

Return the pizzas to the oven and bake for a further 3-4 minutes to warm the topping. Remove from the oven and serve at once.

MAKES FOUR 15-CM (6-INCH) MINI PIZZAS

## AUBERGINE PIZZAS

Fennel Sfincione
Basic Pizza Dough (see page 146)
Cornmeal for dusting
100 ml (3½ fl oz) olive oil
120 ml (4 fl oz) Basic Tomato Sauce (see page 148)
Salt and ground black pepper
100 g (4 oz) feta cheese, crumbled
100 g (4 oz) aubergine
8 sun-dried tomatoes in oil, cut into strips

Prepare the dough as described in the basic recipe. When it is ready for use, divide it into eight equal portions. Roll out pizza dough as described on page 142, make eight 10-cm (4-inch) thin-crust pizza bases. Place bases on baking sheets lightly dusted with cornmeal and brush with 45 ml (3 tbsp) of the olive oil.

Spread 15 ml (1 tbsp) of the tomato sauce over each pizza, leaving a 1.5-cm (½-inch) border. Divide the feta cheese between the pizzas. Slice the aubergine into sixteen very thin slices and brush with the remaining olive oil. Season well and place two slices on each pizza. Top with ground black pepper.

Bake the pizzas in a preheated oven at 240°C (475°F, Gas mark 9) for 8 minutes. Remove from the oven and scatter evenly with the sun-dried tomato strips. Return the pizzas to the oven and bake for a further 5 minutes. Remove from the oven and serve immediately.

MAKES EIGHT 10-CM (4-INCH) MINI PIZZAS

**TOP:** Aubergine Pizzas
**BOTTOM:** Parma Ham & Fig Pizza

## BRIE & CHERRY TOMATO MINI PIZZAS

Basic Pizza Dough (see page 10)
Cornmeal for dusting
90 ml (6 tbsp) olive oil
240 ml (8 fl oz) Fresh Basil Pesto
(see page 16)
550 g (1 lb 4 oz) Brie, sliced thinly
20 cherry tomatoes, halved
Ground black pepper
5 large basil leaves, torn

Prepare the dough. When it is ready for use, divide it into ten equal portions. Roll out or stretch the pizza dough as described on page 6. Make ten 10-cm (4-inch) thin-crust pizza bases. Place the bases on baking sheets lightly dusted with cornmeal and brush them all over with 45 ml (3 tbsp) of the olive oil.

Spread the basil pesto evenly over the pizzas, leaving a 5-mm (¼-inch) border around the edges. Divide the slices of Brie between the pizzas. Place four halves of cherry tomato on each pizza and top with some black pepper. Drizzle over the remaining olive oil.

Bake the pizzas in a preheated oven at 240°C (475°F, Gas mark 9) for 12-13 minutes, until crusts are golden and the cheese has melted. Remove from the oven and sprinkle with basil. Serve at once.

MAKES TEN 10-CM (4-INCH) MINI PIZZAS

## LAMB TIKKA MINI PIZZAS

15 ml (1 tbsp) olive oil
½ onion, chopped
1 clove garlic, crushed
175 g (6 oz) lamb neck fillet, cubed
30 ml (2 tbsp) tikka paste
6 ready-made mini garlic and coriander or
plain naan breads
50 g (2 oz) curd cheese
15 ml (1 tbsp) natural yoghurt
15 ml (1 tbsp) chopped fresh mint

Prepare the lamb tikka. Heat the oil in a saucepan and sauté the onion and garlic for 3 minutes until soft. Add the lamb and cook for a further 3 minutes. Stir in the tikka paste and cook over a medium heat for 10 minutes until the lamb is tender.

Place the naan breads on baking sheets. Mix the curd cheese with the yoghurt and spread over the naan breads, leaving a 1.5-cm (½-inch) border around the edges. Top each naan bread with some of the lamb tikka mixture.

Bake the pizzas in a preheated oven at 180°C (350°F, Gas mark 4) for 6-8 minutes, until they are warmed through. Remove, sprinkle with chopped mint and serve at once.

MAKES SIX MINI PIZZAS

*Variation: If you prefer, substitute diced, skinless, boneless chicken breast or diced monkfish for the lamb. If making fish tikka, cook the monkfish for only 5 minutes instead of the 10 minutes suggested for lamb. Chicken needs the same cooking time as lamb.*

**LEFT:** Brie & Cherry Tomato Mini Pizzas
**RIGHT:** Lamb Tikka Mini Pizzas

## CHEQUERBOARD PIZZA

Basic Pizza Dough, using herby variation
(see page 146)
Cornmeal for dusting
45 ml (3 tbsp) olive oil

### ROASTED PEPPER TOPPING

2 red peppers
1 yellow pepper
60 ml (4 tbsp) olive oil
salt and ground black pepper
120 ml (4 fl oz) Fresh Tomato & Herb Sauce
(see page 148)

### GOAT'S CHEESE AND BLACK OLIVE TOPPING

60 ml (4 tbsp) black olive tapenade
9 thin slices goat's cheese, weighing
about 25 g (1 oz) each
15 ml (1 tbsp) fresh rosemary leaves
15 ml (1 tbsp) fresh thyme leaves
Ground black pepper
30 ml (2 tbsp) olive oil

Prepare the dough as described in the basic recipe. When it is ready for use, divide it into two equal portions and roll out until it is 5-mm (1/4-inch) thick. Cut nine 7.5-cm (3-inch) squares from each portion of dough. Place the eighteen squares of dough on baking sheets lightly dusted with cornmeal. Brush the dough squares all over with the olive oil.

Prepare the roasted pepper topping. Halve the peppers and remove the cores. Place them, skin-side up, under a hot grill and cook for 5-6 minutes until the skins begins to blacken. Remove the peppers from the heat and allow them to cool. Peel off the skins and slice the pepper flesh into thin strips. Mix the sliced peppers with the olive oil and season them well with salt and pepper.

Top nine of the dough squares with pepper topping: divide the Fresh Tomato & Herb Sauce between the squares and spread it over the bases, leaving a 5-mm (1/4-inch) border around the edges. Top each base with some roasted pepper strips.

Top the remaining dough squares with goat's cheese topping. Spread the tapenade over the bases, leaving a 5-mm (1/4-inch) border around the edges, and top each base with a slices of goat's cheese. Sprinkle with the fresh herbs, season with ground black pepper and drizzle with the olive oil.

Bake the pizza squares in a preheated oven at 240°C (475°F, Gas mark 9) for 12-13 minutes, until crusts are golden. Remove from the oven and arrange alternate squares of roast pepper and goat's cheese pizza on a board to produce a chequerboard effect.

MAKES EIGHTEEN MINI PIZZAS

**RIGHT:** Chequerboard Pizza

## FRENCH BREAD PIZZA MARGHERITA

2 pieces French bread, about
12.5cm (5 inches) long
50 g (2 oz) butter
30 ml (2 tbsp) chopped fresh basil
2 large beef tomatoes, weighing about
175 g (6 oz) each
50 g (2 oz) mozzarella cheese, diced
Salt and ground black pepper
15 ml (1 tbsp) grated Parmesan cheese
15 ml (1 tbsp) extra virgin olive oil
4 large basil leaves, coarsely torn

Halve each piece of French bread lengthways. Melt the butter in a small saucepan and stir in the chopped basil. Use this mixture to brush all over the cut sides of the bread. Bake the French bread in a preheated oven at 200°C (400°F, Gas mark 6) for 4 minutes. Remove from the oven and set aside.

Peel and seed the tomatoes and chop them coarsely. Place in a bowl and add the diced mozzarella cheese. Season and mix well to combine. Spoon the tomato and mozzarella mixture evenly over the bread and sprinkle with the Parmesan cheese. Drizzle a little olive oil over each pizza and top with black pepper.

Return the pizzas to the oven and bake for a further 10 minutes, until the topping is bubbling. Remove from the oven and scatter basil leaves over the pizzas. Serve immediately. MAKES FOUR SNACK PIZZAS

## FRENCH BREAD PIZZA WITH GOAT'S CHEESE

60 ml (4 tbsp) hazelnut oil
30 ml (2 tbsp) sunflower oil
20 ml (4 tsp) chopped fresh thyme
4 slices French bread, cut on the diagonal
175 g (6 oz) courgettes
Salt and ground black pepper
275 g (10 oz) goat's cheese
12 toasted hazelnuts, coarsely chopped
10 ml (2 tsp) fresh thyme leaves

Mix together the hazelnut oil, 15 ml (1 tbsp) of the sunflower oil and the chopped thyme. Use this mixture to brush all over the cut sides of the French bread slices. Place the pieces of bread on a baking sheet and bake in a preheated oven at 200°C (400°F, Gas mark 6) for 5 minutes. Remove from the oven and set aside while preparing the topping.

Cut the courgettes into julienne strips and place in a bowl. Season the courgette julienne well and stir in the remaining sunflower oil. Slice the goat's cheese into eight thin circles. Top each piece of French bread with a quarter of the courgette julienne and two slices of goat's cheese. Grind over some black pepper.

Return the pizzas to the oven and bake for 6-8 minutes, until the cheese is bubbling. Remove the pizzas from the oven and scatter with toasted hazelnuts and thyme leaves. Serve immediately.
MAKES FOUR SNACK PIZZAS

**LEFT:** French Bread Pizzas with Goat's Cheese
**RIGHT:** French Bread Pizza Margherita

## PUFF PASTRY PIZZA WITH ROASTED PEPPER & SALAMI

225 g (8 oz) puff pastry
60 ml (4 tbsp) Roasted Pepper Sauce (see page 150)
75 g (3 oz) Italian salami, in one thick slice
ground black pepper
1 egg, beaten
15 ml (1 tbsp) snipped fresh chives

Roll out the puff pastry on a lightly floured surface and cut out six 6.5-cm (2½-inch) diamonds. Prick each pastry diamond with the prongs of a fork and place them on a lightly greased baking sheet.

Spread the pepper sauce evenly between the six pastry diamonds, leaving a 5-mm (¼-inch) border around the edges. Cut the salami into 5-mm (¼-inch) cubes and scatter these over the pepper sauce. Top each pizza with some ground black pepper. Brush the exposed edges of the puff pastry diamonds with the beaten egg.

Bake the pizzas in a preheated oven at 220°C (425°F, Gas mark 7) for 7-8 minutes, until cooked through. Remove the pizzas from the oven and sprinkle with the snipped chives. Serve immediately.

MAKES SIX SNACK PIZZAS

## PUFF PASTRY PIZZA WITH SMOKED SALMON

225 g (8 oz) puff pastry
1 egg, beaten
175 g (6 oz) cream cheese
20 ml (4 tsp) milk
20 ml (4 tsp) lemon juice
Salt and ground black pepper
100 g (4 oz) smoked salmon
20 ml (4 tsp) snipped fresh chervil

Roll out the puff pastry on a lightly floured surface and cut out four 15-cm (6-inch) circles. Prick each pastry circle with the prongs of a fork and place them on lightly greased baking sheets. Brush the circles with beaten egg and bake them in a preheated oven at 220°C (425°F, Gas mark 7) for 10 minutes.

Remove the pastry from the oven and allow to cool slightly. Mix together the cream cheese, milk and lemon juice; season well. Spread the mixture evenly between the four pastry circles, leaving a 1.5-cm (½-inch) border around the edges. Slice the salmon into thick strips and arrange them evenly between the pizzas. Top with black pepper and the snipped chervil. Serve at once.        MAKES FOUR SNACK PIZZAS

**RIGHT:** Puff Pastry Pizzas with Smoked Salmon

## MUSHROOM FOCACCIA PIZZA

1 shop-bought focaccia bread
120 ml (4 fl oz) olive oil
4 cloves garlic, crushed
60 ml (4 tbsp) chopped fresh mixed herbs, such as
parsley, thyme and chives
50 g (2 oz) butter
275 g (10 oz) girolle mushrooms
Salt and ground black pepper

Cut the focaccia bread into six triangles. Mix 90 ml (6 tbsp) of the olive oil with the crushed garlic and chopped herbs. Brush this mixture liberally all over the six focaccia triangles. Place the bread triangles on a baking sheet.

Wipe the mushrooms with damp paper towels and slice any that are large. Heat the butter and the remaining oil in a large heavy-based frying pan, add the prepared mushrooms and sauté over a moderate heat for 4-5 minutes; season generously. Divide the mushrooms evenly over the six bread triangles.

Bake the pizzas in a preheated oven at 200°C (400°F, Gas mark 6) for 7-10 minutes, until warmed through. Remove the pizzas from the oven, top with ground black pepper and serve at once.

MAKES SIX SNACK PIZZAS

Variation: If you prefer, substitute a selection of wild mushrooms or cultivated mixed mushrooms, such as button, field and brown cap, for the girolle mushrooms in this recipe.

## MARINARA FOCACCIA PIZZA

1 shop-bought focaccia bread
90 ml (6 tbsp) extra virgin olive oil
4 cloves garlic, crushed
6 small plum tomatoes
6 black olives, pitted
Salt and ground black pepper
30 ml (2 tbsp) chopped fresh oregano

Cut the focaccia bread into six triangles. Mix 60 ml (4 tbsp) of the olive oil with the crushed garlic. Brush this mixture liberally all over the six focaccia triangles. Place the bread on a baking sheet.

Slice each tomato into three thick slices. Place three slices of tomato on each focaccia triangle. Slice the black olives into rings and scatter these over the pizzas; season and drizzle over the remaining olive oil.

Bake the pizzas in a preheated oven at 200°C (400°F, Gas mark 6) for 7-8 minutes, until the tomato slices have softened and the pizzas are warmed through. Remove from the oven, sprinkle with chopped oregano and serve at once.

MAKES SIX SNACK PIZZAS

Variation: If you prefer, add slivered anchovies to these pizzas before baking them. Allow half an anchovy fillet per pizza triangle.

**RIGHT:** Mushroom Focaccia Pizza,
Marinara Focaccia Pizza

## APRICOT & ALMOND DESSERT PIZZA

4 x 12.5-cm (5-inch) ready-made pizza bases
50 g (2 oz) butter, melted

### TOPPING

100 g (4 oz) ground almonds
100 g (4 oz) caster sugar
2 egg yolks
180 ml (6 fl oz) orange juice
48 dried apricots
60 ml (4 tbsp) Amaretto liqueur
45 ml (3 tbsp) apricot jam

Make the almond topping. Mix together the ground almonds, caster sugar, egg yolks and 60 ml (4 tbsp) of the orange juice. Set aside.

Place the dried apricots in a saucepan with the remaining orange juice for about 15 minutes, until they are plump. Stir in the Amaretto liqueur and simmer over a low heat for 4-5 minutes. Remove from heat and set aside.

Brush the pizza bases with the melted butter and place them on baking sheets. Spread the almond topping evenly over the bases, leaving a 1.5-cm (½-inch) border around the edges. Drain the apricots, reserving liquid. Arrange twelve apricots over each pizza.

Bake the pizzas in a preheated oven at 200°C (400°F, Gas mark 6) for 10-15 minutes until cooked through.

Remove from the oven and allow to cool slightly. Place the reserved liquid from the apricots in a small pan, add the apricot jam and simmer gently to dissolve the jam. Brush the pizzas with the apricot glaze and serve.　　MAKES FOUR DESSERT PIZZAS

## BANANA, RUM & RAISIN PIZZA

4 x 12.5-cm (5-inch) ready-made pizza bases
100 g (4 oz) butter, melted
100 ml (4 oz) mascarpone cheese
100 ml (3½ fl oz) dark rum
60 ml (4 tbsp) soft brown sugar
45 ml (3 tbsp) raisins
4 small bananas, sliced

Brush the pizza bases with half the melted butter and place them on baking sheets. Bake the bases in a pre-heated oven at 200°C (400°F, Gas mark 6) for 10-12 minutes until pale golden. Remove from the oven and set aside.

Mix the mascarpone cheese with 45 ml (3 tbsp) of the rum and spread the mixture evenly over the pizza bases, leaving a 1.5-cm (½-inch) border.

Place the remaining melted butter in a saucepan, add the remaining rum, brown sugar and raisins and cook over a gentle heat for a few minutes until the sugar has dissolved and the mixture is thick and syrupy. Add the sliced bananas and mix through gently. Top each pizza with a quarter of the warm banana mixture and serve at once.

MAKES FOUR DESSERT PIZZAS

**TOP:** Banana, Rum & Raisin Pizza
**BOTTOM:** Apricot & Almond Dessert Pizzas

## APPLE & CINNAMON PUFF PASTRY PIZZA

275 g (10 oz) puff pastry
Milk for brushing
Crème fraîche, to serve

### APPLE PUREE

225 g (8 oz) dessert apples, peeled,
cored and diced
60 ml (4 tbsp) water
45 ml (3 tbsp) soft brown sugar
45 ml (3 tbsp) calvados
25 g (1 oz) unsalted butter

### TOPPING

2 red-skinned apples
20 ml (4 tsp) soft brown sugar
5 ml (1 tsp) ground cinnamon

Roll out the pastry on a lightly floured surface and cut out four oblongs measuring 15 x 10 cm (6 x 4 inches). Place the pastry oblongs on a baking sheet, prick them all over with a fork and brush with a little milk. Bake in a preheated oven at 220°C (425°F, Gas mark 7) for 10 minutes. Remove and reduce the temperature to 200°C (400°F, Gas mark 6).

Make the apple purée. Place the diced apple, water, sugar and calvados in a small pan. Simmer the mixture gently for 10-15 minutes. Stir in the butter. Spread the apple purée evenly over the pastry oblongs, leaving a 1.5-cm (½-inch) border.

Make the topping. Slice the apples very thinly and arrange them over the apple purée. Mix together the brown sugar and cinnamon and sprinkle over the apple slices. Return the pizzas to the oven and bake for 5-8 minutes. Serve warm, accompanied by the crème fraîche.     MAKES FOUR DESSERT PIZZAS

## CALZONE SORPRESA (CHOCOLATE CALZONE)

Basic Pizza Dough
Cornmeal for dusting
25 g (1 oz) butter, melted
A little caster sugar

### FILLING

275 g (10 oz) cream cheese
200 g (7 oz) plain or milk chocolate
65 g (2½ oz) toasted hazelnuts
65 g (2½ oz) candied citrus peel

Prepare the dough as described in the basic recipe. While the dough is proving, make the filling.

Place the cream cheese in a bowl. Chop the chocolate and hazelnuts into small pieces and add them to the cream cheese, together with the citrus peel. Mix until well combined.

When the dough is ready for use, divide it into five equal portions. Roll out each piece of dough to produce an 18-cm (7-inch) circle. Place one-fifth of the cream cheese mixture on one half of each dough circle. Dampen the edges of each circle with water and fold over to produce five semi-circles. Seal the edges well. Place the calzoni on baking sheets lightly dusted with cornmeal and brush with melted butter. Sprinkle with a little caster sugar.

Bake the calzoni in a preheated oven at 240°C (475°F, Gas mark 9) for 15 minutes, until crisp and golden. Remove from the oven, allow to cool slightly, and serve at once.

MAKES FIVE 18-CM (7-INCH) CALZONI

**LEFT:** Calzone Sorpresa
**RIGHT:** Apple & Cinnamon Puff Pastry Pizza

# BURGERS

This section celebrates this favourite food which is a meal in itself – big, juicy burgers – but brings an international flavour to the humble burger by using a wide range of ingredients and seasonings.

Although America is credited with creating the burger, minced beef on bread was a speciality of Hamburg, Germany, which is how the hamburger got its name. The burger as we know it was reputedly first served by German settlers in America during the 1904 St Louis International Exposition. Although minced beef is still the favoured ingredient, fish and vegetarian burgers increasingly have their place in today's healthy lifestyle.

## THE BASIC INGREDIENTS

To many people a burger is synonymous with minced beef; however a wider range of basic ingredients can be made into a patty and eaten as a burger. Minced chicken, pork, lamb, turkey, veal and even venison make wonderfully tasty burgers, and fish and seafood can also be combined for unusual concoctions. For the vegetarian, rice, potato, pulses and grains provide diverse starting points.

Ready-minced beef is easily found in supermarkets, but you may have to visit a butcher for more unusual meats. A good butcher will also grind the meat to order for you. If you have a mincer, you can grind meat at home, but do not try to 'mince' meat in a processor. This will produce a solid texture rather than the ideal grainy-meat burger.

Fish and vegetarian burgers, on the hand, respond well to food processors. The texture of these ingredients is usually more delicate

and so needs a certain amount of processing to make everything bind together.

Good seasoning is vital for all burgers. To your basic ingredient, add generous amounts of complementary spices, herbs and seasonings. Ideally, cook a small amount of the burger mixture in a frying pan, taste it, and adjust the seasoning as necessary before you shape and cook the whole batch of burgers.

After you have combined the basic ingredients, shape your burgers into round patties, handling them as little as possible. This will ensure a lighter textured burger rather than a tough, dense burger. Ideally burgers should be about 2 cm (¾ inch) thick.

## ADVANCED PREPARATION

Meat and fish burgers benefit from being prepared a short while before cooking. If you need to prepare them far in advance, try using one of the marinades on page 220. To do this, place the burgers in a shallow dish, brush them with the marinade, pouring the remaining marinade over, cover with cling film and chill for 2 hours or overnight.

Marinating seafood burgers which contain breadcrumbs or cheese is not recommended, as the burgers will become soggy. Also avoid marinating the vegetarian burgers in the *Meatless Wonders* chapter, as they could disintegrate. Do, however, make the vegetarian burgers several hours in advance and chill them. Refrigeration will help to make them easier to handle during cooking.

**RIGHT:** Grilling or barbecuing gives burgers a charred outside while the inside remains moist.

## STORING BURGERS

Burgers should not be refrigerated for more than 24 hours before cooking. If you absolutely must freeze burgers, arrange the uncooked, prepared patties in a single layer on a tray and freeze them uncovered for 1–2 hours, or until they are hard. Then store the patties in boxes with parchment paper layered between them. Meat and poultry burgers will freeze best, but burgers made from such ingredients as rice and lentils are fragile and will always be better freshly made. Do not freeze burgers for more than three months.

## COOKING BURGERS

Burgers can be cooked in several ways: barbecuing or grilling, pan-frying and deep-frying. The golden rule for cooking burgers is never to press them with a spatula as their flavoursome juices would be lost.

All the meat burgers in this book will barbecue happily, as will those fish and seafood burgers which the recipes say are suitable for pan-frying. However, the fish and seafood burgers need to be handled with extra care. For best results, those fish and seafood burgers for which deep-frying is recommended should only be cooked in this way. Vegetarian burgers will fall apart on a barbecue and must be cooked as directed in the individual recipes.

When barbecuing or grilling, place the burgers on oiled racks and cook them quickly over hot coals or under a hot grill. For barbecuing, ensure that the coals have reached the glowing ash stage. Quick cooking will ensure a charred outside and a moist centre. Of course, non-beef meat or poultry burgers will require longer cooking so that they are well-cooked right through to the centre.

Pan-frying is a quick and easy method that is available the whole year round. Use a heavy-based frying pan that has been well-oiled and cook the burgers over a fairly high heat to achieve similar results to barbecuing or grilling. To deep-fry burgers, pour 7.5-10 cm (3-4 inches) of a good tasteless oil, such as corn, sunflower or vegetable oil, in a deep pan. To test if the oil is hot enough, drop a breadcrumb into the oil. If it floats and bubbles appear, the oil is the correct temperature.

As a general guideline for minced beef burgers, barbecue, grill or pan-fry the burgers for 4 minutes on each side for a medium-rare burger. Allow 5 minutes per side for a medium burger and 6 minutes for a well-done burger. These guidelines will need to be adjusted according to the size of your burgers and the cooking heat.

## BREAD, BUNS & ACCOMPANIMENTS

The obvious partner to a burger is a sesame seed bun; however many unusual breads and buns are recommended in the following recipes. For example, focaccia and ciabatta bread complement Italian-style burgers while pitta breads can be used for Mediterranean-style burgers. Chinese pancakes, crepes and soft flour tortillas make interesting choices, as do muffins and bagels. But none of the suggestions on the following pages is set in stone. Experiment with the breads available to you to create your own combinations.

Because many people prefer to eat accompaniments alongside their burgers, a selection of recipes for salads, chips and crisps have been included in the last chapter, *Side Orders*.

**RIGHT:** Choose from a range of international breads bought from your local supermarket, speciality shop or those you have made yourself.

# MARINADES & CONDIMENTS

Burgers can be given exciting flavours by marinating them prior to cooking, and condiments, such as salsas and relishes, add a different texture to a burger in a bun. The recipes in this chapter are referred to in the specific burger recipes throughout the book, and all the marinades are of sufficient quantity for four burgers. Because tomato sauce and mustard are in stock in most households, more exotic recipes are included here, such as Pumpkin Relish and Tropical Mango Salsa, along with suggested flavourings for mayonnaise.

## LEMON MARINADE

180 ml (6 fl oz) sunflower oil
Grated zest and juice of 1 small lemon
2.5 ml (½ tsp) cracked black pepper
30 ml (2 tbsp) chopped fresh dill

To make the marinade, place all the ingredients in a bowl and mix well to combine. Use as required to marinate burgers. Repeat this process for all the marinade variations opposite.

### TANGY MARINADE

180 ml (6 fl oz) grapeseed oil
Grated zest and juice of 1 lime
45 ml (3 tbsp) finely chopped coriander

### MEDITERRANEAN MARINADE

180 ml (6 fl oz) olive oil
15 ml (1 tbsp) sun-dried tomato paste
2 cloves garlic, crushed
5 ml (1 tsp) chopped fresh oregano
15 ml (1 tbsp) chopped fresh thyme

### CHINESE MARINADE

15 ml (1 tbsp) sesame oil
45 ml (3 tbsp) sunflower oil
60 ml (4 tbsp) soy sauce
30 ml (2 tbsp) clear honey
10 ml (2 tsp) Chinese five-spice powder
2 cloves garlic, crushed
1 stalk fresh lemon grass, finely chopped

### TANDOORI MARINADE

100 g (4 oz) thin natural yoghurt
10 ml (2 tsp) garam masala
5 ml (1 tsp) ground cumin
2.5 ml (½ tsp) chilli powder
2.5 ml (½ tsp) turmeric
45 ml (3 tbsp) chopped fresh mint

**CLOCKWISE AND CENTRE:** Tandoori Marinade, Tangy Marinade, Mediterranean Marinade, Chinese Marinade, Lemon Marinade

## MAYONNAISE

2 egg yolks
5 ml (1 tsp) Dijon mustard
Salt and ground black pepper
Pinch of caster sugar
300 ml (½ pint) olive oil
30 ml (2 tbsp) white wine vinegar

Place the egg yolks in a bowl and whisk until thick. Stir in the mustard, seasoning and sugar; beat to combine.

Add the oil, drop by drop, whisking well between each addition. Each drop of oil should be thoroughly absorbed before more is added. As the mayonnaise thickens and becomes shiny, the oil may be added in a thin stream. Finally, blend in the vinegar.

If you prefer, make the mayonnaise in a food processor by blending together the egg and seasonings, then pouring in the oil in a steady stream until the mayonnaise is thick and shiny. Lastly, blend in the vinegar.

Store the mayonnaise in a covered jar in the refrigerator and use as required.

## SWEET PEPPER MAYONNAISE

90 ml (6 tbsp) mayonnaise
45 ml (3 tbsp) diced mixed-coloured peppers
15-30 ml (1-2 tbsp) chopped fresh coriander

Mix all the ingredients together. Cover and chill until needed. Use as required. Follow this method for all the variations below.

### CHILLI MAYONNAISE

120 ml (4 fl oz) mayonnaise
½ red chilli, seeded and chopped
½ green chilli, seeded and chopped
5 ml (1 tsp) chilli sauce

### GARLIC MAYONNAISE

120 ml (4 fl oz) mayonnaise
2 cloves garlic, crushed

### HERB MAYONNAISE

120 ml (4 fl oz) mayonnaise
30 ml (2 tbsp) chopped mixed herbs, or use a single herb of your choice

### MUSTARD MAYONNAISE

120 ml (4 fl oz) mayonnaise
30 ml (2 tbsp) Dijon or coarse-grain mustard

### SESAME MAYONNAISE

120 ml (4 fl oz) mayonnaise
5 ml (1 tsp) sesame oil
2.5 ml (½ tsp) sesame seeds, toasted

### TOMATO MAYONNAISE

120 ml (4 fl oz) mayonnaise
10 ml (2 tsp) sun-dried tomato paste

**CLOCKWISE:** Chilli Mayonnaise, Herb Mayonnaise, Sesame Mayonnaise, Sweet Pepper Mayonnaise, Mustard Mayonnaise

## TANGY TOMATO SALSA

2 ripe beef tomatoes
½ small green pepper, seeded
1 small shallot, very finely chopped
30 ml (2 tbsp) chopped fresh coriander
Freshly squeezed juice of 1 lime
Salt and ground black pepper
Pinch of caster sugar

Cut the tomatoes into small cubes and place them in a bowl. Dice the pepper finely and add this to the bowl of tomatoes, together with the other ingredients. Toss gently to combine. Cover and chill for 1 hour before serving to allow the flavours to develop.
SERVES 4-6

## TROPICAL MANGO SALSA

1 small mango, peeled and finely chopped
75 g (3 oz) black grapes, seeded and
roughly chopped
2 slices fresh pineapple, finely diced
Pulp of 1 passion fruit
1 fresh green chilli, seeded and sliced
Grated zest and juice of 1 lime

Place all the ingredients in a bowl and toss gently to combine. Chill the mango salsa for 2-3 hours before serving to allow the flavours to develop.
SERVES 4-6

## CRANBERRY RELISH

100 g (4 oz) cranberry sauce
15 ml (1 tbsp) sultanas
15 ml (1 tbsp) chopped fresh thyme
1 orange, segmented and coarsely chopped

Place all the ingredients in a bowl and toss gently to combine. Chill and use as required.     SERVES 4-6

## CUCUMBER RELISH

½ cucumber, peeled and thinly sliced
1 large red chilli, seeded and sliced
1 shallot, finely chopped
30 ml (2 tbsp) rice wine vinegar
5 ml (1 tsp) caster sugar

Place all the ingredients in a bowl and toss gently to combine. Chill and use as required.     SERVES 4-6

**CLOCKWISE:** Tropical Mango Salsa, Cranberry Relish, Cucumber Relish, Tangy Tomato Salsa

## TOMATO RELISH

900 g (2 lb) ripe tomatoes
50 g (2 oz) onion
5 ml (1 tsp) allspice berries, cracked
8 whole celery leaves
100 ml (3½ fl oz) red wine vinegar
5 ml (1 tsp) cayenne pepper
15 ml (1 tbsp) mustard seeds
100 g (4 oz) soft brown sugar
Salt to taste

Wash and quarter the tomatoes and place them in a heavy-based saucepan. Dice the onion and separate it into layers. Add these to the pan, together with the allspice berries and celery leaves. Cover the pan and cook the tomato mixture over a gentle heat for 45 minutes.

Uncover the pan and add the vinegar, cayenne, mustard seeds, sugar and salt to the cooked tomatoes. Stir gently to mix in these ingredients and cook the relish, uncovered, for a further 35 minutes until it is pulpy and the juices are reduced and thickened.

Pour the hot relish into warmed, sterilized jars, allow to cool slightly, then seal and label. This relish will keep well for a month. Once opened, store in the refrigerator.      MAKES ABOUT 900 G (2 LB)

## PUMPKIN RELISH

1.5 kg (3 lb) pumpkin, peeled, seeded and cubed
Salt
5-cm (2-inch) piece fresh ginger, peeled
and grated
225 g (8 oz) shallots, peeled and sliced
225 g (8 oz) soft brown sugar
1 small green pepper, seeded and cubed
1 small red pepper, seeded and cubed
225 g (8 oz) cooking apples, peeled, cored and
chopped
100 g (4 oz) raisins
300 ml (½ pint) cider vinegar
2.5 ml (½ tsp) cracked black pepper

Place the pumpkin in a bowl, sprinkle over some salt to coat the pumpkin cubes and leave overnight.

The next day, drain off the liquid and rinse the pumpkin in cold water. Place the pumpkin in a large preserving pan with the remaining ingredients. Bring the mixture to the boil, then reduce the heat and simmer for about 1 hour, until the mixture is soft and pulpy.

Cool the mixture slightly, then pack the relish into warmed, sterilized jars and seal and label. The relish will keep for several months. Once opened, store in the refrigerator.      MAKES ABOUT 1.5 KG (3 LB)

**TOP:** Pumpkin Relish
**BOTTOM:** Tomato Relish

# CLASSIC BURGERS

*The recipes in this chapter all owe their inspiration to American-style burgers. Along with the standard Cheeseburger, there are more varied burgers, such as the Hickory Barbecue Burger and the Chilli Burger. All of the recipes contain minced beef as their main ingredient. The best beef burgers are made with beef that has a little fat included, which creates juicy burgers.*

## CLASSIC HAMBURGERS

700 g (1½ lb) medium- or coarse-ground beef
Salt and ground black pepper
4 sesame seed buns, split lengthways
A little butter, softened
Sliced onion
Shredded iceberg lettuce
Dijon mustard, dill pickles and tomato ketchup,
to serve.

Place the beef and seasoning in a bowl and combine. Divide the mixture into four equal portions and shape into patties to fit the buns.

Prepare a barbecue, grill or pan for cooking the burgers. Brush the rack or pan with a little oil and cook the burgers, turning once with a large spatula. Cook for 4 minutes on each side for a medium-rare burger or longer. Towards the end of cooking, butter the cut sides of the buns and grill to toast lightly.

To serve, divide the onion slices and lettuce between the four bottom bun halves. Place a burger on each and finish with the bun tops. Pass condiments separately. SERVES 4

## CHEESEBURGERS

700 g (1½ lb) medium- or coarse-ground beef
Salt and ground black pepper
20 ml (4 tsp) Worcestershire sauce
4 slices American or Cheddar cheese
A little butter, softened
4 sesame seed buns, split lengthways
Soft lettuce leaves
Sliced dill pickles
Sliced tomatoes
Onion rings
Tomato ketchup

Place the beef, seasoning and Worcestershire sauce in a bowl and mix well to combine. Divide the mixture into four equal portions and shape into patties to fit the buns.

Prepare a barbecue, grill or pan for cooking the burgers. Brush the rack or pan with a little oil and cook the burgers, turning once with a large spatula. Cook for 4 minutes on each side for a medium-rare burger or longer if a more thoroughly cooked burger is required. Just before the burgers are ready, top each one with a slice of cheese and allow to melt.

Towards the end of cooking, butter the cut sides of the buns and grill to toast lightly.

To serve, divide the lettuce between the four bottom halves of the buns. Place a burger on each, top with sliced dill pickles, sliced tomatoes, onion rings and ketchup and finish with the bun tops. Serve at once. SERVES 4

**RIGHT:** Classic Hamburger

# BACON CHEESEBURGERS

700 g (1½ lb) medium- or coarse-ground beef
Salt and ground black pepper
20 ml (4 tsp) Worcestershire sauce
8 rindless rashers smoked streaky bacon
4 x 25 g (1 oz) slices Emmental cheese
Sliced white onion
Soft lettuce leaves
4 small tomatoes
Sliced dill pickles
A little butter, softened
4 sesame seed buns, halved lengthways
Yellow mustard, tomato ketchup and Mayonnaise
(see page 222)

Place the beef, seasoning and Worcestershire sauce in a bowl and mix well to combine. Divide the mixture into four equal portions. Shape into patties to fit the buns. Cover and leave in a cool place until required. Cook the bacon until crisp and keep it warm.

Prepare the barbecue, grill or pan for cooking the burgers. Brush the rack or pan with a little vegetable oil and cook the burgers, turning once. Cook for 4 minutes on each side for a medium-rare burger or longer if a more thoroughly cooked burger is required. Just before the burgers are ready, top each one with a slice of cheese and allow to melt. Towards the end of cooking, butter the cut sides of the buns and grill to toast lightly.

To serve, divide the onion, lettuce, tomatoes and dill pickles between the four bottom halves of the buns. Place a burger on each and top each burger with two rashers of crispy bacon and a bun top. Serve the condiments separately. SERVES 4

# BACON & BLUE CHEESE BURGERS

700 g (1½ lb) medium- or coarse-ground beef
Salt and ground black pepper
4 x 25 g (1 oz) Slices Dolcelatte cheese
Sliced plum tomatoes
Soft lettuce leaves
4 ciabatta buns, split lengthways
Olive oil for brushing
4 slices cooked pancetta (Italian cured 'bacon'), halved

Place the beef and seasoning in a bowl and mix well to combine. Divide the mixture into four equal portions and shape into patties.

Prepare the barbecue, grill or pan for cooking the burgers. Brush the rack or pan with a little oil and cook the burgers, turning once with a large spatula. Cook for 4 minutes on each side for a medium-rare burger or longer if a more thoroughly cooked burger is required. Towards the end of cooking, top each burger with a slice of cheese and allow to melt. Brush the cut sides of the buns with olive oil and toast them lightly.

To serve, divide the lettuce and sliced tomatoes between the four bottom halves of the buns. Place a cheeseburger on each and top each burger with a slice of cooked pancetta. Finish with the bun tops and serve at once. SERVES 4

**TOP:** Bacon Cheeseburger
**BOTTOM:** Bacon & Blue Cheese Burger

## BURGERS WITH MUSHROOM TOPPING

700 g (1½ lb) lean minced beef
Salt and ground black pepper
1 small onion, very finely chopped
4 wholemeal hamburger buns, split lengthways
Frisée lettuce leaves

### MUSHROOM TOPPING

75 g (3 oz) butter
45 ml (3 tbsp) vegetable oil
225 g (8 oz) mixed mushrooms, such as brown cap,
field, oysters and girolles, sliced
Salt and ground black pepper

Place the beef, seasoning and onion in a bowl and mix well to combine. Divide the mixture into four equal portions and shape into patties to fit the buns.

Prepare a barbecue, grill or pan for cooking the burgers. Brush the rack or pan with a little oil and cook the burgers, turning once. Cook for 4 minutes on each side for a medium-rare burger or longer if a more thoroughly cooked burger is required.

When the burgers are half-cooked, start cooking the mushroom topping. Heat half the butter and half the oil in a large frying pan and sauté half the mushrooms for about 2 minutes until lightly cooked. Season well and keep warm while cooking the second batch of mushrooms.

Toast the wholemeal buns and place a little frisée lettuce on the four bottom halves of the buns. Place a burger on each, top each burger with a quarter of the cooked mushrooms and finish with the bun tops. Serve at once. SERVES 4

## ONION & MUSTARD BURGERS

700 g (1½ lb) lean minced beef
Salt and ground black pepper
10 ml (2 tsp) mustard powder
60 ml (4 tbsp) Mayonnaise (see page 222)
20 ml (4 tsp) American mustard
A little butter, softened
4 floury white buns, split lengthways

### CARAMELIZED ONIONS

2 large onions, sliced into rings
45 ml (3 tbsp) vegetable oil
10 ml (2 tsp) soft brown sugar

Place the beef and seasoning in a bowl and mix well to combine. Divide the mixture into four equal portions and shape into patties

Prepare the caramelized onions. Heat the oil in a pan and add the onion rings. Cook over a gentle heat for about 8-10 minutes until the onions are really soft. Stir in the sugar and cook for a further 2 minutes. Set aside.

Prepare a barbecue, grill or pan for cooking the burgers. Brush the rack or pan with a little oil and cook the burgers, turning once. Cook for 4 minutes on each side for a medium-rare burger or longer if desired.

Mix together the mayonnaise and American mustard and set aside. Butter the cut sides of the buns sparingly and grill to toast lightly.

To serve, divide the mayonnaise between the four bottom halves of the buns. Place a burger on each, then top with the caramelized onions and bun tops. Serve immediately. SERVES 4

**RIGHT:** Burger with Mushroom Topping

## CHILLI BURGERS

30 ml (2 tbsp) vegetable oil
1 onion, finely chopped
2 cloves garlic, crushed
15 ml (1 tbsp) crushed chilli flakes
10 ml (2 tsp) ground cumin
700 g (1½ lb) minced beef
30 ml (2 tbsp) sun-dried tomato paste
60 ml (4 tbsp) chopped fresh coriander
Salt and ground black pepper
4 wheat tortillas, warmed through
Cos lettuce leaves, onion rings and sliced tomato,
to serve

Heat the oil in a pan and cook the onion and garlic for 3 minutes until soft. Add the crushed chilli flakes and cumin and cook for a further 2 minutes. Set aside to cool.

Place the beef in a bowl. Add the cooked onion mixture, sun-dried tomato paste, coriander and seasoning, and mix well to combine. Divide the mixture into four equal portions and shape into patties.

Prepare a barbecue, grill or pan for cooking the burgers. Brush the rack or pan with a little oil and cook the burgers, turning once. Cook for 4 minutes on each side for a medium-rare burger or longer if a more thoroughly cooked burger is required.

Serve each burger in a warm tortilla with lettuce, onion and tomato. SERVES 4

## HICKORY BARBECUE BURGERS

700 g (1½ lb) ground sirloin steak
1 small onion, finely chopped
60 ml (4 tbsp) good quality barbecue sauce
30 ml (2 tbsp) chopped fresh parsley
Salt and ground black pepper
A little butter, softened
4 hamburger buns, split lengthways
Salad garnish to include lettuce, tomato and sliced green peppers
Sliced dill pickles
Extra barbecue sauce

Place the beef, onion, barbecue sauce, parsley and seasoning in a bowl and mix well to combine. Divide the mixture into four equal portions and shape into patties to fit the buns.

Prepare a barbecue, grill or pan for cooking the burgers. Brush the rack or pan with a little oil and cook the burgers, turning once. Cook for 4 minutes on each side for a medium-rare burger or longer if a more thoroughly cooked burger is required. Butter the cut sides of the buns sparingly and toast them lightly.

To serve, divide the salad garnish between the four bottom halves of the buns. Place a burger on each, top with dill pickles and then with the bun tops. Serve at once, passing extra barbecue sauce separately. SERVES 4

**TOP:** Hickory Barbecue Burger
**BOTTOM:** Chilli Burger

## DOUBLE-DECKER BURGERS

### HERB BURGERS

450 g (1 lb) lean minced beef
5 ml (1 tsp) mixed dried herbs
Salt and ground black pepper

### BEEF AND MUSHROOM BURGERS

50 g (2 oz) butter
100 g (4 oz) button mushrooms, chopped
450 g (1 lb) lean minced beef
Salt and ground black pepper

4 wholemeal hamburger buns, each sliced in three
horizontal layers
Soft lettuce leaves
Yellow American mustard
Sliced onion
Tomato Relish (see page 226)

Place the beef, herbs and seasoning for the herb burgers in a bowl and mix well to combine. Divide the mixture into four equal portions and shape into patties and set aside.

Prepare the beef and mushroom burgers. Melt the butter in a pan and sauté the mushrooms for 3-4 minutes. Cool slightly and then add to the minced beef and seasoning. Mix well and shape into four patties.

Prepare the barbecue, grill or pan for cooking the burgers. Brush the rack or pan with a little oil and cook the burgers, turning once. Cook for 2½ minutes on each side for a medium-rare burger or longer if desired.

To serve, divide the soft lettuce between the four bun bottoms. Place a mushroom burger on each and top with the middle bun layers. Place a herb burger on each bun and top with mustard, onion and Tomato Relish. Finish with the bun tops and serve.   SERVES 4

## HAWAIIAN BURGERS

700 g (1½ lb) medium- or coarse-ground minced beef
Salt and ground black pepper
30 ml (2 tbsp) chopped fresh parsley
4 sesame seed buns, split lengthways
Mayonnaise (see page 222)
Cos lettuce leaves
4 slices honey-roast ham
4 slices canned or fresh pineapple

Place the beef, seasoning and parsley in a bowl and mix well to combine. Divide the mixture into four equal portions and shape into patties to fit the buns.

Prepare the barbecue, grill or pan for cooking the burgers. Brush the rack or pan with a little oil and cook the burgers, turning once. Cook for 4 minutes on each side for a medium-rare burger or longer if a more thoroughly cooked burger is required. Toast the cut sides of the buns lightly.

To serve, top the four bottom halves of the buns with a dollop of mayonnaise, followed by pieces of cos lettuce leaves and a slice of ham. Place a burger on each and top with a slice of pineapple. Finish with the bun tops and serve at once, passing extra mayonnaise separately.   SERVES 4

**RIGHT:** Hawaiian Burger

# FROM THE TURF

*The following recipes use a wide variety of meats to create internationally flavoured burgers, such as the Chinese Burger. The unusual Croque Monsieur and 'Café Parisien' burgers are French-bistro inspired. Along with beef, chicken, pork and lamb, some of the other meats used in this chapter are venison, veal, turkey and sausage.*

## RIO GRANDE BURGERS

700 g (1½ lb) coarse-ground beef
75 g (3 oz) onion, finely chopped
Salt and ground black pepper
2.5 ml (½ tsp) ground cumin
2.5 ml (½ tsp) ground coriander
2 cloves garlic, crushed
A little butter, softened
4 granary buns, halved lengthways
1 large jalapeño chilli, thinly sliced
Batavia lettuce leaves
1 onion, sliced into rings
Sweet Pepper Mayonnaise (see page 222)

Place the beef, onion, seasoning, spices and garlic in a bowl and mix well. Divide the mixture into four and shape into patties.

Prepare the barbecue, grill or pan for cooking the burgers. Brush the rack or pan with a little oil and cook the burgers, turning once. Cook for 4 minutes on each side for a medium-rare burger or longer. Towards the end of cooking, butter the cut sides of the buns and grill to toast.

To serve, divide the chilli, lettuce and onion between the four bottom halves of the buns. Place a burger on each and top with a spoonful of Sweet Pepper Mayonnaise. Finish with the bun tops and serve at once. SERVES 4

## HERBED BEEF PATTIES

700 g (1½ lb) coarse-ground beef
60 ml (4 tbsp) chopped fresh mixed herbs, such as parsley, chives, oregano and thyme
Salt and ground black pepper
Lemon Marinade (see page 220)
8 slices cornbread
lettuce
Onion rings
Garlic Mayonnaise (see page 222)
Halved cherry tomatoes, to serve

Place the beef, herbs and seasoning in a bowl and mix well to combine. Divide the mixture into four and shape into patties. Place the patties in a single layer in a glass dish and pour over the marinade. Cover and chill for at least 2 hours or, preferably, overnight.

Either barbecue or pan-fry the patties, basting each one well before starting to cook them. Cook for 4 minutes on each side for a medium-rare patty or longer if a more thoroughly cooked patty is required. Towards the end of cooking, toast the slices of corn-meal bread lightly.

To serve, divide the lettuce and onion rings between the four slices of bread, top each with a patty and spoon over a dollop of Garlic Mayonnaise. Finish with the remaining slices of bread and serve at once with cherry tomatoes. SERVES 4

**RIGHT:** Rio Grande Burger

## ITALIAN BURGERS

700 g (1½ lb) coarse-ground beef

100 g (4 oz) full-flavoured Italian salami, finely chopped

60 ml (4 tbsp) chopped fresh oregano

Salt and ground black pepper

Mediterranean Marinade (see page 220)

225 g (8 oz) mozzarella cheese, cut into 4

4 pieces focaccia bread, halved lengthways

Oak leaf lettuce

Sliced beef tomatoes

Sliced red onions

Place the beef, salami, oregano and seasoning in a bowl and mix well to combine. Divide the mixture into four equal portions and shape into patties. Place the patties in a single layer in a glass dish and pour over the marinade. Cover and chill for at least 2 hours or overnight.

Either grill or barbecue the burgers. Cook them for 5 minutes on one side, basing with reserved marinade, and then turn them over and cook for a further 5 minutes, continuing to baste. Top each burger with a slice of mozzarella for the last 1½ minutes of cooking. These times will produce a medium-rare burger; adjust cooking times to suit personal preference. Toast the cut sides of the focaccia bread lightly.

To serve, divide the lettuce and tomato between the four bottom pieces of bread. Place a burger on each and top with red onion slices. Finish with the top slices of bread and serve immediately.      SERVES 4

## BEEF, BASIL & TOMATO BURGERS

700 g (1½ lb) ground beef or sirloin

30 ml (2 tbsp) sun-dried tomatoes in oil, drained and chopped

30 ml (2 tbsp) shredded fresh basil

60 ml (4 tbsp) grated Parmesan cheese

Salt and ground black pepper

4 ciabatta buns, halved lengthways

Olive oil for brushing

100 g (4 oz) mixed Italian salad leaves

Fresh basil leaves

Sun-dried tomato strips

Mayonnaise (see page 222)

Place the ground beef, sun-dried tomato, basil, Parmesan and seasoning in a bowl and mix well to combine. Divide the mixture into four equal portions and shape into patties. Cover and chill until required.

These burgers may be grilled, barbecued or pan-fried. Brush the grill rack or pan with olive oil and cook the burgers, turning once. Cook for 4 minutes on each side of a medium-rare burger or longer if a more thoroughly cooked burger is required. Towards the end of cooking, brush the cut sides of the buns with olive oil and grill to toast lightly.

To serve, place a small amount of the mixed salad leaves on the bottom half of each bun. Place a burger on each and top with fresh basil, sun-dried tomato strips and a dollop of mayonnaise. Finish with the bun tops and divide the remaining salad between four plates.      SERVES 4

**TOP:** Italian Burger

**BOTTOM:** Beef, Basil & Tomato Burger

# BOMBAY BURGERS

30 ml (2 tbsp) vegetable oil

I onion, finely chopped

25ml curry powder

5 ml (I tsp) turmeric

700 g (1½ lb) minced lamb

45 ml (3 tbsp) cooked green peas

Salt and ground black pepper

Tandoori Marinade (see page 220)

4 mini naan breads, split lengthways

Cos lettuce leaves

Greek-style natural yoghurt

Tropical Mango Salsa (see page 224)

Heat the oil in a pan and cook the onion and spices for 3-4 minutes until soft. Cool this mixture, then add the minced lamb, peas and seasoning, and mix well to combine. Divide the mixture into four equal portions and shape into patties. Place the patties in a single layer in a glass dish and pour over the marinade. Cover and chill for at least 2 hours, preferably, overnight.

Pan-fry the burgers; cook them over a fairly low heat for 7 minutes on each side until they are cooked all the way through. Warm the naan breads.

To serve, divide the lettuce between the four bottom halves of bread. Dollop a spoonful of yoghurt over each bed of lettuce and top with a burger. Spoon over some mango salsa and finish with the naan tops. Serve at once with extra salsa and yoghurt.       SERVES 4

# MOROCCAN BURGERS

30 ml (2 tbsp) olive oil

3 cloves garlic, crushed

30 ml (2 tbsp) pine nuts

15 ml (I tbsp) ground coriander

10 ml (2 tsp) ground cumin

700 g (1½ lb) minced lamb

60 ml (4 tbsp) finely chopped dried apricots

Salt and ground black pepper

4 pitta breads, split lengthways

Shredded iceberg lettuce

## CUCUMBER AND MINT YOGHURT

175 g (6 oz) natural yoghurt

100 g (4 oz) cucumber, finely diced

15 ml (I tbsp) chopped fresh mint

Heat the oil in a pan and cook the garlic for 2-3 minutes until soft. Add the pine nuts and cook for a further minute. Stir in the spices and cook them briefly. Cool the mixture slightly.

Place the lamb, apricots and seasoning in a bowl. Add the cooled garlic mixture and mix well to combine. Divide the mixture into four equal portions and shape into patties.

Prepare a barbecue, grill or pan for cooking the burgers. Brush the rack or pan with a little oil and cook the burgers for 6-7 minutes on each side until cooked through.

Mix together the yoghurt, cucumber and chopped mint. Warm the pitta bread.

To serve, place some lettuce and a burger in each pocket, spoon over some yoghurt and serve at once, passing extra yoghurt separately.       SERVES 4

**RIGHT:** Bombay Burger

## CHINESE BURGERS

700 g (1½ lb) minced pork
3 spring onions, finely chopped
15 ml (1 tbsp) grated fresh ginger
30 ml (2 tbsp) soy sauce
16 water chestnuts, finely chopped
Chinese Marinade (see page 220)
8 Chinese pancakes, available from Oriental
supermarkets
Chilli sauce, to serve

### BEANSPROUT SALAD

150 g (5 oz) beansprouts
6 radishes, sliced
50 g (2 oz) cucumber, cut into thin strips
1 green chilli, seeded and sliced
45 ml (3 tbsp) chopped fresh coriander

Place the pork, spring onion, ginger, soy sauce and water chestnuts in a bowl and mix well to combine. Divide the mixture into four equal portions and shape into patties. Place the patties in a single layer in a glass dish and pour over the marinade. Cover and chill for at least 2 hours, preferably, overnight.

Either grill or barbecue these burgers, cooking them for 5-6 minutes on each side, basting with the reserved marinade during cooking.

Place the ingredients for the salad in a bowl and toss well. Warm the Chinese pancakes.

To serve, place some salad on two pancakes, top with a burger and fold pancakes over. Repeat for the remaining burgers. Serve at once, passing the chilli sauce separately. SERVES 4

## MARINATED PORK BURGERS

*Use quick-polenta or traditional cornmeal in this recipe. Follow the packet instructions to cook polenta, then proceed as described in the recipe.*

700 g (1½ lb) minced pork
60 ml (4 tbsp) chopped fresh coriander
2 cloves garlic, crushed
Salt and ground black pepper
Tangy Marinade (see page 220)
4 circles of cooked polenta, cut to fit the burgers
A little olive oil fro brushing
Frisée and radicchio leaves, to serve

Place the pork, coriander, garlic and seasoning in a bowl and mix well to combine. Divide the mixture into four equal portions and shape into patties. Place the patties in a single layer in a glass dish and pour over the marinade. Cover and chill for at least 2 hours, preferably, overnight.

Either grill or barbecue the burgers, cooking them for 4 minutes on one side, basting with the reserved marinade. Turn them over, baste again, and cook for a further 4 minutes until cooked through.

Brush the circle of polenta with olive oil and grill or barbecue them for 3 minutes on each side until they are pale golden.

To serve, place a burger on each circle of polenta and serve at once, garnished with the salad leaves.
SERVES 4

**TOP:** Marinated Pork Burger
**BOTTOM:** Chinese Burger

## SPICY CHICKEN & CORN BURGERS

30 ml (2 tbsp) olive oil

I onion, finely chopped

2 cloves garlic, crushed

15 ml (I tbsp) paprika

700 g (I ½ lb) minced chicken

100 g (4 oz) canned sweetcorn kernels, drained

Salt and ground black pepper

4 hamburger buns, split lengthways

150 g (5 oz) mature Gouda cheese, grated

Little Gem lettuce leaves

Red pepper rings

Mayonnaise (see page 222)

Tomato Relish (see page 226), to serve

Heat the oil in a pan and cook the onion and garlic for 4 minutes until soft. Stir in the paprika and cook for a further minute. Cool the mixture slightly and then combine it with the chicken, corn and seasoning. Divide into four portions and shape into patties.

Prepare a barbecue, grill or pan for cooking the burgers. Brush the rack or pan with a little oil and cook the burgers for 5 minutes on each side until cooked through.

Grill the cut sides of the burger buns to toast lightly. Turn the four tops of the buns over and sprinkle with the grated cheese. Grill the cheesy bun tops for a further I ½ minutes until the cheese is melted.

To serve, divide the lettuce between the four bottom halves of bun, top with red pepper rings and the burgers, spoon over some mayonnaise and finish with the bun tops. Serve at once, accompanied by Tomato Relish. SERVES 4

## CHICKEN BURGERS WITH TARRAGON & PROSCIUTTO

30 ml (2 tbsp) vegetable oil

I red onion, finely chopped

2 cloves garlic, crushed

700 g (I ½ lb) minced chicken

Salt and ground black pepper

100 g (4 oz) prosciutto (Parma ham), cut into thin strips

30 ml (2 tbsp) chopped fresh tarragon

A little butter, softened

4 mixed-grain buns, split lengthways

Lettuce leaves

Marinated artichokes and marinated green olives, to serve

Heat the oil in a pan and cook the onion and garlic for 3 minutes until soft. Cool the mixture and place it in a bowl with the chicken and seasoning; mix well to combine. Divide into eight equal portions and shape into patties. Place a quarter of the prosciutto and tarragon in the centre of the four of the patties. Place the other four patties over these and reshape to make four stuffed burgers.

Prepare a barbecue, grill or pan for cooking the burgers. Brush the rack or pan with a little oil and cook the burgers for 4½ minutes on each side until cooked through. Butter the cut sides of the buns and toast them lightly.

To serve, divide the lettuce between the four bottom halves of bun. Top with a burger and finish with the bun tops. Serve at once with marinated artichokes and olives. SERVES 4

**TOP:** Spicy Chicken & Corn Burger
**BOTTOM:** Chicken Burger with
Tarragon & Prosciutto

## TURKEY, ORANGE & THYME BURGERS

700 g (1½ lb) minced turkey
1 shallot, finely chopped
30 ml (2 tbsp) chopped fresh thyme
30 ml (2 tbsp) grated orange zest
Salt and ground black pepper
8 slices sourdough rye bread
Lamb's lettuce (corn salad)
Mayonnaise (see page 222)
Cranberry Relish (see page 224)

Place the turkey, shallot, thyme, orange zest and seasoning in a bowl and mix well to combine. Divide the mixture into four portions and shape into patties.

Prepare a barbecue, grill or pan for cooking the burgers. Brush the rack or pan with a little oil and cook the burgers for 4 minutes on each side until cooked through. Toast the slices of bread lightly.

To serve, divide the lamb's lettuce between four slices of bread, top with mayonnaise and a burger and place a spoonful of relish on each burger. Top the burgers with the remaining slices of bread and serve at once with extra relish and mayonnaise.     SERVES 4

## TURKEY TIKKA BURGERS

700 g (1½ lb) minced turkey
40ml tikka paste
60 ml (4 tbsp) chopped fresh coriander
Salt and ground black pepper
4 mini naan breads, split lengthways
Red onion slices
Cos lettuce leaves
Lemon wedges, to serve

### MINT RAITA
175 g (6 oz) natural yoghurt
45 ml (3 tbsp) chopped fresh mint
Pinch of paprika

Place the turkey, tikka paste, coriander and seasoning in a bowl and mix well to combine. Divide the mixture into four equal portions and shape into patties.

Prepare a barbecue, grill or pan for cooking the burgers. Brush the rack or pan with a little oil and cook the burgers for 3½ minutes on each side until cooked through.

Place the ingredients for the raita in a bowl and mix well to combine.

To serve, divide the onion and lettuce between the four bottom halves of the naan breads and top each with a burger, followed by a spoonful of raita. finish with the naan tops and serve at once with lemon wedges, passing extra raita separately.     SERVES 4

**RIGHT:** Turkey, Orange & Thyme Burger

## GREEK BURGERS

60 ml (4 tbsp) olive oil
1 onion, finely chopped
3 cloves garlic, crushed
450 g (1 lb) minced beef
450 g (1 lb) minced lamb
60 ml (4 tbsp) chopped fresh parsley
24 calamata olives, stoned and chopped
Salt and ground black pepper
225 g (8 oz) feta cheese, cubed
4 pitta breads, split lengthways
Lettuce leaves
Sliced beef tomatoes
Greek-style pickled green chillies, to serve

Heat half of the oil in a pan and cook the onion and garlic for 4 minutes until soft. Cool this mixture and then place in a bowl with the minced meats, parsley, olives and seasoning and mix well. Divide into four equal portions and shape into patties.

Brush the burgers with the remaining oil and grill under a medium-hot grill for 6 minutes on each side. Two or three minutes before the end of cooking time, divide the cheese cubes between the four burgers and return to the grill to cook the cheese until it turns a golden colour. (The grill rack may need to be inverted when cooking the cheese, so it is not so close to the heat.) Warm the pitta breads.

To serve, divide the lettuce and tomato between the pitta breads and top each with a burger. Serve with pickled green chillies. SERVES 4

## LAMB & HAZELNUT BURGERS WITH GOAT'S CHEESE

45 ml (3 tbsp) olive oil
3 shallots, finely chopped
2 cloves garlic, crushed
700 g (1½ lb) minced lamb
15 ml (1 tbsp) chopped fresh rosemary
15 ml (1 tbsp) chopped fresh thyme
25 g (1 oz) toasted hazelnuts, chopped
Salt and ground black pepper
150 g (5 oz) goat's cheese, sliced into 4
4 slices olive ciabatta bread or focaccia bread
Continental salad leaves
Sliced plum tomatoes

Heat 30 ml (2 tbsp) of the oil in a pan and cook the shallots and garlic for 4 minutes until soft. Cool the mixture and then place it in a bowl with the lamb, herbs, nuts and seasoning. Mix well, divide into four equal portions and shape into patties.

Brush the burgers with the remaining oil and grill under a medium-hot grill for 4½ minutes on each side. Two minutes before the end of cooking time, place a slice of goat's cheese on each burger and return to the grill to melt the cheese. (The grill rack may need to be inverted when cooking the cheese so it is not so close to the heat.) Toast the bread lightly.

To serve, place a burger on each piece of bread and garnish with the salad leaves and tomato slices. SERVES 4

**TOP:** Lamb & Hazelnut Burger with Goat's Cheese
**BOTTOM:** Greek Burger

## VEAL & SAGE BURGERS

25 g (1 oz) dried cep mushrooms

450 g (1 lb) minced veal

2 shallots, finely chopped

15 ml (1 tbsp) red wine

15 ml (1 tbsp) chopped fresh sage

Salt and ground black pepper

A little butter, softened

4 pieces French bread, split lengthways

Green salad and Herb Mayonnaise with sage
(see page 222), to serve

Soak the cep mushrooms in hot water for 10 minutes, then drain and chop finely. Place the ceps in a bowl with the veal, shallots, wine, sage and seasoning, and mix well to combined. Divide the mixture into four equal portions and shape into patties.

Prepare a barbecue, grill or pan for cooking the burgers. Brush the rack or pan with a little oil and cook the burgers for 4 minutes on each side until cooked through. Butter the cut sides of the French bread and grill until they are lightly toasted.

To serve, place the burgers between the slices of toasted bread and serve with green salad and Herb Mayonnaise.                     SERVES 4

## VENISON BURGERS WITH SPICED APPLES

450 g (1 lb) minced veal

15 ml (1 tbsp) chopped fresh thyme

15 ml (1 tbsp) chopped fresh parsley

Salt and ground black pepper

8 rashes streaky bacon, rinds removed

2 large red-skinned apples

50 g (2 oz) butter

2.5 ml (½ tsp) ground cinnamon

Good pinch of grated nutmeg

4 hamburger buns, split lengthways

Soft lettuce leaves

Place the venison, herbs and seasoning in a bowl and mix well to combine. Divide the mixture into four equal portions and shape into patties. Wrap two rashers of bacon around each burger and secure with cocktail sticks.

Grill or barbecue the burgers. Brush the rack or pan with a little oil and cook the burgers for 6 minutes on each side until cooked through. Toast the cut sides of the buns lightly.

While the burgers are cooking, prepare the spiced apples. Core the apples and slice them into thick rings. Heat half the butter in a large pan and cook half the apple slices for 4-5 minutes until tender. Sprinkle over half the spices and keep apples warm while cooking the second batch in the remaining butter.

To serve, place some soft lettuce on the bottom halves of the buns, top with some apple slices and a burger. Finish with the bun tops and serve at once.
SERVES 4

**RIGHT:** Venison Burger with Spiced Apples

## SANTIAGO BURGERS

450 g (1 lb) minced pork

100 g (4 oz) spicy Chorizo sausage, finely chopped

225 g (8 oz) cooked chick-peas, mashed

½ small green pepper, finely chopped

Salt and ground black pepper

8 slices Spanish country bread

Olive oil for brushing

Lettuce leaves

Onion rings and black olives, to serve

Place the pork, chorizo, chick-peas, pepper and seasoning in a bowl and mix well to combine. Divide the mixture into four portions and shape into patties.

Prepare a barbecue, grill or pan for cooking the burgers. Brush the rack or pan with a little vegetable oil and cook the burgers for 5 minutes on each side until cooked through. Brush the cut bread slices with olive oil and toast them lightly.

To serve, divide the lettuce between the four slices of the bread, top each with a burger and the remaining slices of bread. Serve at once, accompanied by onion rings and black olives.                    SERVES 4

## SATAY BURGERS

75 ml (5 tbsp) groundnut oil

2 shallots, finely chopped

3 cloves garlic, crushed

5 ml (1 tsp) ground coriander

5 ml (1 tsp) ground cumin

2.5 ml (½ tsp) turmeric

450 g (1 lb) minced chicken

8 slices white bread

Cucumber Relish (see page 224), to serve

### SPICY PEANUT SAUCE

15 ml (1 tbsp) vegetable oil

1 clove garlic, crushed

10 ml (2 tsp) crushed dried chillies

10 ml (2 tsp) dark soy sauce

30 ml (2 tbsp) soft brown sugar

90 ml (6 tbsp) crunchy peanut butter

150 ml (¼ pint) water

Heat 15 ml (1 tbsp) of the oil in a pan and cook the shallots and garlic for 3 minutes until soft. Stir in the spices and cook for a further minute. Cool the mixture and then mix it in a bowl with the minced chicken and seasoning. Divide into four and shape into patties.

Prepare the peanut sauce. Cook the garlic in the oil over a low heat for 2 minutes. Add the chillies and cook for a further minute. Stir in the remaining ingredients and simmer the sauce gently for 3 minutes. Keep warm.

Pan-fry the burgers in the remaining oil, cooking them for 4½ minutes on each side until cooked through. Toast the bread lightly.

To serve, place each burger between two slices of toast. Serve accompanied by the peanut sauce and Cucumber Relish.                    SERVES 4

**RIGHT:** Santiago Burger

## BURGERS 'CAFE PARISIEN'

4 x 100 g (4 oz) sirloin or rump steaks
Salt and ground black pepper
Olive oil for brushing
4 pieces French baguette, split
Dijon mustard, to taste
Frisée lettuce tossed in vinaigrette

Trim the steaks of all fat and season them well. Brush each steak with olive oil and grill for about 4½ minutes on each side under a moderately hot grill. This will produce a medium-rare steak – adjust the cooking times accordingly to suit personal preferences. Toast the French baguette lightly.

To serve, spread mustard on the cut sides of the toasted bread and sandwich the steaks between the pieces of baguette. Serve at once with the dressed frisée lettuce, passing extra mustard if desired.

SERVES 4

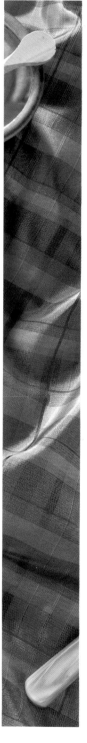

## CROQUE-MONSIEUR BISTRO BURGERS

4 x 75 g (3 oz) ham steaks
175 g (6 oz) Cantal or Cheddar cheese, grated
4 eggs, fried
4 thick slices French country bread
A little butter, softened
Sautéed mushrooms or grilled tomatoes,
to serve (optional)

Grease a large frying pan lightly and cook the ham steaks on one side for 3 minutes. Turn them over, sprinkle with the grated cheese and continue cooking for a further 3 minutes until the steaks are cooked and the cheese has begun to melt. Toast the bread lightly.

To serve, butter one side of the toasted bread slices and place a cheese and ham steak on each slice. Top each steak with a fried egg and serve at once with sautéed mushrooms or grilled tomatoes, if desired.

SERVES 4

**TOP:** Croque-Monsieur Bistro Burger
**BOTTOM:** Burger 'Café Parisien'

# FROM THE SURF

*Fish and seafood form the basic ingredients for the burgers in this chapter. Along with simple Tuna & Sweetcorn Burgers are exotic Acapulco Crab Burgers as well as highly unusual burgers, such as sesame-coated Spicy Thai Fish Patties and sushi-inspired Osaka Fish Cakes.*

## SALMON & DILL BURGERS

450 g (1 lb) skinless, boneless salmon, minced
100 g (4 oz) mashed potato
60 ml (4 tbsp) chopped fresh dill
30 ml (2 tbsp) chopped gherkins
5 ml (1 tsp) green peppercorns in brine, crushed
Salt to taste
120 ml (4 fl oz) sunflower oil
4 bagels, split lengthways
60 ml (4 tbsp) cream cheese
Watercress sprigs
Sliced dill pickles
Potato Salad (see page 282), to serve

Place the minced salmon, potato, dill, gherkins, peppercorns and salt in a bowl and mix well. Divide into four and shape into patties.

Heat the sunflower oil in a large frying pan and cook the burgers over a moderately low heat for 4½ minutes on each side, until cooked through. Toast the bagels lightly.

To serve, spread 15 ml (1 tbsp) cream cheese on the bottom half of each bagel, top with some watercress and a burger. Finish with sliced dill pickles and bagel tops. Serve at once, accompanied by Potato Salad. SERVES 4

## POTATO LATKES

4 x 175 g (6 oz) baking potatoes, peeled and grated
4 small shallots, finely chopped
1 egg, beaten
Salt and ground black pepper
180 ml (6 fl oz) olive oil
4 slices light rye bread
60 ml (4 tbsp) soured cream
20 ml (4 tsp) snipped fresh chives
20 ml (4 tsp) salmon caviar or cod's roe
100 g (4 oz) smoked salmon, cut into strips
Salad garnish of chicory, radicchio and frisée

Squeeze the moisture out of the grated potatoes so they are as dry as possible. Place them in a bowl with the shallots, beaten egg and seasoning. Mix thoroughly to combine and divide the mixture into four patties.

Heat half the oil in a large frying pan and cook two of the latkes over a medium-low heat for 5 minutes on each side until golden and cooked through. Remove and drain on paper towels. Repeat with the remaining oil and latkes. Toast the rye bread lightly.

To serve, place a latke on each slice of toasted rye bread and top each one with a quarter of the soured cream, chives, caviar or cod's roe and smoked salmon. Garnish with the mixed salad leaves and serve at once. SERVES 4

**RIGHT:** Salmon & Dill Burger

# LOCH FYNE BURGERS

450 g (1 lb) skinless kippers, minced
175 g (6 oz) mashed potato
20 ml (4 tsp) horseradish sauce
20 ml (4 tsp) chopped fresh chervil
Ground black pepper
100 g coarse oatmeal
120 ml (4 fl oz) sunflower oil
4 Staffordshire oatcakes (oatmeal pancakes),
warmed through
Sliced tomatoes
Mixed salad leaves

## HORSERADISH MAYONNAISE
60 ml (4 tbsp) Mayonnaise (see page 222)
30 ml (2 tbsp) horseradish sauce

Place the minced kippers, potato, horseradish sauce, chervil and pepper in a bowl and mix well to combine. (These burgers do not need salt, as the kippers are very salty.) Divide the mixture into four equal portions and shape into patties. Roll the patties in the oatmeal to coat thoroughly.

Heat the sunflower oil in a large frying pan and cook the burgers over a moderately low heat for 5 minutes on each side until cooked through.

Make the horseradish mayonnaise by mixing the ingredients thoroughly.

To serve, place each burger in an oatcake, topped with a slice of tomato and a few mixed salad leaves. Pass the horseradish mayonnaise separately.

SERVES 4

# ENGLISH FISH CAKES

1 onion, finely chopped
30 ml (2 tbsp) vegetable oil
450 g (1 lb) skinless, boneless haddock, minced
175 g (6 oz) mashed potato
20 ml (4 tsp) chopped fresh parsley
Grated zest of 1 lemon
20 ml (4 tsp) lemon juice
Salt and ground black pepper
1 egg, beaten
100 g (4 oz) dried breadcrumbs
Vegetable oil for deep-frying
4 muffins, split lengthways
A little butter, softened
Soft lettuce leaves
Sliced shallot
Tartar sauce

Heat 30 ml (2 tbsp) oil in a saucepan and sauté the onion for 3 minutes until soft. Cool and add to the haddock, potato, parsley, lemon zest and juice and seasoning, and mix well to combine. Divide the mixture into four equal portions and shape into patties.

Dip a fish cake in the beaten egg and then in the breadcrumbs to coat thoroughly. Repeat with the remaining fish cakes.

Heat the oil for deep-frying. (It is hot enough when a cube of bread dropped into the oil floats and bubbles at the surface.) Fry the fish cakes in batches, if necessary, for 6 minutes until cooked through. Remove and drain on paper towels. Toast the cut sides of the muffins lightly and butter them sparingly.

To serve, divide the lettuce and shallot between the four bottom halves of the muffins, top with a fish cake, a spoonful of tartar sauce and the muffin tops. Serve at once.

SERVES 4

**TOP:** English Fish Cake
**BOTTOM:** Loch Fyne Burger

## ACAPULCO CRAB BURGERS

350 g (1 lb) white crabmeat
225 g (8 oz) mashed potato
20 ml (4 tsp) chopped fresh coriander
5 ml (1 tsp) chopped fresh red chilli
2.5 ml (½ tsp) grated lime zest
10 ml (2 tsp) freshly squeezed lime juice
Salt and ground black pepper
1 egg, beaten
175 g (6 oz) fresh white breadcrumbs
Vegetable oil for deep-frying
4 granary buns, split lengthways
A little butter, softened
Lettuce leaves
Tangy Tomato Salsa (see page 224)
Herb Mayonnaise, with coriander (page 222)

Squeeze any excess moisture from the crabmeat and place in a bowl with the potato, coriander, chilli, lime zest and juice, and seasoning. Mix well to combine. Divide into four equal portions and shape into patties.

Dip a burger in the beaten egg and then in bread-crumbs to coat well. Repeat with remaining burgers.

Heat the oil for deep-frying. (It is hot enough when a cube of bread dropped into the oil floats and bubbles at the surface.) Deep-fry over a medium-low heat for 10 minutes until golden and cooked through. Remove and drain on paper towels. Toast the cut sides of the buns and butter sparingly.

To serve, divide the lettuce between the four bottom halves of bun, top with a burger and a spoonful of tomato salsa and coriander mayonnaise and finish with the bun tops. Serve the remaining salsa separately

SERVES 4

## OSAKA FISH CAKES

15 g (½ oz) dried arame seaweed, soaked in
600 ml (1 pint) water for 1 hour
5 ml (1 tsp) wasabi powder
5 ml (1 tsp) water
15 ml (1 tbsp) tamari soy sauce
15 ml (1 tbsp) sunflower oil
5 ml (1 tsp) sesame oil
10 ml (2 tsp) mirin
175 g (6 oz) cooked white rice
225 g (8 oz) smoked tuna
8 strips Japanese pink pickled ginger
8 Japanese rice cakes

### CUCUMBER AND RADISH SALAD

¼ cucumber, sliced and cut into matchsticks
8 radishes, sliced and cut into matchsticks
15 ml (1 tbsp) rice wine vinegar
2.5 ml (½ tsp) caster sugar

Drain the soaked arame and lay it on paper towels to absorb excess moisture. Place the wasabi powder, water and soy sauce in a small bowl and mix. Heat the two oils in a frying pan, add the arame and wasabi mixture and cook gently for 2 minutes. Allow to cool.

Mix the mirin into the cooked rice. Divide the smoked tuna into four equal portions and lay flat on a board. Divide the rice between the tun, spreading in a thin layer. Divide the arame between the portions and spread over. Lay two strips of pickled ginger down the centre of each pile and roll the rice portions up. Place the salad ingredients in a bowl and toss.

To serve, slice each sushi roll in half, on the diagonal, and place a cut roll on each rice cake. Serve each person two sushi rolls and rice cakes, accompanied by the salad.

SERVES 4

**RIGHT:** Acapulco Crab Burger

## SPICY THAI FISH PATTIES

450 g (1 lb) skinless, boneless cod, minced
225 g (8 oz) cooked, shelled prawns, minced
4 spring onions, finely chopped
10 ml (2 tsp) grated fresh root ginger
5 ml (1 tsp) finely chopped lime leaves
Salt and ground black pepper
1 egg, beaten
175 g (6 oz) white sesame seeds
Vegetable oil for deep-frying
4 slices white bread, crusts removed
Salad garnish of cos lettuce, coriander, sliced chilli and cucumber
Thai sweet chilli sauce, to serve

Place the cod, prawns, spring onion, ginger, lime leaves and seasoning in a bowl and mix well to combine. Divide the mixture into eight equal portions and shape into patties.

Dip a patty in the beaten egg and then in the sesame seeds to coat. Repeat with remaining patties.

Heat the oil for deep-frying. (It is hot enough when a cube of bread dropped into the oil floats and bubbles at the surface.) Deep-fry the patties over a medium-low heat, in batches if necessary, for 8 minutes until golden and cooked through. Remove with a slotted spoon and drain on paper towels. Deep-fry the bread in the hot oil for a few minutes until pale golden. Remove and drain on paper towels.

To serve, place two fish patties on each piece of fried bread and garnish with the salad. Pass Thai sweet chilli sauce separately.                    SERVES 4

## VALENCIA BURGERS

450 g (1 lb) skinless, boneless cod, minced
225 g (8 oz) cooked, shelled prawns, minced
100 g (4 oz) canned clams in brine, drained and finely chopped
1 shallot, finely chopped
2.5 ml (½ tsp) chopped saffron, infused in 15 ml (1 tbsp) hot water for 10 minutes
Salt and ground black pepper
Vegetable oil for deep frying
4 chunks ciabatta bread, split lengthways
A little olive oil for brushing
Lettuce leaves
Sliced tomato
Sliced orange pepper

### LEMON AIOLI
60 ml (4 tbsp) Mayonnaise (see page 222)
1 clove garlic, crushed
Grated zest of 1 lemon
20 ml (4 tsp) lemon juice

Place the cod, prawns, clams, shallot, infused saffron and seasoning in a bowl and mix well. Divide into four equal portions and shape into patties.

Place the ingredients for the lemon aïoli in a small bowl and mix well to combine.

Heat the oil for deep-frying. Fry the burgers over a medium-low heat for about 9-10 minutes until cooked through. Remove and drain on paper towels. Brush the cut sides of the bread with olive oil and grill to toast lightly.

To serve, divide the lettuce, sliced tomato and pepper between the four bottom halves of bun, top each with a burger, a spoonful of aïoli and the bun tops. Serve at once.                    SERVES 4

**TOP:** Valencia Burger
**BOTTOM:** Spicy Thai Fish Patties

## TUNA & SWEETCORN BURGERS

450 g (1 lb) canned tuna, drained
175 g (6 oz) canned sweetcorn kernels, drained
1 small onion, finely chopped
½ small red pepper, finely chopped
225 g (8 oz) fresh white breadcrumbs
15 ml (1 tbsp) chopped fresh parsley
Salt and ground black pepper
1 egg, beaten
Vegetable oil for deep-frying
4 hamburger buns, split lengthways
Crisp lettuce leaves
Coleslaw (see page 282), to serve

Place the tuna in a bowl and mash it really thoroughly until no lumps remain. Add the sweetcorn, onion, red pepper, half the breadcrumbs, parsley and seasoning and mix well to combine. Divide into four equal portions and shape into patties.

Dip a patty in the beaten egg and then in the sesame seeds to coat. Repeat with remaining patties.

Dip each burger in the beaten egg and then in the remaining breadcrumbs to coat well.

Heat the oil for deep-frying. (It is hot enough when a cube of bread dropped into the oil floats and bubbles at the surface.) Fry the burgers, in batches if necessary, for 6 minutes until golden and warmed through. Remove with a slotted spoon and drain on paper towels. Toast the buns lightly.

To serve, divide the lettuce between the four bottom halves of the buns, top each with a burger and finish with the bun tops. Serve at once with a helping of Coleslaw on each plate. SERVES 4

## KEDGEREE PATTIES

350 g (12 oz) skinless, boneless smoked haddock, minced
100 g (4 oz) cooked rice
4 spring onions, finely chopped
10 ml (2 tsp) chopped fresh parsley
Freshly grated nutmeg
Salt and ground black pepper
120 ml (4 fl oz) sunflower oil
4 soda bread farls (buns), split lengthways
A little butter, softened
Crisp lettuce leaves
Sliced tomato

### EGG AND CAYENNE MAYONNAISE

2 hard-boiled eggs, peeled and chopped
60 ml (4 tbsp) Mayonnaise (see page 222)
10 ml (2 tsp) cayenne pepper

Place the haddock, rice, spring onion, parsley, nutmeg and pepper in a bowl and mix well. Divide into four and shape into patties.

Place the ingredients for the egg mayonnaise in a small bowl and mix well to combine. Chill.

Heat the sunflower oil in a large frying pan and cook the patties over a low heat for 5 minutes on each side until golden and cooked through. Alternatively, cook the patties on a barbecue, on an oiled rack, for about 4-5 minutes on each side. Toast the cut sides of the soda farls and butter them lightly.

To serve, divide the lettuce and tomato between the four bottom halves of the farls, top each with a patty and a spoonful of mayonnaise and finish with the tops of the farls. Serve at once, passing extra mayonnaise separately. SERVES 4

**RIGHT:** Tuna & Sweetcorn Burger

# MEATLESS WONDERS

The following vegetarian recipes use ingredients such as potato, pumpkin, parsnip, rice, chick-peas, nuts, bulghur wheat and beans and lentils to make a firm burger. Breadcrumbs and eggs are used to bind the patties in many of the recipes, and most of the burgers benefit from an hour's refrigeration prior to cooking to help hold them together.

## ROSTI BURGERS

225 g (8 oz) potato, peeled and grated
225 g (8 oz) courgettes, grated
1 small red onion, peeled and grated
100 g (4 oz) Gruyère cheese, grated
1 egg, beaten
Salt and ground black pepper
180 ml (6 fl oz) vegetable oil
4 mixed-grain buns, split lengthways
A little butter, softened
Soft lettuce leaves
Tomato Relish (see page 226)

Squeeze out all the excess moisture from the potatoes and courgettes. Place in a bowl with the onion, cheese, egg and seasoning. Mix well and divide into four. Shape into patties.

Heat the oil in a large pan and cook two burgers over a medium-low heat for 5 minutes on each side until crisp. Cook the remaining burgers. Toast the cut sides of the buns and butter lightly.

To serve, divide the lettuce leaves between the four bottom bun halves and top each with a burger, a spoonful of relish and a bun top. Serve at once.

SERVES 4

## ROOT BURGERS

350 g (12 oz) parsnip purée (steam parsnips before puréeing)
100 g (4 oz) carrot, grated
4 spring onions, thinly sliced
Salt and ground black pepper
175 g (6 oz) sunflower seeds
180 ml (6 fl oz) sunflower oil
4 floury hamburger buns, split lengthways
A little butter, softened
Cos lettuce leaves

### TANGY DRESSING

120 ml (4 fl oz) crème fraîche
20 ml (4 tsp) snipped fresh chives
Grated zest of 1 small orange

Place the parsnip purée, carrot, spring onion and seasoning in a bowl and mix well. Divide the mixture into four equal portions and shape into patties. Coat each patty in sunflower seeds and chill for at least 1 hour before cooking.

Place the ingredients for the dressing in a bowl and mix well to combine. Chill until needed.

Heat the oil in a large frying pan and cook the burgers over a medium-low heat for 5 minutes on each side until golden and cooked through. Toast the cut sides of the buns and butter them sparingly.

To serve, divide the lettuce between the four bottom halves of the buns and top each with a burger. Finish with the bun tops and serve at once with the dressing.

SERVES 4

**RIGHT:** Rosti Burger

## RICE & SPINACH BURGERS

225 g (8 oz) cooked mixed long-grain rice
and wild rice
350 g (12 oz) cooked fresh spinach, squeezed of all
excess moisture
½ red pepper, chopped
100 g (4 oz) Cheddar cheese, grated
1 small egg, beaten
Salt and ground black pepper
A good pinch freshly grated nutmeg
75 g (3 oz) dried white breadcrumbs
60 ml (4 tbsp) grated Parmesan cheese
180 ml (6 fl oz) vegetable oil
A little butter, softened
8 slices light rye bread
Sliced tomato
Lettuce leaves and onion rings, to serve

Place the rice, spinach, red pepper, cheese, egg and seasoning in a food processor and process briefly to combine. Divide the mixture into four equal portions and shape into patties. Mix together the dried bread-crumbs and Parmesan cheese and coat the burgers with this mixture. Chill the burgers for at least 1 hour before cooking them.

Heat the oil in a large frying pan and cook the burgers over a medium-low heat for 5 minutes on each side until cooked through.

To serve, butter one side of each piece of bread. Divide the tomato slices between four slices of the bread, top each with a burger and finish with the remaining bread. Serve the burgers garnished with the lettuce leaves and onion rings.          SERVES 4

## SPICY PUMPKIN BURGERS

450 g (1 lb) mashed pumpkin (steam pumpkin before
mashing)
2 shallots, finely chopped
½ red pepper, finely chopped
½ green pepper, finely chopped
60 ml (4 tbsp) sultanas
100 g (4 oz) cooked rice
Salt and ground black pepper
175 g (6 oz) pumpkin seeds
180 ml (6 fl oz) olive oil
4 slices cornbread
Olive oil for brushing
Mixed green salad leaves
Mayonnaise (see page 222), to serve

Place the mashed pumpkin, shallots, peppers, sultanas and seasoning in a bowl and mix well to combine. Divide the mixture into four equal portions and shape into patties. Coat each patty in pumpkin seeds and chill for at least 1 hour before cooking.

These burgers are very soft and fragile and they need to be cooked over a very low heat so the pumpkin seeds do not burn. Heat the oil in a large pan and cook the burgers very gently for 4-5 minutes on each side until golden and cooked through. Brush the corn-bread with olive oil and toast it lightly.

To serve, divide the salad leaves between the four slices of bread and top each with a burger. Serve at once with the mayonnaise.          SERVES 4

**TOP:** Spiced Pumpkin Burger
**BOTTOM:** Rice & Spinach Burger

## AUBERGINE CHEESE PARCELS

1 large aubergine
45 ml (3 tbsp) extra virgin olive oil
Salt and ground black pepper
2 ripe plum tomatoes
100 g (4 oz) mozzarella cheese
30 ml (2 tbsp) chopped fresh basil
60 ml (4 tbsp) extra virgin olive oil
4 chunks ciabatta bread, split lengthways

Preheat the oven to 180°C (350°F, Gas mark 4). Remove the stalk from the aubergine and slice it lengthways into four long slices, discarding the two outer edges – you should be left with four flat pieces. Brush each piece on both sides with the 45 ml (3 tbsp) of olive oil and season well. Grill the aubergine slices under a moderate grill for 5 minutes on each side until they are pale golden and soft.

Slice each tomato into four and cut the mozzarella into four thick slices. Mix together the basil and the 60 ml (4 tbsp) of oil and use this to brush the cut sides of the bread.

Layer the tomato and mozzarella to produce four stacks, each consisting of one piece of cheese sandwiched between two slices of tomato. Wrap a slice of aubergine around each cheese and tomato stack and place each parcel between two slices of ciabatta bread. Bake the cheese and bread parcels in the oven for 10 minutes until the bread is warmed through and the cheese has begun to melt. Serve at once.   SERVES 4

## MUSHROOM BURGERS

700 g (1½ lb) mixed mushrooms, such as field, chestnut and oyster
180 ml (6 fl oz) olive oil
50 g (2 oz) butter
4 shallots, finely chopped
15 ml (1 tbsp) chopped fresh thyme
15 ml (1 tbsp) Madeira
225 g (8 oz) fresh white breadcrumbs
Salt and ground black pepper
6 hamburger buns, split lengthways
A little butter, softened
Lettuce leaves
Onion rings
Sliced tomato
Herb Mayonnaise (see page 12), to serve

Place the mushrooms in a food processor and process briefly until chopped. Heat 60 ml (4 tbsp) of the oil and all the butter in a large frying pan and sauté the shallots for 2 minutes. Add the mushrooms and sauté for a further 4 minutes. Cool the mixture, then stir in the thyme, Madeira, breadcrumbs and seasoning, and mix well. Divide into six equal portions and shape into patties. Chill for at least 1 hour.

Heat half the remaining oil in a large frying pan and cook the burgers in two batches over a medium-low heat for 5 minutes on each side until golden and cooked through. Toast the cut sides of the buns and butter sparingly.

To serve, divide the lettuce and onion between the six bottom halves of the buns, top each with a burger, some sliced tomato and a bun top. Serve at once, passing Herb Mayonnaise separately.   SERVES 6

**RIGHT:** Aubergine Cheese Parcel

# FALAFEL BURGERS

450 g (1 lb) cooked chick-peas
120 ml (4 fl oz) light tahini
60 ml (4 tbsp) freshly squeezed lemon juice
60 ml (4 tbsp) chopped fresh parsley
5 ml (1 tsp) ground cumin
10 ml (2 tsp) ground coriander
2.5 ml (½ tsp) turmeric
Salt and ground black pepper
75 g (3 oz) wholemeal flour
180 ml (6 fl oz) vegetable oil
4 pitta breads, warmed and split lengthways
Lettuce leaves
Sliced tomato
Sliced red onion
Garlic Mayonnaise (see page 12)
Lemon wedges, to serve

Place the chick-peas in a food processor and process briefly. Add the tahini, lemon juice, parsley, spices and seasoning, and process again until well combined. Divide the mixture into four equal portions and shape into patties. Roll each patty in wholemeal flour to coat and chill for at least 1 hour before cooking.

Heat the oil in a large frying pan and cook the burgers over a medium-low heat for 5 minutes on each side until golden and cooked through.

To serve, fill each pitta bread with lettuce, tomato and onion and top with a burger and a spoonful of mayonnaise. Serve at once with lemon wedges, passing extra mayonnaise separately. SERVES 4

# LEBANESE BURGERS

350 g (12 oz) prepared bulghur wheat
350 g (12 oz) cooked cannellini beans
1 clove garlic, crushed
60 ml (4 tbsp) chopped fresh parsley
30 ml (2 tbsp) chopped fresh mint
Salt and ground black pepper
180 ml (6 fl oz) vegetable oil
4 pitta breads, warmed and split lengthways
Soft lettuce leaves
Halved cherry tomatoes and marinated black olives, to serve

### YOGHURT DRESSING

90 ml (6 tbsp) natural yoghurt
20 ml (4 tsp) chopped fresh parsley
5 ml (1 tsp) chopped fresh mint
10 ml (2 tsp) lemon juice
1 clove garlic, crushed

Place the bulghur wheat, cannellini beans, garlic, herbs and seasoning in a food processor and process briefly until combined. Divide into four equal portions and shape into patties. Chill for at least 1 hour before cooking.

Place the ingredients for the dressing in a bowl and mix to combine. Chill until needed to allow the flavours to develop.

Heat the oil in a large frying pan and cook the burgers over a low heat for 6 minutes on each side until golden and cooked through.

To serve, place lettuce leaves and a burger in each pitta pocket and top with a spoonful of dressing. Serve at once with cherry tomatoes and black olives.
SERVES 4

**TOP:** Lebanese Burger
**BOTTOM:** Falafel Burger

## POLENTA & MUSHROOM BURGERS

*Either use quick-cooking polenta or traditional cornmeal for these burgers. Follow the packet instructions to cook polenta and then stamp out circles from the prepared slab as instructed below.*

90 ml (6 tbsp) extra virgin olive oil
4 x 10 cm (4 inch) circles of cooked polenta, about 1.5cm (½ inch) thick
Continental salad leaves tossed in vinaigrette, to serve

### WILD MUSHROOM TOPPING
350 g (12 oz) wild mushrooms
75 g (3 oz) butter
3 shallots, sliced
Salt and ground black pepper
10 ml (2 tsp) lemon juice
30 ml (2 tbsp) chopped fresh parsley
30 ml (2 tbsp) snipped fresh chives

Heat half the oil in a large frying pan and cook two polenta circles over a moderate heat for about 7 minutes on each side, until the polenta is golden on the outside and warmed through. Repeat with the remaining oil and polenta, and keep warm.

To make the mushroom topping, clean the mushrooms and slice any that are large. Heat half the butter in a large frying pan and sauté half the shallots for 2 minutes. Tip in half the mushrooms and sauté for a further 2 minutes. Season well and stir in half the lemon juice and herbs. Keep warm while cooking the second batch.

To serve, top each polenta burger with a quarter of the mushroom topping and serve at once with the salad garnish. SERVES 4

## PUTTANESCA BURGERS

450 g (1 lb) cooked green lentils, mashed
60 ml (4 tbsp) sun-dried tomato paste
20 ml (4 tsp) capers, chopped
30 ml (2 tbsp) chopped black olives
10 ml (2 tsp) chilli powder
Salt and ground black pepper
100 g (4 oz) dried white breadcrumbs
180 ml (6 fl oz) olive oil
4 chunks focaccia bread, split lengthways
Olive oil for brushing
Lettuce leaves
Sliced shallot
Pickled sweet cherry peppers, to serve

Place the lentils, tomato paste, capers, olives, chilli powder and seasoning in a bowl and mix well to combine. Divide the mixture into four equal portions and shape into patties. Roll the patties in the breadcrumbs to coat. Chill for at least 1 hour.

Heat the oil in a large frying pan and cook the burgers over a medium-low heat for 5 minutes on each side until golden and cooked through. Brush the cut sides of the focaccia bread with olive oil and grill to toast lightly.

To serve, divide the lettuce and shallot slices between the four bottom halves of the bread, top with burgers and the bread tops. Serve at once with cherry peppers. SERVES 4

**RIGHT:** Polenta & Mushroom Burger

## VEGETARIAN CHILLI BURGERS

450 g (1 lb) cooked red kidney beans
225 g (8 oz) cooked black-eye beans
10 ml (2 tsp) cayenne pepper
5 ml (1 tsp) ground cumin
½ fresh green chilli, finely chopped
Salt and ground black pepper
1 egg, beaten
175 g (6 oz) tortilla chips, coarsely crunched
180 ml (6 fl oz) vegetable oil
8 slices cornbread
Crisp lettuce
Chilli Mayonnaise (see page 222)
Pickled jalapeño chillies, to serve

Place the beans, spices, green chilli and seasoning in a food processor and process until mixture is combined but the beans are still fairly coarse. Divide the mixture into four equal portions and shape into patties. Dip each patty into egg and then coat in crushed tortilla chips. Chill for at least 1 hour before cooking.

Heat the oil in a large frying pan and cook the burgers over a medium-low heat for 5 minutes on each side until golden and cooked through. Toast the cornbread lightly.

To serve, divide the lettuce between four slices of the bread, top each with a burger, followed by a spoonful of Chilli Mayonnaise; finish with the remaining bread. Serve at once with pickled jalapeño chillies.

SERVES 4

## THREE-NUT BURGERS

275 g raw cashew nuts, chopped
175 g (6 oz) walnut pieces
225 g (8 oz) red Leicester cheese, grated
100 g (4 oz) fresh white breadcrumbs
30 ml (2 tbsp) snipped fresh chives
2 eggs
Salt and ground black pepper
175 g (6 oz) flaked almonds, coarsely crushed
Oil for deep-frying
8 wholemeal buns, split lengthways
Mixed salad leaves
Pumpkin Relish (see page 226), to serve

Place the nuts, cheese, breadcrumbs, chives, one beaten egg and seasoning in a food processor and process until combined. Divide the mixture into eight equal portions and shape into patties. Dip each patty into the second beaten egg and then coat in flaked almonds. Chill for at least 1 hour before cooking.

Heat the oil for deep-frying. (It is hot enough when a cube of bread dropped into the oil floats and bubbles at the surface.) Fry the burgers in batches for 7-8 minutes until golden and cooked through. Remove with a slotted spoon and drain on paper towels. Toast the buns lightly.

To serve, divide the salad between the bottom halves of the buns. Top each with a burger and finish with the bun tops. Serve at once with Pumpkin Relish.

SERVES 4

**TOP:** Three-Nut Burger
**BOTTOM:** Vegetarian Chilli Burger

# SIDE ORDERS

Accompaniments to burgers make the meal complete, and the recipes in this chapter are suggestions you may like to try. Along with salads, there are deep-fried chips made from potatoes and sweet potatoes, as well as vegetable crisps made from beetroot and carrot. Of course, the simplest accompaniments are ones you may have at home, such as gherkins and olives which complement the heartiness of burgers made with meat.

## ITALIAN SALAD

4 celery sticks, sliced on the diagonal
I small red pepper, cut into diamonds
I small green pepper, cut into diamonds
30 ml (2 tbsp) flat-leafed parsley, coarsely chopped
9 black olives and 9 green olives

### DRESSING

90 ml (6 tbsp) extra virgin olive oil
30 ml (2 tbsp) red wine vinegar
5 ml (I tsp) fennel seeds, lightly crushed
I clove garlic, crushed
Pinch of caster sugar
Salt and ground black pepper

Place the salad ingredients in a bowl. Place the ingredients for the dressing in a screw-topped jar and shake well to combine. Taste and adjust seasoning.

Pour the dressing over the salad and toss well to combine. Cover the salad and chill for 30 minutes before serving to allow the flavours to develop.

SERVES 6

## ARTICHOKE SALAD WITH BLUE CHEESE DRESSING

400 g (14 oz) canned artichoke hearts in brine, drained and halved
½ small iceberg lettuce, torn into bite-sized pieces
12 cherry tomatoes, halved
30 ml (2 tbsp) snipped fresh chives

### BLUE CHEESE DRESSING

50 g (2 oz) Dolcelatte cheese, mashed
Pinch of caster sugar
Pinch of cayenne pepper
Salt and ground black pepper
90 ml (6 tbsp) sunflower oil
30 ml (2 tbsp) white wine vinegar
30 ml (2 tbsp) soured cream

Divide the prepared salad ingredients between four individual bowls and set aside until required.

Place the cheese in a food processor with the sugar, cayenne and seasoning, and process briefly to form a smooth paste. Add the oil in a steady stream with the processor running to produce a creamy-textured mixture. Add the vinegar and soured cream and pulse again briefly until combined. Taste and adjust seasoning if necessary.

Spoon some dressing over each salad and serve, passing extra dressing separately.       SERVES 4

**TOP:** Italian Salad
**BOTTOM:** Artichoke Salad with Blue Cheese Dressing

## POTATO SALAD

450 g (1 lb) new potatoes
90 ml (6 tbsp) Mayonnaise (see page 12)
60 ml (4 tbsp) thick natural yoghurt
Salt and ground black pepper
2 spring onions, thinly sliced

Scrub or peel the potatoes and cut them into bite-sized chunks. Cook them for about 5 minutes in boiling, salted water until they are just tender. Drain and refresh in cold water.

Mix together the mayonnaise, yoghurt and seasoning. Fold this mixture into the cooked potatoes, together with the spring onions. Cover the salad and chill until required.                    SERVES 4-6

## COLESLAW

½ small white cabbage, finely shredded
75 g (3 oz) carrot, peeled and grated
2 spring onions, sliced into long, thin strips
1 red-skinned apple, cut into matchsticks
75 ml (5 tbsp) Mayonnaise (see page 12)
60 ml (4 tbsp) Greek-style yoghurt
Salt and ground black pepper

Place the prepared vegetables and the apple in a mixing bowl. Mix together the mayonnaise and yoghurt, and season well.

Stir the mayonnaise mixture into the prepared vegetables and toss gently to coat. Cover the coleslaw and chill until required.                    SERVES 6

**TOP:** Potato Salad
**BOTTOM:** Coleslaw

## FRENCH FRIES

175 g (6 oz) baking potatoes per person
Vegetable oil for deep-frying
Salt for sprinkling

Old or baking potatoes will produce the best results. Peel the required quantity of potatoes, and cut them into 1.5-cm (½-inch) wide strips.

Pour oil into a pan to a depth of about 7.5cm (3 inches). Using a cooking thermometer, heat until the oil reaches a temperature of 130°C (250°F) – this is a fairly low heat. Alternatively, use a deep-fat fryer, following the manufacturer's cooking instructions.

Cook the potatoes, in batches if necessary, for 9 minutes until they are partially cooked but are still very pale. Remove the potatoes from the oil with a slotted spoon and drain on paper towels.

Just before serving, heat the oil to 150°C (300°F) and return the potatoes to the oil. Cook them in batches for about 10 minutes until crisp and golden. Remove the potatoes from the oil and drain on paper towels. Sprinkle with salt and serve at once.

## GRATED CHILLI FRIES

50 g (2 oz) baking potatoes per person
Vegetable oil for deep-frying
2.5 ml (½ tsp) chilli powder
Pinch of dried chilli flakes
15 ml (1 tbsp) sea salt, crushed

Coarsely grate the potatoes or cut them into julienne strips. Squeeze the potato of all excess moisture and pat it dry on paper towels.

Pour oil into a pan to a depth of about 7.5 cm (3 inches). Heat until a cube of bread dropped into the oil floats and bubbles on the surface. Alternatively, test the oil with a thermometer; when it reaches 190°C (375°F), it is hot enough. Fry the potatoes, in batches if

necessary, for a few seconds until pale golden and crisp. Remove the potatoes with a slotted spoon and drain on paper towels.

Mix the chilli powder, flakes and salt together and sprinkle on the fries.

## SWEET POTATO FRIES

175 g (6 oz) sweet potatoes per person
Vegetable oil for deep-frying
Salt for sprinkling

Peel the required quantity of sweet potatoes and cut them into 1.5-cm (½-inch) wide strips.

Pour oil into a pan to a depth of about 7.5 cm (3 inches). Using a cooking thermometer, heat until the oil reaches a temperature of 130°C (250°F) – this is a fairly low heat. Cook the sweet potatoes, in batches if necessary, for 9 minutes until they are partially cooked but are still pale. Remove from the oil with a slotted spoon and drain on paper towels.

Just before serving, heat the oil to 150°C (300°F) and return the potatoes to the oil. Cook them for about 3 minutes until crisp and golden. Remove the potatoes from the oil with a slotted spoon and drain on paper towels. Sprinkle with salt and serve at once.

**TOP TO BOTTOM:** Sweet Potato Fries, Grated Chilli Fries, French Fries

# VEGETABLE CRISPS

*The recipes below describe how to make parsnip, carrot, beetroot and potato crisps. Choose your own combination or cook a mixture of them all.*

### PARSNIP CRISPS

50 g (2 oz) parsnips per person
Oil for deep-frying
Salt for sprinkling

Peel the parsnips and slice them very, very thinly. The ideal way of doing this is to use a mandoline. Place the sliced parsnips on paper towels and pat to remove all excess moisture.

Pour oil into a pan to a depth of 7.5 cm (3 inches). Test the oil with a thermometer; when it reaches 190°C (375°F), it is hot enough.

Fry the crisps, in batches if necessary, for 1½ minutes until crisp and golden. Remove the crisps with a slotted spoon and drain on paper towels. Sprinkle with salt and serve at once, or store in an airtight container until required.

### CARROT CRISPS

75 g (3 oz) carrots per person
Oil for deep-frying
Salt for sprinkling

Follow the instructions for Parsnip Crisps, above, except heat the oil to the slightly lower temperature of 180°C (350°F).

### BEETROOT CRISPS

75 g (3 oz) beetroot per person
Oil for deep-frying
Salt for sprinkling

Follow the instructions for Parsnip Crisps, above, except heat the oil to the slightly lower temperature of 180°C (350°F) and fry the crisps for the longer time of 3 minutes.

### POTATO CRISPS

50 g (2 oz) potatoes per person
Oil for deep-frying
Salt for sprinkling

These crisps need to be double-fried to make them extra crisp. Follow the instructions for Parsnip Crisps, left, up to the point where the crisps are drained on paper towels. Reheat the oil to 190°C (375°F) and re-fry the crisps for a further 1½ minutes until crisp and dark golden. Remove from the oil with a slotted spoon and drain again on fresh paper towels. Sprinkle with salt before serving.

# FRIED GREEN TOMATOES

30 ml (2 tbsp) plain flour
Salt and ground pepper
5 ml (1 tsp) cayenne pepper
4 firm green tomatoes, thickly sliced
50 g (2 oz) butter
15 ml (1 tbsp) chopped fresh parsley

Mix together the flour, seasoning and cayenne pepper. Toss the tomato slices in the flour mixture.

Melt the butter in a large frying pan and cook the tomatoes for 3 minutes on each side. Stir in the parsley and cook the tomatoes for a further 3 minutes until they are tender. Serve at once.          SERVES 4

**CLOCKWISE:** Potato Crisps, Assorted Vegetable Crisps, Green Fried Tomatoes

## POTATO SKINS WITH SOURED CREAM DRESSING

4 large baking potatoes, weighing about
225 g (8 oz) each
Oil for deep-frying

### SOURED CREAM DRESSING

150 ml (¼ pint) soured cream
60 ml (4 tbsp) snipped fresh chives
2.5 ml (½ tsp) lemon juice
Pinch of cayenne pepper
Salt and ground black pepper

Preheat the oven to 200°C (400°F, Gas mark 6). Wash the potatoes and place them on a baking tray. Bake in the oven for 40-45 minutes until they are just cooked. Remove the potatoes from the oven and allow to cool.

Meanwhile, prepare the dressing. Place the soured cream, chives, lemon juice, cayenne and seasoning in a bowl and mix thoroughly to combine. Set aside.

Cut each cooled potato into six to eight wedges. Cut away most of the potato flesh, leaving about 1.5 cm (½ inch) of potato with the skin attached. Discard the potato flesh or reserve for use in another recipe.

Heat some oil in a deep-frying pan to a temperature of 180°C (350°F) using a cooking thermometer. Deep-fry the potato skins in batches for 3-5 minutes until they are crisp and golden. Remove from the oil with a slotted spoon and drain on paper towels.

Serve the potato skins at once, accompanied by the dressing. SERVES 4-6

## ROSEMARY & GARLIC POTATO WEDGES

4 large baking potatoes, weighing about
225 g (8 oz) each
240 ml (8 fl oz) extra virgin olive oil
10 ml (2 tsp) paprika
4 cloves garlic, crushed
45 ml (3 tbsp) chopped fresh rosemary
Sea salt and freshly ground black pepper
Chilli or Herb Mayonnaise (see page 12) or
Tomato Relish (see page 16), to serve

Preheat the oven to 200°C (400°F, Gas mark 6). Cut each potato into eight thin wedges and place them on a large baking tray. Mix together the oil, paprika, garlic and rosemary; pour over the potatoes. Season the potatoes with salt and pepper, and toss well to make sure the potatoes are thoroughly coated in oil.

Bake the potatoes in the oven for 45 minutes, basting occasionally, until they are crisp and golden. Remove from the oven.

Serve at once with flavoured mayonnaise or Tomato Relish. SERVES 4-6

**TOP:** Rosemary & Garlic Potato Wedges
**BOTTOM:** Potato Skins with
Soured Cream Dressing

# BARBECUES

This selection of barbecue recipes offers inspiration for outdoor cooking, whatever the occasion. Contrary to the popular belief that barbecues cater primarily for the meat-eater, barbecuing is evolving fast to suit all contemporary tastes. The recipes in these chapters demonstrate the versatility of barbecues with an entire chapter devoted to imaginative vegetable-based dishes.

Historically, barbecuing was the original style of cooking, with our ancestors of centuries ago spit-roasting whole animals over live coals. In more recent times, the art of barbecuing has evolved to become, in modern societies, a popular way of eating 'al fresco'.

## CHARCOAL OR WOOD BARBECUES

Whether they are permanent features, made from a brick base, or portable, most barbecues are designed for just grilling food. They consist of a firebox that holds the fuel and an adjustable rack, which enables you to place food at different heights above the fuel.

There are two types of coal fuel that can be used: lumpwood charcoal is cheaper, easier to light and burns hotter than its alternative, pressed briquettes. However, once briquettes have been lit they last a lot longer.

Fire lighters or lighting ignition fluid are also essential to start the barbecue. Fire lighters should be placed in the bottom of the firebox, and a 7.5-cm (3-inch) pyramid of charcoal constructed over the top. The fire lighters are then ignited with a taper to start the fire. Use ignition fluid to help the fire, if necessary.

Once the barbecue is lit, it can take up to one hour to reach the 'ashen coal or wood

stage', which means the barbecue is ready to cook on. Please remember to follow the manufacturer's instructions carefully if you are using ignition fluid. Ensure the hot coals are spread out evenly. To maintain the heat, gradually add fresh coal around the outer edges.

Wood can also be used as a fuel, but is more difficult to start. If you use wood, use hardwoods which burn longer. Allow the flames to die right down before cooking. Wood barbecues will take 30-45 minutes to reach the point where they are ready for cooking.

Aromatic wood chips are available for use on barbecues to impart flavours to the food. Oak and hickory wood chips are especially popular and there are also more unusual ones, like mesquite and cherry. Wood chips should be soaked for about 30 minutes in cold water, then drained and placed on the ashen coals.

## GAS BARBECUES

These barbecues only need 5 or 10 minutes to heat and the temperature can be easily controlled. Gas barbecues either have vaporizer bars or lava rocks that are heated up by gas burners. The cooking rack is set above these. Moisture drips from the cooking food on to the bars and vaporizes to give the food an aromatic smoked flavour. Pre-soaked wood chips can also be placed in a foil container on the vaporizer bar, or on the heated lava rocks, but do not put food too near the container.

**RIGHT:** Fish, seafood, vegetables, meat and even certain cheeses barbecue well, and you may want to try the Mushroom & Mozzarella Brochettes (see page 348), pictured here.

## GENERAL SAFETY

Always place the barbecue on even ground and away from trees, buildings or fences. Once the barbecue is alight, do not leave it unattended, and keep children away from it.

Allow embers to cool completely before disposing. They will take several hours to cool. Allow transportable barbecues to cool completely before packing them away. Always use long-handled tongs when handling food on the barbecue. Never use petrol or similar flammable liquids to light a barbecue and keep matches well away from the barbecue. Have a bottle of water handy to douse the flames if they become too unruly.

## FOOD SAFETY AND COOKING

Keep raw food out of the sun. Make sure that pieces of meat and sausages are well cooked. Adequate lighting around a barbecue is essential at night to check whether food is properly cooked. Never cook frozen food on a barbecue – it must always be thoroughly defrosted.

All the recipes should be cooked over a medium-hot barbecue, unless otherwise indicated. Barbecuing is a rather unpredictable cooking method, and you will need to adjust the cooking times according to the intensity of your barbecue. If you find the barbecue is becoming too hot, simply raise the grill to the next setting on your barbecue.

## EQUIPMENT

There is a large array of barbecue equipment for sale these days, but there are a few essential pieces. Wear an apron to prevent splatters on clothes and use well-padded oven gloves to handle hot metal skewers and griddle plates. Long-handled tongs, a fork and a fish slice are

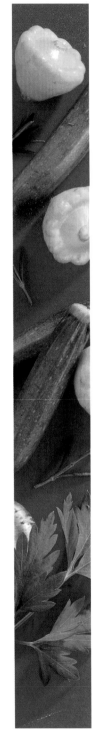

essential for turning food. Use metal skewers for more robust food, oiling them first. Wood skewers should be used for delicate foods. Soak them in cold water before use to prevent them catching fire. When barbecuing food in foil parcels, use heavy-duty foil.

A wide range of hinged wire racks are available for barbecuing. These are especially useful for fish and fragile food. Metal griddle plates that can be heated on the barbecue are useful for cooking fragile foods that would otherwise be tricky to cook on a barbecue. Always oil the heated griddle plate before placing food on it. A stiff wire brush is essential for brushing down the grill bars after use and use a metal scraper for removing any burnt food.

## MARINADES

Marinating plays a vital part in barbecuing, as it adds extra depth of flavour. Fish and shellfish generally require a shorter marinating time than meat. If food has been marinated in the refrigerator, allow it to come back to room temperature before cooking.

Marinades that contain acidic elements, like vinegar or citrus juice, will tenderize the food. Oils in marinades help prevent food from sticking and herbs and spices create mouthwatering flavours. All in all, marinating can turn the simplest cut of meat or piece of fish or vegetable into something more special.

Barbecuing should be an enjoyable way of cooking, so do not rush. Above all, relax, enjoy this sociable way of cooking and eating, and savour the tantalizing aromas and tastes that barbecuing produces.

**RIGHT:** Using marinades to brush meat and vegetables while barbecuing adds extra flavour.

# QUICK BARBECUES

*A range of 'fuss-free' recipes are included in this chapter, all which take a minimum of time to prepare and would be suitable for impromptu summer meals or weekday family meals. Although certain recipes, such as Spare Ribs with Tangy BBQ Sauce and Horseradish Steaks, benefit from being marinated for several hours before cooking, as this provides a better depth of flavour, the end result will still be tasty if you do not have the time to marinate.*

## TERIYAKI RIBS

1.4 kg (3 lb) meaty pork spare ribs
Salad and crusty bread, to serve (optional)

### MARINADE
90 ml (6 tbsp) clear honey
45 ml (3 tbsp) dark soy sauce
90 ml (6 tbsp) tomato ketchup
7.5 ml (1½ tsp) cracked black pepper
10 ml (2 tsp) Chinese five-spice powder
Grated zest and juice of 1 large orange

Mix the marinade ingredients together in a bowl. Place the spare ribs in a large glass dish and pour the marinade over them. Turn the ribs to coat evenly. Cover and refrigerate for 2-3 hours, if time permits.

Remove the ribs from the marinade, reserving the marinade for basting. Cook the ribs on a prepared barbecue for about 20 minutes, basting frequently. Serve with salad and crusty bread, if desired.   SERVES 4-6

## SPARE RIBS WITH TANGY BBQ SAUCE

1.4 kg (3 lb) meaty pork spare ribs

### TANGY BBQ SAUCE
2 cloves garlic, crushed
90 ml (6 tbsp) clear honey
30 ml (2 tbsp) tomato purée
30 ml (2 tbsp) chilli sauce
30 ml (2 tbsp) Worcestershire sauce
30 ml (2 tbsp) soy sauce
20 ml (4 tsp) American yellow mustard
Juice of 1 lemon

Mix the sauce ingredients together in a bowl. Place the spare ribs in a large glass dish and pour the sauce over the ribs, turning the ribs to coat evenly. Cover and refrigerate for 2 hours, if time permits.

Remove ribs from the barbecue sauce and pour the remaining sauce into a small saucepan. Cook the ribs on a prepared barbecue for about 20 minutes, turning frequently. Just before serving, reheat the sauce. Bring the sauce to the boil and boil rapidly for 2-3 minutes. Serve the ribs hot, passing the sauce separately.

SERVES 4-6

**RIGHT:** Teriyaki Ribs

## HORSERADISH STEAKS WITH BBQ VEGETABLES

4 sirloin steaks, weighing about 150 g (5 oz) each

### MARINADE
30 ml (2 tbsp) horseradish sauce
30 ml (2 tbsp) cracked black pepper
60 ml (4 tbsp) vegetable oil
Pinch of salt

### HORSERADISH SAUCE
60 ml (4 tbsp) soured cream
15 ml (1 tbsp) horseradish sauce
Salt and ground black pepper

### BBQ VEGETABLES
4 medium courgettes, halved lengthways
2 red peppers, cored, seeded and quartered
4 shallots, unpeeled and halved
Salt and ground black pepper
Oil for brushing

Mix the marinade ingredients together in a bowl. Place the steaks in a shallow glass dish and pour over the marinade. Turn the steaks to coat evenly, cover and refrigerate for 2 hours.

Mix the sauce ingredients together in a bowl, cover and refrigerate until required.

Season the vegetables and brush them liberally with oil. Cook them on a prepared barbecue, turning occasionally and basting with oil. The courgettes require about 12 minutes to cook, the peppers 10 minutes, and the shallots 8 minutes. Keep all the vegetables warm while cooking the steaks.

Cook the steaks on the barbecue, brushing them occasionally with the marinade. For a medium-cooked steak, cook for about 3 minutes each side. Decrease or increase the cooking time if a rare or well-done steak is required. Serve the steaks hot with the Horseradish Sauce and the BBQ Vegetables. SERVES 4

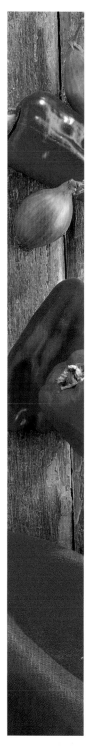

## COFFEE BEAN & MOLASSES RIBS

1.4 kg (3 lb) pork spare ribs
45 ml (3 tbsp) molasses or treacle
60 ml (4 tbsp) vegetable oil
120 ml (8 tbsp) coarsely ground coffee beans
Salad and jacket potatoes, to serve (optional)

Place the spare ribs in a large glass dish. Mix the molasses, oil and coffee beans together in a bowl and pour over the ribs, turning the ribs to coat evenly. Cover and refrigerate for 2-3 hours, if time permits.

Remove the ribs from the dish, reserving any remaining mixture for basting. Cook the ribs on a prepared barbecue for about 20 minutes, turning and basting them frequently. Serve with salad and jacket potatoes, if desired. SERVES 4-6

**TOP:** Coffee Bean & Molasses Ribs
**BOTTOM:** Horseradish Steaks with BBQ Vegetables

## LIVER & BACON BROCHETTES WITH GRILLED RED ONION

450 g (1 lb) lamb's liver
16 rashers streaky bacon
8 wooden or metal skewers
60 ml (4 tbsp) chopped fresh sage
90 ml (6 tbsp) olive oil
Sea salt and ground black pepper
4 small red onions, unpeeled and halved
Salad and potatoes, to serve (optional)

Cut the lamb's liver into fairly large chunks. Remove the rind from the bacon rashers and roll up each rasher. Thread the liver chunks and two bacon rolls on to each skewer.

Mix together the sage and oil, season, and brush the oil all over the prepared brochettes and the halved onions. Cook the onions on a prepared barbecue for about 8 minutes on each side, brushing occasionally with the sage oil.

Cook the liver and bacon brochettes on the barbecue for 4-5 minutes on each side, brushing frequently with the sage oil. Serve at once with salad and potatoes, if desired.                    SERVES 4

## LAMB CHOPS WITH GARLIC, LEMON & OREGANO

4 cloves garlic
20 ml (4 tsp) chopped fresh oregano
Grated zest and juice of 2 small lemons
60 ml (4 tbsp) sunflower oil
Sea salt and ground black pepper
8 lamb chops

Preheat an oven grill to hot. Place the garlic cloves under the grill for 8-10 minutes, turning them occasionally, until the skins are charred and the garlic cloves feel soft. Squeeze the roasted garlic out of its skin into a bowl, and mash to a paste. Add the oregano, lemon zest and juice, oil and seasoning. Mix well to combine thoroughly.

Place the lamb chops in a shallow bowl and pour over the roasted garlic mixture. Cover and refrigerate for 2 hours, if time permits.

Remove the chops from the garlic mixture, reserving the remaining mixture. Cook the chops on a prepared barbecue for about 5 minutes on each side. Just before serving, heat up the reserved garlic mixture in a small saucepan and pour it over the barbecued chops. Serve at once.                    SERVES 4

**RIGHT:** Liver & Bacon Brochettes with Grilled Red Onion

## BEEF & BEAN BURGERS

450 g (I lb) minced beef
225 g (8 oz) canned red kidney beans, drained
and chopped
I small onion, finely chopped
2 cloves garlic, crushed
5 ml (I tsp) chilli powder
Salt and ground black pepper
A little oil for brushing
50 g (2 oz) crisp green lettuce leaves
4 thick slices avocado
I red onion, sliced into rings
60 ml (4 tbsp) coriander leaves
4 flour tortillas, warmed
60 ml (4 tbsp) soured cream
Pickled Mexican chillies, to serve

Place the beef, beans, onion, garlic, chilli powder and salt and pepper in a bowl and mix well to combine. Divide the mixture into four and shape into equal-sized patties. Chill until required.

Just before cooking, brush each burger with a little oil. Cook on a prepared barbecue for about 6 minutes on each side for a medium-cooked burger. Decrease or increase the cooking time for either a rare or well-done burger.

Divide the lettuce, avocado, sliced onion and coriander between the tortillas. Top each with a burger and spoon some soured cream on each one. Serve the burgers with pickled chillies. SERVES 4

## CALIFORNIA DOGS

4 large frankfurters
4 plain or granary hot dog rolls, split lengthways
A little softened butter
6 Cos lettuce leaves, torn into bite-sized pieces
4 small tomatoes, sliced
I small onion, sliced into rings

### SWEETCORN SALSA
198-g (7-oz) can sweetcorn kernels, drained
¼ green pepper, finely diced
4 radishes, thinly sliced
½ red onion, finely diced
I clove garlic, crushed
Juice of ½ lemon
15 ml (I tbsp) chopped fresh parsley
Salt and ground black pepper

Place the ingredients for the salsa in a bowl and mix together gently to combine. Cover and refrigerate.

Make several diagonal slashes in each frankfurter and cook them on a prepared barbecue for 4 minutes on each side. Place the hot dog rolls, cut-side down, on the barbecue to toast them lightly. Spread a little softened butter on the rolls.

Divide the lettuce, tomato and onion between the four rolls and top each with a frankfurter. Serve them at once with the Sweetcorn Salsa. SERVES 4

**TOP:** California Dog
**BOTTOM:** Beef & Bean Burger

## MEDITERRANEAN CHARGRILLED SARDINES

*The sardines in this recipe are cooked on pairs of skewers, but you could also use a metal fish rack that holds 6 or 12 sardines.*

12 sardines
12 small lemon zest strips
12 small rosemary sprigs
8 long bamboo skewers, soaked in cold water for 2 hours
4 lemon wedges

### HERB AND LEMON OIL
60 ml (4 tbsp) extra virgin olive oil
10 ml (2 tsp) grated lemon zest
Juice of 1 lemon
15 ml (1 tbsp) chopped fresh rosemary
15 ml (1 tbsp) chopped fresh thyme
Salt and ground black pepper

Using a pair of small scissors, slit the bellies of the sardines and discard the guts. Wash the sardines and dry them on kitchen paper. Stuff a small strip of lemon zest and a rosemary sprig into the cavity of each sardine.

Thread three sardines on to each pair of skewers by pushing one skewer through a sardine just below the head and pushing the second skewer in just above the tail. Thread on the other two sardines in the same way, then repeat the process with the remaining sardines and skewers.

Mix the ingredients for the herb oil together, and brush liberally over the sardines. Cook the sardines on a prepared, very hot barbecue for 3-4 minutes on each side, basting with more oil while they are cooking.

Slide the cooked sardines off the skewers and serve at once with lemon wedges.          SERVES 4

## SALMON WITH CAPERS & GAZPACHO SALSA

4 salmon steaks, weighing about 100 g (4 oz) each

### MARINADE
45 ml (3 tbsp) olive oil
Zest and juice of 1 lime
15 ml (1 tbsp) capers in brine, drained
Pinch of sea salt

### GAZPACHO SALSA
4 small tomatoes, peeled, seeded and diced
150 g (5 oz) cucumber, diced
½ onion, diced
½ red pepper, diced
15 ml (1 tbsp) chopped fresh parsley
20 ml (4 tsp) chopped fresh coriander
5 ml (1 tsp) caster sugar
30 ml (2 tbsp) red wine vinegar
Salt and ground black pepper

Mix the marinade ingredients together in a bowl. Place the salmon steaks in a shallow dish and pour over the marinade. Cover and refrigerate the salmon for 2 hours, if time permits.

Place the ingredients for the salsa in a bowl and mix together gently to combine. Cover and refrigerate until required.

Remove the salmon steaks from the marinade and press a few capers into the flesh of each piece of salmon. Reserve the remaining marinade for basting. Cook the salmon on a prepared barbecue for 4-5 minutes on each side, turning the fish once and basting occasionally. Serve the salmon hot with the salsa.

SERVES 4

**TOP:** Mediterranean Chargrilled Sardines
**BOTTOM:** Salmon with Capers & Gazpacho Salsa

# GRILLED TUNA WITH TOMATO & OLIVE SALSA

4 tuna steaks, weighing about 150 g (5 oz) each

### OLIVE MARINADE
60 ml (4 tbsp) green olive purée
120 ml (8 tbsp) olive oil
3 cloves garlic, crushed
Salt and ground black pepper

### TOMATO AND OLIVE SALSA
15 black olives, stoned and sliced
4 tomatoes, peeled, seeded and sliced
75 g (3 oz) sun-dried tomatoes in oil,
drained and sliced
4 spring onions, sliced
14 basil leaves, torn
Pinch of sugar

Mix the marinade ingredients together in a large shallow dish. Add the tuna steaks, turning to coat evenly. Cover and refrigerate for 2 hours, if time permits.

Make the salsa by combining all the ingredients together. Refrigerate until required.

Remove the tuna steaks from the marinade, reserving the marinade for basting. Cook the steaks on a prepared barbecue for about 5 minutes on each side, basting occasionally. Serve the grilled tuna at once with the salsa. SERVES 4

# MESQUITE-SMOKED FISH

*Use a solid-fleshed fish for this recipe, such as catfish or monkfish.*

4 pieces catfish or monkfish tail with the bone, weighing about 200 g (7 oz) each
About 1 cup mesquite chips, soaked in cold water for 1 hour
Skewered New Potatoes, to serve (see page 358)

### MARINADE
120 ml (8 tbsp) extra virgin olive oil
60 ml (4 tbsp) white wine vinegar
4 cloves garlic, crushed
10 ml (2 tsp) tropical peppercorns, crushed
10 ml (2 tsp) chopped fennel fronds (optional)
A little sea salt

Mix the marinade ingredients together in a bowl. Place the fish portions in a shallow dish and pour over the marinade, turning the fish to coat evenly. Cover and refrigerate for 2 hours, if time permits.

Drain the soaked mesquite chips and scatter them over the hot coals of a prepared barbecue. Remove the fish from the marinade, reserving the marinade for basting. Cook the fish on the barbecue for about 15 minutes, or until cooked through, turning and basting occasionally. Serve at once with some Skewered New Potatoes, if desired. SERVES 4

**RIGHT:** Grilled Tuna with Tomato & Olive Salsa

## TIGER PRAWNS WITH CORIANDER MAYONNAISE

16 raw tiger prawns in their shells, with
heads removed
4 wooden or metal skewers

### MARINADE

120 ml (8 tbsp) sweet chilli sauce
60 ml (4 tbsp) tomato purée
20 ml (4 tsp) lemon juice
4 cloves garlic, crushed
20 ml (4 tsp) sesame oil

### CORIANDER MAYONNAISE

90 ml (6 tbsp) mayonnaise
½ fresh red chilli, seeded and finely chopped
½ small red onion, finely chopped
30 ml (2 tbsp) chopped fresh coriander
30 ml (2 tbsp) lemon juice
Salt and ground black pepper

Mix the marinade ingredients together in a bowl. Add
the prawns to the marinade and toss to coat evenly.
Cover and refrigerate for 2 hours, if time permits.

Mix the mayonnaise ingredients together, cover
and refrigerate until required.

Thread four prawns on to each skewer and cook
them on a prepared barbecue for 4-5 minutes on each
side, turning them once. To serve, remove prawns
from skewers, if preferred, and serve with the Coriander Mayonnaise.                    SERVES 2

## CHARGRILLED LOBSTER WITH HERB BUTTER

*Ask your fishmonger to split the lobsters in
half, ready for the barbecue. Otherwise, kill each
lobster by piercing with a knife at the central point
where the head meets the body. Halve the head
and split in half along the body.*

2 raw lobsters, each weighing about 450 g (1 lb),
split in half lengthways with claws cracked
Salt and ground black pepper

**HERB BUTTER**

40 g (1½ oz) butter, softened
15 ml (1 tbsp) chopped fresh chervil
5 ml (1 tsp) snipped fresh chives
5 ml (1 tsp) finely chopped shallot
Squeeze of lemon juice
Salt and ground black pepper

Place the ingredients for the Herb Butter in a bowl
and beat together to combine. Place the flavoured
butter in a sausage shape on a piece of greaseproof
paper or cling film. Roll up the butter to produce a
cylinder and refrigerate to harden the butter.

Season the lobster flesh lightly with salt and pepper
and cook the lobster halves, cut-side down, on a prepared barbecue for 8-10 minutes, until the flesh has
become opaque and the shells have turned orange.

Cook the claws separately. They are cooked when
the shells have turned bright orange. Serve the freshly
grilled lobster with discs of Herb Butter.   SERVES 2

**TOP:** Chargrilled Lobster with Herb Butter
**BOTTOM:** Tiger Prawns with
Coriander Mayonnaise

# SPICY & EXOTIC BARBECUES

*Influenced by the cuisines of Mexico, the Mediterranean and the Far East, the recipes in this chapter are robustly flavoured. Chillies, coriander, ginger, lime and sesame are ingredients that feature predominantly in the recipes. An exciting selection of chicken, meat, fish and seafood dishes are included, from the spicy Turmeric Prawn & Pineapple Skewers to the unusual Halibut Chargrilled in Banana Leaves.*

## MUSTARD-GLAZED CHICKEN DRUMSTICKS

8 chicken drumsticks

### MUSTARD MARINADE
30 ml (2 tbsp) clear honey
10 ml (2 tsp) English mustard
10 ml (2 tsp) coarse-grain mustard
10 ml (2 tsp) Worcestershire sauce
Juice of 1 orange
2 cloves garlic, crushed
½ onion, very finely chopped

Make several deep slashes through the skin of each drumstick and place the chicken in a shallow glass dish.

Mix the marinade ingredients together and pour over the drumsticks. Turn the drumsticks so they are evenly coated in marinade. Cover and refrigerate for 2-3 hours or overnight.

Remove the drumsticks from the marinade, reserving the marinade for basting, and cook the chicken on a prepared barbecue for about 20 minutes, turning occasionally and basting during cooking. To test that the chicken is cooked, pierce the flesh with a skewer. If the juices run clear, the chicken is ready to serve.

SERVES 4

## BARBECUED CHICKEN WITH CHILLI & LIME

6 boneless chicken breasts

### MARINADE
20 ml (4 tsp) chilli oil
30 ml (2 tbsp) clear honey
60 ml (4 tbsp) chopped fresh coriander
2 cloves garlic, crushed
Grated zest and juice of 2 limes

### CORIANDER AND CHILLI YOGHURT
120 ml (8 tbsp) Greek yoghurt
2.5 ml (½ tsp) chilli oil
Grated zest and juice of 1 lime
60 ml (4 tbsp) chopped fresh coriander
1 small fresh red chilli, seeded and finely chopped
A little salt

Place the marinade ingredients in a shallow glass dish and mix well to combine. With a sharp knife, make several deep slashes in each chicken and place the chicken breasts in the marinade, turning to coat well. Cover and refrigerate for 3-4 hours.

Mix the yoghurt ingredients together in a bowl. Cover and refrigerate until required.

Remove the chicken from the marinade, reserving the marinade for basting. Place the chicken, skin-side up, on a prepared, medium-hot barbecue. Cook the chicken breasts for 10 minutes, brushing occasionally with the marinade, then turn over and cook for a further 10 minutes. To test if the chicken is cooked, pierce the thickest part of the breast with a skewer. If the juices are still pink, cook until the juices run clear. Serve at once with the yoghurt.

SERVES 6

**RIGHT:** Barbecued Chicken with Chilli & Lime

## MEXICAN FISH KEBABS

550 g (1¼ lb) red snapper fillets, cut into chunks
4 mini red peppers, halved, or 8 pickled
cherry peppers
2 onions, cut into 8 wedges each
8 wooden or metal skewers
Spicy Rice, to serve (see page 356)

### MARINADE
60 ml (4 tbsp) chopped fresh coriander
60 ml (4 tbsp) olive oil
Juice of 3 limes
20 ml (4 tsp) paprika
1 fresh red chilli, seeded and finely chopped

### GUACAMOLE
2 avocados
Juice of 1 large lime
½ onion, finely chopped
90 ml (6 tbsp) torn coriander leaves
Salt and ground black pepper

Place the marinade ingredients in a shallow glass bowl and mix well to combine. Add the chunks of fish and turn to coat evenly. Cover and refrigerate for 2 hours.

Make the Guacamole. Mash the avocados with the lime juice. Stir in the other ingredients, taste and adjust seasoning, and refrigerate until required.

Thread the marinated fish on to the skewers, alternating with the peppers and onion wedges. Reserve the marinade for basting. Cook the kebabs on a prepared barbecue for about 10 minutes, turning and brushing them with the reserved marinade. Serve at once with the Guacamole and Spicy Rice.  SERVES 4

## HALIBUT CHARGRILLED IN BANANA LEAVES

*Galangal is used in this recipe for its exotic taste, but you can substitute fresh root ginger. Heavy-duty foil can also be substituted for the banana leaves, but the foil will not need to be oiled.*

450-g (1-lb) piece skinless, boneless halibut, cut into
2.5-cm (1-inch) cubes
4 pieces banana leaf, about 31 cm (12 inches) square
Oil for brushing
Cocktail sticks

### SPICY PASTE
1 large dried red chilli
5-cm (2-inch) piece galangal, peeled and chopped
2 stalks lemon grass, finely chopped
2 cloves garlic, crushed
1 shallot, finely chopped
2 Kaffir lime leaves, finely chopped
15 ml (1 tbsp) Thai fish sauce
45 ml (3 tbsp) groundnut oil

Prepare the Spicy Paste. Soak the red chilli in hot water for 10 minutes, then drain and chop finely. Place the chilli and the remaining ingredients in a spice grinder or food processor and blend to a smooth paste.

Transfer the paste to a shallow glass dish, add the cubed fish and toss the fish to coat evenly. Cover and refrigerate for 2 hours.

Brush the banana leaves with a little oil and divide the marinated fish between them. Wrap up to form parcels and secure with cocktail sticks. Brush the outside of the parcels with a little oil and cook the fish parcels on a prepared barbecue for about 10 minutes, until the fish is cooked through.  SERVES 4

**TOP:** Halibut Chargrilled in Banana Leaves
**BOTTOM:** Mexican Fish Kebabs

## SCALLOP BROCHETTES WITH GINGER & ORANGE

16 large scallops
4 long strips of orange zest
350 g (12 oz) courgettes, canelled and cut
into 12 chunks
4 metal skewers

### MARINADE

Juice of 2 oranges
20 ml (4 tsp) grated fresh root ginger
60 ml (4 tbsp) vegetable oil
4 spring onions, finely chopped
2 cloves garlic, crushed
Salt and ground black pepper

### GINGER AND ORANGE BUTTER

100 g (4 oz) butter, softened
15 ml (1 tbsp) grated fresh root ginger
15 ml (1 tbsp) grated orange zest
15 ml (1 tbsp) orange juice
Salt and ground black pepper

Mix the marinade ingredients together in a large, shallow bowl. Add the scallops to the marinade and turn to coat evenly. Cover and refrigerate for 2 hours.

Mix the ingredients for the butter together and place the butter in a sausage shape on a piece of greaseproof paper or cling film. Roll up to form a cylinder and refrigerate until the butter hardens.

Remove the scallops from the marinade, reserving the marinade for basting. Thread four scallops, a strip of orange zest and three chunks of courgette on to each skewer. Cook the brochettes on a prepared, medium-hot barbecue for 8-10 minutes, turning and brushing them frequently with the marinade. Serve the hot brochettes with discs of flavoured butter, so the butter melts over the scallops and courgettes.

SERVES 4

## TURMERIC PRAWN & PINEAPPLE SKEWERS

24 raw tiger prawns, peeled but with tails intact
8 wooden or metal skewers
225 g (8 oz) fresh pineapple, cut into 16 chunks
16 bulbous white parts of spring onion

### TURMERIC MARINADE

1 stalk lemon grass, finely chopped
2.5-cm (1-inch) piece fresh root ginger, peeled and grated
2 cloves garlic, crushed
30 ml (2 tbsp) groundnut oil
15 ml (1 tbsp) lemon juice
5 ml (1 tsp) turmeric
Pinch of sugar
Salt and ground black pepper

Place the marinade ingredients in a food processor and blend to a paste. Transfer the paste to a large bowl, add the prawns and turn to coat evenly. Refrigerate for 2-3 hours or overnight.

Thread the marinated prawns on to the skewers, alternating with the pineapple chunks and spring onions. Reserve the marinade for basting. Cook the prawn skewers on a prepared barbecue for 8-10 minutes, turning and basting them while they cook. Serve at once. SERVES 4

**LEFT:** Turmeric Prawn & Pineapple Skewers
**RIGHT:** Scallop Brochettes with
Ginger & Orange

## MALAYSIAN FISH WITH SPICY PEANUT SAUCE

6 medium mackerel, weighing about 200 g (7 oz)
each, gutted and cleaned
A wire frame for cooking the fish

### MARINADE
60 ml (4 tbsp) sambal oelek (hot pepper condiment)
60 ml (4 tbsp) groundnut oil
10 ml (2 tsp) soft brown sugar
2 cloves garlic, crushed
Juice of 2 limes

### SPICY PEANUT SAUCE
15 ml (1 tbsp) tamarind concentrate, mixed with
120 ml (8 tbsp) water
20 ml (4 tsp) soft brown sugar
2 spring onions, chopped
1 stalk lemon grass, chopped
1 clove garlic, crushed
15 ml (1 tbsp) sambal oelek (hot pepper condiment)
75 g (3 oz) salted peanuts, coarsely ground
150 ml (¼ pint) coconut milk

Mix the marinade ingredients together in a bowl. Make several deep slashes in the flesh of each mackerel and place the fish in a large, shallow dish. Pour over the marinade and turn the fish around, coating well. Cover and refrigerate for at least 2 hours.

Make the peanut sauce. Place the first six ingredients in a saucepan, bring to the boil, then reduce the heat and simmer for 5 minutes. Add the peanuts and cook for a further minute, then stir in the coconut milk and simmer for a further 3 minutes. Set aside.

Remove the mackerel from the marinade, reserving the marinade for basting. Cook the fish in a wire frame on a prepared barbecue for about 15 minutes, turning and basting as they cook. Serve the fish with the warm Spicy Peanut Sauce. SERVES 6

## PHUKET CRAB CAKES

25 g (1 oz) butter
25 g (1 oz) flour
150 ml (¼ pint) milk
450 g (1 lb) fresh or canned crabmeat, drained
and flaked
175 g (6 oz) fresh white breadcrumbs
60 ml (4 tbsp) chopped fresh coriander
30 ml (2 tbsp) grated lime zest
45 ml (3 tbsp) freshly squeezed lime juice
45 ml (3 tbsp) grated fresh root ginger
20 ml (4 tsp) soy sauce
1 fresh red chilli, seeded and finely chopped
Salt and ground black pepper
60 ml (4 tbsp) vegetable oil for brushing
A barbecue griddle plate for cooking
Salad and hot chilli sauce, to serve (optional)

Melt the butter in a saucepan and stir in the flour to make a roux. Gradually add the milk, whisking well between each addition, and boil for 2-3 minutes to form a thick white sauce.

Remove the sauce from the heat and stir in the crab, breadcrumbs, coriander, lime zest and juice, ginger, soy sauce, chilli and seasoning. Leave to cool.

When the mixture is cool, shape it into eight cakes. Refrigerate the crab cakes for at least 2 hours before cooking them.

Oil the griddle and heat it on a prepared barbecue. Brush the crab cakes with some oil and cook on the griddle for 4-5 minutes. Brush with more oil, turn them over and cook for a further 4-5 minutes. Serve at once with a salad and chilli sauce, if desired.

SERVES 4

**RIGHT:** Malaysian Fish with Spicy Peanut Sauce

# PORK BROCHETTES WITH CITRUS SALSA

450 g (1 lb) pork tenderloin, cut into 4-cm
(1½-inch) cubes
8 wooden or metal skewers
2 small yellow peppers, cored, seeded and chopped
8 small onions, halved
16 bay leaves

### MARINADE

60 ml (4 tbsp) dry sherry or rice wine
60 ml (4 tbsp) ground coriander
60 ml (4 tbsp) sunflower oil
4 cloves garlic, finely chopped
6 Kaffir lime leaves, finely chopped
Salt and ground black pepper

### CITRUS SALSA

2 oranges
2 pink grapefruit
10 ml (2 tsp) chopped fresh thyme
20 ml (4 tsp) snipped fresh chives
4 Kaffir lime leaves, very finely chopped
Salt and ground black pepper

Mix the marinade ingredients together in a glass bowl. Add the cubed pork and mix to coat evenly. Cover and refrigerate for 4 hours.

Thread the marinated pork on to the skewers, alternating with the peppers, onions and bay leaves. Reserve the marinade for basting.

For the salsa, peel the oranges and grapefruit and cut in between the membranes to produce segments. Chop the segments roughly. Place in a bowl with the remaining ingredients and toss gently to combine.

Cook the brochettes over a prepared medium-hot barbecue for about 15 minutes, turning frequently and brushing them with the marinade. Serve hot, accompanied by the Citrus Salsa. SERVES 4

# THAI-STYLE SKEWERED CHICKEN

4 skinless, boneless chicken breasts, weighing
150 g (5 oz) each
8 wooden or metal skewers
Lime wedges, to serve
Jasmine and Sesame Rice, to serve (see page 356)

### THAI MARINADE

30 ml (2 tbsp) Thai red curry paste
30 ml (2 tbsp) ground coriander
45 ml (3 tbsp) groundnut oil
10 ml (2 tsp) ground cumin
10 ml (2 tsp) caster sugar
2 stalks lemon grass, very finely chopped
Juice of 2 limes

Mix the marinade ingredients together in a large bowl. Cut the chicken into 2.5-cm (1-inch) cubes and add to the marinade. Turn to coat evenly, cover and refrigerate for 2-3 hours or overnight.

Thread the marinated chicken on to the skewers and reserve the marinade for basting. Cook the chicken on a prepared, medium-hot barbecue for about 7 minutes on each side, basting with the reserved marinade while cooking. Serve with lime wedges and Jasmine and Sesame Rice, if desired.

SERVES 4

**TOP:** Thai-style Skewered Chicken
**BOTTOM:** Pork Brochettes with Citrus Salsa

# CHARGRILLED SQUID WITH SESAME & CASHEW

30 ml (2 tbsp) cornflour, sifted
2 egg whites, beaten
10 ml (2 tsp) light soy sauce
5 ml (1 tsp) sesame oil
175 g (6 oz) raw cashew nuts, finely chopped
60 ml (4 tbsp) sesame seeds
12 prepared baby squid tubes
Cocktail sticks
A barbecue griddle plate for cooking
Thai sweet chilli sauce, to serve
Julienne of spring onion and cucumber, to serve

### STUFFING

350 g (12 oz) cooked white rice
4 spring onions, finely chopped
10 ml (2 tsp) finely chopped fresh root ginger
5 ml (1 tsp) finely chopped fresh red chilli
10 ml (2 tsp) light soy sauce

Place the stuffing ingredients in a food processor and blend briefly until well combined. Stuff the cavities of the squid with the mixture.

Mix the cornflour, egg whites, soy sauce and sesame oil together. Mix the cashew nuts and sesame seeds together and spread them out on a plate. Dip each stuffed squid tube in the egg mixture and then roll in the cashew nut mixture to coat evenly. Secure the end of each squid tube with a cocktail stick to hold in the stuffing. Chill the coated squid tubes in the refrigerator for 2 hours.

Oil the griddle plate and heat it on a prepared barbecue. Cook the squid on the griddle for about 8 minutes, turning occasionally until golden. Serve hot with chilli sauce and vegetable julienne.    SERVES 4

# CHINESE-STYLE SPARE RIBS

1.4 kg (3 lb) meaty pork spare ribs

### SZECHUAN MARINADE

4 stalks lemon grass, very finely chopped
60 ml (4 tbsp) Szechuan peppercorns, crushed
60 ml (4 tbsp) dried chilli flakes
60 ml (4 tbsp) groundnut oil
45 ml (3 tbsp) soft brown sugar
20 ml (4 tsp) ground coriander
20 ml (4 tsp) sesame oil

Place the marinade ingredients in a food processor or spice grinder and blend to a paste. Transfer the marinade to a large bowl.

Cut the spare ribes into 10-cm (4-inch) lengths and add to the bowl of marinade. Turn to coat evenly, cover and refrigerate for 2-3 hours or overnight.

Remove the ribs from the marinade, reserving the marinade for basting. Cook the ribs on a prepared barbecue for 15-20 minutes, turning and basting them occasionally. Serve at once.    SERVES 4-6

**RIGHT:** Chargrilled Squid with Sesame & Cashew

## LAMB & APRICOT SKEWERS

550 g (1¼ lb) lamb fillet, cut into 24 pieces
4 shallots
4 firm, ripe apricots, halved
16 bay leaves
8 wooden or metal skewers
Barbecued Artichokes, to serve (optional)

### MARINADE
45 ml (3 tbsp) apricot jam
30 ml (2 tbsp) soy sauce
60 ml (4 tbsp) vegetable oil
30 ml (2 tbsp) cider vinegar
3 ml (¾ tsp) cayenne
2 large cloves garlic, crushed
Ground black pepper

Mix the marinade ingredients together in a shallow glass dish. Add the lamb pieces, toss to coat evenly, cover and refrigerate for 2 hours.

Blanch the shallots in boiling water for 4 minutes, then remove and peel and halve them.

Remove the lamb from the marinade, reserving the marinade for basting. Thread three chunks of meat, a shallot half, an apricot half and two bay leaves on to each skewer. Cook the lamb skewers on a prepared barbecue for about 15 minutes, turning and basting them while cooking. Serve hot with Barbecued Artichokes, if desired. SERVES 4

## BARBECUED ARTICHOKES

4 small globe artichokes
60 ml (4 tbsp) olive oil
Juice of ½ lemon
Salt and ground black pepper

Trim the artichoke stalks close to the base and cook them in boiling, salted water for 20-25 minutes.

Halve the artichokes and scoop out the hairy chokes. Mix together the oil, lemon juice and seasoning. Brush the artichokes all over with the oil mixture and cook on a prepared barbecue for 10-15 minutes, turning occasionally, until they are lightly charred. Serve hot. SERVES 4

## SPICY BEEF KEBABS

550 g (1¼ lb) fillet or rump steak, cut into
bite-sized cubes
1 red pepper
1 green pepper
1 yellow pepper
16 cherry tomatoes
8 metal skewers

### GINGER MARINADE
30 ml (2 tbsp) vegetable oil
60 ml (4 tbsp) red wine
120 ml (8 tbsp) balsamic vinegar
45 ml (3 tbsp) grated fresh root ginger
10 ml (2 tsp) paprika
10 ml (2 tsp) cayenne
Salt and ground black pepper

Mix the marinade ingredients together in a shallow glass dish. Add the cubed beef and toss to coat evenly. Cover and refrigerate for 2-3 hours or overnight.

Halve and remove the cores and seeds from the peppers. Cut the peppers into 2.5-cm (1-inch) cubes.

Remove the beef from the marinade, reserving the marinade for basting. Thread the beef, peppers and cherry tomatoes on to the skewers. Cook the kebabs on a prepared barbecue for 10-12 minutes, turning and basting them while they are cooking. SERVES 4

**TOP:** Barbecued Artichokes
**BOTTOM:** Lamb & Apricot Skewers,
Spicy Beef Kebabs

# AROMATIC BARBECUES

*The blends of herbs and spices used in the recipes in this chapter evoke the warmth of the Mediterranean. Chicken Bagna Cauda combines the classic Southern Italian ingredients of anchovies, sun-dried tomatoes, garlic and olive oil, while the Eastern Mediterranean Kofta Kebabs use mint, garlic, cumin and coriander to reproduce the aromatic flavours of that region. Sage, thyme, rosemary, saffron, cayenne and peppercorns are used liberally in the recipes to produce enticing aromas guaranteed to whet most appetites.*

## SURF & TURF GRILL

450 g (I lb) fillet steak, cut into 2.5-cm
(I-inch) cubes
8 medium scallops
8 raw tiger prawns, shelled but with tails left intact
4 long metal skewers
Herby rice and salad, to serve (optional)

### MARINADE
60 ml (4 tbsp) corn oil
60 ml (4 tbsp) Bourbon whiskey
Grated zest and juice of 2 limes
Salt and ground black pepper

Place the marinade ingredients in a shallow glass dish and mix well. Add the steak, scallops and prawns to the marinade, cover and refrigerate for 4 hours.

Remove the marinated food from the marinade, reserving the marinade for basting, and thread the steak, scallops and prawns on to the skewers.

Cook the skewers on a prepared barbecue for 8-10 minutes, basting them while they are cooking. Serve with herby rice and a salad, if desired.    SERVES 4

## BLACKENED SEA BASS

4 sea bass fillets, weighing 150 g (5 oz) each
50 g (2 oz) butter, melted
Lemon wedges, to serve
Skewered New Potatoes, to serve (see page 358).

### SPICE MIX
5 ml (I tsp) salt
5 ml (I tsp) garlic granules
5 ml (I tsp) dried parsley
5 ml (I tsp) chilli powder
2.5 ml (½ tsp) ground bay leaves
15 ml (I tbsp) cayenne
Ground black pepper

### BUTTER SAUCE
45 ml (3 tbsp) dry white wine
30 ml (2 tbsp) white wine vinegar
50 g (2 oz) butter, cubed
150 ml (¼ pint) double cream
15 ml (I tbsp) chopped fresh parsley
15 ml (I tbsp) snipped fresh chives

Mix the spice mix ingredients together and place on a plate. Brush the sea bass fillets all over with melted butter, then place on the spice mix and turn to coat evenly. Cover and refrigerate the fillets for I hour.

Cook the fish on the oiled rack of a prepared barbecue for 3-4 minutes on each side.

Just before serving, make the sauce. Place the wine and vinegar in a saucepan and boil rapidly for 1-2 minutes to reduce it by half. Then whisk in the butter, a cube at a time, over a low heat. Add the cream and whisk for 1-2 minutes. Stir in the herbs and serve with the sea bass, lemon and potatoes.    SERVES 4

**RIGHT:** Blackened Sea Bass

## SEAFOOD BROCHETTES

350 g (12 oz) skinless, boneless salmon steak
350 g (12 oz) skinless, boneless monkfish
16 large raw prawns
8 metal skewers

### CHERVIL MARINADE
60 ml (4 tbsp) sunflower oil
120 ml (8 tbsp) chopped fresh chervil
Salt and ground black pepper

### SAFFRON SAUCE
15 ml (1 tbsp) sunflower oil
2 shallots, finely chopped
600 ml (1 pint) dry white wine
Scant 2.5 ml (½ tsp) saffron strands, soaked in
30 ml (2 tbsp) boiling water
300 ml (½ pint) single cream
30 ml (2 tbsp) chopped fresh chervil
30 ml (2 tbsp) snipped fresh chives
Salt and ground black pepper

Cut the salmon and monkfish into 16 chunks each. Place the fish and prawns in a shallow glass dish. Mix the marinade ingredients together and pour over. Toss to coat evenly, cover and refrigerate for 2 hours.

Make the Saffron Sauce. Heat the oil in a saucepan and sauté the shallots for 3 minutes. Add the wine and saffron with the water, bring to the boil and boil steadily for 10-12 minutes, until liquid has reduced to about one-quarter of its original amount. Add the cream and reduce again for 4-5 minutes. Add the herbs and seasoning and heat for a further 30 seconds. Set aside.

Remove the fish and prawns from the marinade, reserving the marinade for basting, and divide them equally between the skewers. Cook on the oiled rack of a prepared barbecue for 8-10 minutes, turning and brushing with marinade. Reheat the sauce and serve it at once with the brochettes. SERVES 4

## CRUMBED OYSTERS WITH PIQUANT TOMATO DIP

16 fresh oysters
50 g (2 oz) butter
65 g (2½ oz) fresh white breadcrumbs
2 spring onions, finely chopped
15 ml (1 tbsp) chopped fresh thyme
Generous pinch of paprika
Salt and ground black pepper

### PIQUANT TOMATO DIP
450 g (1 lb) tomatoes, roughly chopped
4 spring onions, finely chopped
20 ml (4 tsp) horseradish sauce
10 ml (2 tsp) Worcestershire sauce
5 ml (1 tsp) sugar
Few drops Tabasco sauce
Salt and ground black pepper

Prepare the tomato dip. Place the tomatoes in a food processor and blend briefly to produce a thick purée. Transfer the tomatoes to a saucepan, add the remaining ingredients and bring to the boil. Boil steadily for about 10 minutes to produce a thick sauce. Taste and adjust seasoning, if necessary, and set aside.

Open the oysters, leaving them on the half shell. Melt the butter in a frying pan, add the breadcrumbs and cook for 1 minute. Stir in the remaining ingredients and cook for 3-4 minutes, stirring constantly.

Top each oyster with a little of the crispy breadcrumb mixture, making sure the coating covers the oysters. Cook the oysters on a prepared barbecue for 4-5 minutes, until the oysters are lightly cooked and heated through. Reheat the tomato dip and serve it with the oysters. SERVES 4 AS A STARTER

**TOP:** Crumbed Oysters with Piquant
Tomato Dip
**BOTTOM:** Seafood Brochettes

## CAJUN TURKEY KEBABS

550 g (1¼ lb) turkey breast, cut into 2.5-cm
(1-inch) cubes
8 wooden or metal skewers
8 baby sweetcorn, blanched for 1 minute
8 shallots, blanched for 5 minutes and peeled
1 large green pepper, cored, seeded and chopped
16 bay leaves
30 ml (2 tbsp) corn oil
Saffron rice, to serve

### MARINADE

1 small onion, chopped
2 cloves garlic, chopped
15 ml (1 tbsp) chopped fresh oregano
15 ml (1 tbsp) chopped fresh thyme
7.5 ml (1½ tsp) paprika
2.5 ml (½ tsp) cayenne
Juice of ½ lemon
60 ml (4 tbsp) corn oil
Salt and ground black pepper

Place the marinade ingredients in a food processor and blend to a smooth paste. Pour the marinade into a glass bowl and add the cubed turkey, turning to coat well. Cover and refrigerate for 4 hours.

Thread the marinated turkey on to the skewers, alternating with the sweetcorn, shallots, peppers and bay leaves.

Add the corn oil to the remaining marinade in the dish and brush over the kebabs while cooking them.

Cook the kebabs on a prepared, medium-hot barbecue for about 7 minutes on each side, brushing them with the reserved marinade. Serve at once with the saffron rice. SERVES 4

## CREOLE-STYLE PORK SKEWERS

550 g (1¼ lb) pork tenderloin, cut into 24 pieces
8 wooden or metal skewers
1 large red onion, cut into 8 wedges
1 large yellow pepper, cored, seeded and cut
into chunks

### MARINADE

60 ml (4 tbsp) olive oil
30 ml (2 tbsp) sun-dried tomato paste
30 ml (2 tbsp) tomato ketchup
30 ml (2 tbsp) lemon juice
2 cloves garlic, crushed
2 small pickled green chillies, chopped
Salt and ground black pepper

Mix all the marinade ingredients together. Pour the marinade into a shallow glass dish and add the pork pieces, turning to coat well. Cover and refrigerate for 4 hours.

Remove the pork from the marinade, reserving the marinade for basting, and thread the pork on to the skewers with the onions and peppers.

Cook the pork skewers on a prepared, medium-hot barbecue for 12-15 minutes, basting them with the reserved marinade while they are cooking. SERVES 4

**RIGHT:** Cajun Turkey Kebabs

## CHICKEN PINWHEELS

4 skinless, boneless chicken breasts, weighing
150 g (5 oz) each
100-g (4-oz) piece leek, cut into 2 lengths
45 ml (3 tbsp) olive oil for brushing
Rice, to serve (optional)

### STUFFING

25 g (1 oz) pistachio nuts, finely chopped
25 g (1 oz) fresh white breadcrumbs
50 g (2 oz) butter, melted
24 basil leaves, torn
Salt and ground black pepper

### BASIL CREAM SAUCE

300 ml (½ pint) single cream
16 large basil leaves, torn
Ground black pepper

Place the stuffing ingredients in a bowl and mix well.

Place a chicken breast between two pieces of grease-proof paper and pound with a rolling pin or mallet to flatten. Repeat with the remaining chicken breasts.

Blanch the leeks for 3 minutes, then drain and refresh in cold water. Slice each piece of leek in half lengthways. Dry the pieces of leek on kitchen paper.

Spread one-quarter of the stuffing on to each chicken breast, leaving a 1.5-cm (½-inch) border around the edges. Place a piece of leek in the centre, then roll up to enclose the stuffing. Secure with string. Repeat with the remaining chicken. Refrigerate for 2 hours.

Brush the pinwheels with a little olive oil and cook on a prepared barbecue for 20-25 minutes, turning and brushing them with more oil as they cook.

Make the sauce. Place the cream, basil and seasoning in a saucepan and bring to the boil. Boil rapidly for 4-5 minutes, until the sauce has reduced slightly. To serve, slice the chicken pinwheels thickly and serve with some sauce and rice.                    SERVES 4

## CHICKEN BAGNA CAUDA

4 boneless chicken breasts with skin, weighing about
175 g (6 oz) each
60 ml (4 tbsp) chopped fresh parsley
60 ml (4 tbsp) olive oil
4 cloves garlic, crushed
Salt and ground black pepper
Polenta or pasta, to serve (optional)

### ANCHOVY SAUCE

240 ml (8 fl oz) olive oil
4 cloves garlic, crushed
8 anchovy fillets, finely chopped
12 halves sun-dried tomatoes in oil, drained and finely chopped
30 ml (2 tbsp) chilli sauce
30 ml (2 tbsp) chopped fresh parsley
Ground black pepper

Make several deep slashes through the skin and flesh of each chicken breast. Mix the chopped parsley, oil, garlic and seasoning together. Work this mixture into the slashes and over the surface of each chicken breast. Place the chicken in a shallow dish, pour over any remaining mixture, cover and refrigerate for 2 hours.

Make the sauce. Heat the oil in a saucepan and sauté the garlic for 1 minute. Add the remaining ingredients and simmer gently for 3-4 minutes. Set the sauce aside until required.

Remove the chicken from the dish, reserving any remaining mixture for basting. Cook the chicken breasts on a prepared barbecue for about 20 minutes, turning and basting occasionally. Test the chicken with a skewer: if juices run clear, the chicken is cooked.

Reheat the sauce and serve it with the cooked chicken and the cooked polenta or pasta.   SERVES 4

**TOP:** Chicken Pinwheels
**BOTTOM:** Chicken Bagna Cauda

## AROMATIC DUCK BREASTS WITH PORT & CHERRIES

4 duck breasts, weighing 200 g (7 oz) each
New potatoes, to serve (optional)

### MARINADE
60 ml (4 tbsp) chopped fresh rosemary
20 ml (4 tsp) ground cinnamon
10 ml (2 tsp) ground allspice
5 ml (1 tsp) soft brown sugar
45 ml (3 tbsp) vegetable oil

### PORT AND CHERRY SAUCE
360 ml (12 fl oz) ruby port
120 ml (8 tbsp) red wine vinegar
20 ml (4 tsp) soft brown sugar
225 g (8 oz) fresh cherries, halved, or
175 g (6 oz) stoned whole canned cherries
Salt and ground black pepper

Make several deep slashes through the skin and flesh of each duck breast. Mix the marinade ingredients together and work this mixture into the slashes and surface of the duck breasts. Cover and refrigerate for at least 2 hours.

Make the sauce. Place the port, vinegar and sugar in a saucepan and bring to the boil. Boil the sauce for 4-5 minutes to reduce it, then add the cherries. Reduce the heat and cook very gently for a further 6-8 minutes. Taste and adjust seasoning, if necessary, and set the sauce aside until required.

Cook the duck breasts on a prepared, medium-hot barbecue for about 10 minutes on each side, until cooked through. Reheat the sauce. Slice the duck breasts and serve them with the Port and Cherry Sauce and potatoes, if desired.          SERVES 4

## BBQ DUCK WITH SAGE & ORANGE STUFFING

4 leg portions of duck

### SAGE AND ORANGE STUFFING
60 ml (4 tbsp) butter, softened
10 ml (2 tsp) dry mustard powder
60 ml (4 tbsp) very finely chopped celery
8 sage leaves, chopped
Grated zest of 1 large orange
Salt and ground black pepper

### MARINADE
Juice of 1 large orange
2 sage leaves, chopped
60 ml (4 tbsp) orange marmalade
15 ml (1 tbsp) vegetable oil

Mix the ingredients for the stuffing together in a bowl. Loosen the skin of the duck portions by easing it away from the leg meat. Divide the stuffing between the duck portions, placing it between the skin and leg meat, and spreading it out as much as possible.

Mix together the marinade ingredients. Place the duck portions in a shallow glass dish, pour over the marinade, then cover and refrigerate for at least 2 hours or overnight.

Remove the duck from the marinade, reserving the marinade for basting. Cook the duck on a prepared barbecue for 20-25 minutes, turning and basting the duck while it is cooking. Serve at once.     SERVES 4

**TOP:** Aromatic Duck Breasts with Port & Cherries
**BOTTOM:** BBQ Duck with Sage & Orange Stuffing

## KOFTA KEBABS

350 g (12 oz) minced lamb

4 slices crustless white bread, crumbled

1 onion, finely chopped

4 cloves garlic, crushed

60 ml (4 tbsp) chopped fresh mint

30 ml (2 tbsp) chopped fresh parsley

60 ml (4 tbsp) pine nuts, toasted

30 ml (2 tbsp) raisins

30 ml (2 tbsp) cumin seeds, lightly toasted

5 ml (1 tsp) ground coriander

1 egg, beaten

Salt and ground black pepper

4 metal skewers

Oil for brushing

50 g (2 oz) iceberg lettuce, shredded

2 tomatoes, cut into wedges

1 onion, sliced

12 black olives

Warm pitta bread and lemon wedges, to serve

### MINT DRESSING

160 ml (5½ fl oz) Greek-style yoghurt

60 ml (4 tbsp) chopped fresh mint

Pinch of cayenne

Salt and ground black pepper

Place the first 12 ingredients in a food processor and process briefly to combine. Divide the mixture into 12 portions and shape each portion into an oval-shaped patty. Refrigerate for 2 hours.

Mix the Mint Dressing ingredients together in a bowl and refrigerate until required.

Thread three koftas on to each skewer and brush with a little oil. Cook on a prepared barbecue for 6 minutes on each side, turning and brushing with oil.

Divide the lettuce, tomato, onion and olives between four plates. Add the kebabs and serve at once with the dressing, pitta and lemon.      SERVES 4

## PEPPERED STEAKS WITH HERB COUS-COUS

4 fillet steaks, weighing 150 g (5 oz) each

20 ml (4 tsp) olive oil

60 ml (4 tbsp) tropical peppercorns, crushed

### HERB COUS-COUS

175 g (6 oz) cous-cous

480 ml (16 fl oz) boiling water

30 ml (2 tbsp) olive oil

4 spring onions, finely chopped

120 ml (8 tbsp) chopped fresh parsley

Finely grated zest of 1 large lemon

20 ml (4 tsp) lemon juice

1 red pepper, grilled, skinned and diced

Salt and ground black pepper

Brush each steak with a little olive oil and press the crushed peppercorns on to the surfaces.

Place the cous-cous in a bowl with a little salt and pour over the boiling water. Leave the cous-cous to stand for 5-10 minutes, until the water has been absorbed and the grains have swelled up.

Cook the peppered steaks on the oiled rack of a prepared barbecue for about 5 minutes on each side, turning them halfway through cooking.

Just before serving, finish the cous-cous by heating the oil in a large saucepan, adding the cous-cous and all the remaining ingredients, and stirring to combine and heat through. Serve the peppered steaks with the cous-cous.      SERVES 4

**RIGHT:** Kofta Kebabs

## BBQ VEAL ROLLS

4 veal escalopes, weighing 150 g (5 oz) each
50 g (2 oz) fresh spinach
15 ml (1 tbsp) olive oil
2 large cloves garlic, chopped
30 ml (2 tbsp) finely chopped red onion
100 g (4 oz) ricotta cheese
20 ml (4 tsp) pine nuts, toasted
Salt and ground black pepper
Barbecued Artichokes, to serve (see page 320)

### MARINADE

90 ml (6 tbsp) white wine
45 ml (3 tbsp) olive oil
Pinch of nutmeg
Ground black pepper

Place a veal escalope between two pieces of grease-proof paper and pound with a rolling pin or mallet to flatten. Repeat with the remaining veal escalopes.

Steam the spinach, then lay the leaves on kitchen paper to remove any excess moisture. Heat the oil in a saucepan, add the garlic and onion and sauté for 1-2 minutes until soft. Transfer to a large bowl and stir in the ricotta cheese, pine nuts and seasoning.

Season a veal escalope, then place one-quarter of the spinach in a layer over the veal, leaving a 1.5-cm (½-inch) border around the edges. Season again and spread one-quarter of the ricotta mixture over the spinach. Roll the veal escalope up to completely enclose the filling. Secure with string. Repeat with the remaining veal, spinach and ricotta mixture.

Place the marinade ingredients in a shallow glass dish and mix well. Add the veal rolls to the dish and turn to coat evenly. Cover and refrigerate for 2 hours.

Remove the veal rolls from the marinade, reserving the marinade for basting. Cook on a prepared barbecue for about 20 minutes, turning and basting. Serve at once with Barbecued Artichokes.          SERVES 4

## PECAN NUT TURKEY ESCALOPES

4 turkey escalopes, weighing 100 g (4 oz) each
30 ml (2 tbsp) Dijon mustard
30 ml (2 tbsp) soured cream
100 g (4 oz) pecan nuts, coarsely ground
Oil for brushing
Lemon wedges, to serve

### SOURED CREAM DIP

90 ml (6 tbsp) soured cream
30 ml (2 tbsp) snipped fresh chives
10 ml (2 tsp) Dijon mustard
Lemon juice to taste
Salt and ground black pepper

Place the turkey escalopes between two pieces of greaseproof paper and pound them with a rolling pin or mallet to flatten.

Mix together the Dijon mustard and soured cream and place the ground pecans on a flat plate. Dip an escalope in the mustard mixture and then place it on the plate of pecans and turn to coat evenly. Repeat with the remaining turkey escalopes. Cover and refrigerate for at least 2 hours before barbecuing.

Mix the ingredients for the dip together, cover and refrigerate until required.

Brush the pecan-coated turkey escalopes with a little oil and cook them on a prepared barbecue for 6-7 minutes on each side, until they are golden and cooked through. Serve hot with lemon wedges and the Soured Cream Dip.          SERVES 4

**TOP:** Pecan Nut Turkey Escalopes
**BOTTOM:** BBQ Veal Rolls

# VEGETABLE BARBECUES

Recipes for starters, side dishes and main courses are included in this chapter, enabling you to create a totally vegetarian meal, if so desired. Although some of the recipes would not immediately be associated with barbecues, they work very well. For example, the Savoy Cabbage Parcels and the Vine Leaves with Feta, Olives & Tomato are novel barbecue ideas, but delicious. Some recipes will require a little extra care with handling, as the ingredients are more fragile than traditional barbecue ingredients.

## SPICED CORN ON THE COB

4 corn on the cob, husks removed
30 ml (2 tbsp) olive oil
2.5 ml (½ tsp) cayenne
Salt and ground black pepper

### CHILLI BUTTER
75 g (3 oz) butter, softened
30 ml (2 tbsp) coarsely chopped fresh coriander
10 ml (2 tsp) finely chopped fresh red chilli
Salt and ground black pepper

Prepare the Chilli Butter. Mix the ingredients together until thoroughly combined. Place the butter in a sausage shape on a piece of cling film or greaseproof paper. Roll up to form a cylinder and refrigerate to harden the butter.

Cook the corn in plenty of boiling, salted water for about 15 minutes, until it is tender. Drain, then toss the corn in the olive oil, cayenne and seasoning to coat.

Cook the corn on a prepared barbecue for 10-15 minutes, turning occasionally while cooking. They are ready to serve when they are slightly charred. Serve at once with discs of Chilli Butter.          SERVES 4

## MEDITERRANEAN VEGETABLES

The quantity of herb oil in this recipe is sufficient to cook the vegetables listed below. Vegetables may be varied according to preference.

4 corn on the cob
8 baby fennel bulbs
4 plum tomatoes
2 red onions
2 peppers, any colour

### HERB AND GARLIC OIL
150 ml (¼ pint) extra virgin olive oil
30 ml (2 tbsp) balsamic vinegar
2 cloves garlic, crushed
120 ml (8 tbsp) chopped fresh mixed herbs, such as fennel fronds, chives, parsley and basil
Salt and ground black pepper

Prepare the vegetables for barbecuing. Peel back the husks from the corn and knot them at the base. Remove all the threads from the sweetcorn and discard. Trim the baby fennel and halve the tomatoes. Halve the onions, leaving the skins intact. Halve the peppers lengthways and remove the cores and seeds, leaving the stalks intact.

Mix the ingredients for the Herb and Garlic Oil together. To cook the vegetables, brush them liberally with the herb oil and cook on a prepared barbecue, turning and brushing frequently until they are cooked through and slightly charred. The corn on the cob will take about 20 minutes to cook, the onions 15-20 minutes, and the fennel, tomatoes and peppers about 10 minutes.          SERVES 4-6

**RIGHT:** Mediterranean Vegetables

# HALLOUMI, COURGETTE & MUSHROOM SKEWERS

*These cheese and vegetable skewers make a satisfying vegetarian main course when served with a tomato and olive salad and warm pitta bread.*

350 g (12 oz) halloumi cheese
1 red pepper, halved, cored and seeded
175 g (6 oz) courgettes, cut into 8 chunks
8 large mushrooms, halved
120 ml (8 tbsp) extra virgin olive oil
30 ml (2 tbsp) chopped fresh thyme
2 cloves garlic, chopped
Ground black pepper
8 wooden or metal skewers

Cut the cheese and red pepper into 2.5-cm (1-inch) squares. Place them in a shallow dish with the courgettes and mushrooms. Mix the olive oil, thyme, garlic and pepper together and pour over the vegetables. Toss gently to coat evenly, then thread the cheese and vegetables on the skewers. Brush with any remaining oil mixture.

Cook on the oiled rack of a prepared barbecue for about 8 minutes, turning occasionally and brushing with any remaining oil mixture. The skewers are ready to serve when the cheese is golden and the vegetables are tender. SERVES 4

# SPICY POTATO, SHALLOT & FENNEL KEBABS

*Baby fennel bulbs are used in this recipe, but if they are unavailable, substitute small wedges of fennel.*

24 baby new potatoes
8 small shallots
16 baby fennel bulbs, about 275 g (10 oz) in total weight
20 ml (4 tsp) mustard seeds
20 ml (4 tsp) cumin seeds
20 ml (4 tsp) garam masala
10 ml (2 tsp) turmeric
20 ml (4 tsp) lemon juice
120 ml (8 tbsp) groundnut oil
Salt and ground black pepper
8 wooden or metal skewers

Cook the potatoes in boiling, salted water for about 12 minutes until tender. Drain and transfer to a large mixing bowl. Cook the shallots in boiling water for 4 minutes, drain and, when cool enough to handle, peel them. Add to the potatoes, along with the fennel.

Crush the mustard and cumin seeds lightly and place them in a bowl with the garam masala, turmeric, lemon juice, groundnut oil and some seasoning. Mix to combine, then pour over the prepared vegetables and toss to coat well. Cover and refrigerate for 2 hours, if time permits.

Remove the vegetables from the mixture, reserving any remaining mixture for basting, and thread the vegetables evenly between the skewers. Cook the kebabs on a prepared barbecue for about 12 minutes, turning and basting while cooking. SERVES 4

**TOP:** Spicy Potato, Shallot & Fennel Kebabs
**BOTTOM:** Halloumi, Courgette & Mushroom Skewers

## GRILLED VEGETABLES WITH TAHINI DRESSING

350 g (12 oz) sweet potato, peeled and cut
into 4 slices
450 g (1 lb) celeriac, peeled and cut into 4 slices
350 g (12 oz) pumpkin, peeled and cut
into 4 wedges
2 medium parsnips, peeled and halved lengthways
90 ml (6 tbsp) olive oil for brushing
Sea salt and ground black pepper

### TAHINI DRESSING
60 ml (4 tbsp) light tahini
60 ml (4 tbsp) mayonnaise
45 ml (3 tbsp) olive oil
1.25 ml (¼ tsp) paprika
2 cloves garlic, crushed
2 spring onions, chopped
10 ml (2 tsp) lemon juice
Salt and ground black pepper

Mix the ingredients for the dressing together in a bowl and refrigerate until required.

Cook the different types of root vegetables individually in boiling, salted water until they are just tender. The celeriac will take about 12 minutes to cook, the sweet potato 10 minutes, the parsnip 8 minutes and the pumpkin 6 minutes.

Drain the cooked vegetables and dry them on kitchen paper. Brush them all over with olive oil and season generously with salt and pepper.

Cook the vegetables on the oiled rack of a prepared barbecue for about 6 minutes on each side, turning them halfway through cooking and brushing occasionally with oil. Serve the barbecued vegetables with the Tahini Dressing.       SERVES 4

## CHARGRILLED YAMS & PLANTAINS WITH HOT PEPPER MAYONNAISE

*Green, unripe plantains can be substituted for the half-ripe plantains in this recipe, but they will take longer to cook.*

4 × 150-g (5-oz) slices yam, peeled
4 × 75-g (3-oz) thick slices half-ripe plantain, with skins left intact
Corn oil for brushing
Salt and ground black pepper

### HOT PEPPER MAYONNAISE
90 ml (6 tbsp) mayonnaise
30 ml (2 tbsp) chopped fresh thyme
5 ml (1 tsp) seeded and finely chopped hot Jamaican chilli
20 ml (4 tsp) freshly squeezed lime juice
Salt and ground black pepper

Cook the yam slices in boiling, salted water for 15 minutes or until tender. Drain and set aside until required. Mix the mayonnaise ingredients together and refrigerate until required.

Brush the yam and plantain slices all over with corn oil and season with salt and pepper. Cook on a prepared barbecue, turning occasionally until they are tender and charred on the outside. The yams will be ready to serve in 15 minutes and the plantains in about 12 minutes. Serve at once with the Hot Pepper Mayonnaise.       SERVES 4 AS A STARTER

**TOP:** Chargrilled Yams & Plantains with Hot
Pepper Mayonnaise
**BOTTOM:** Grilled Vegetables with
Tahini Dressing

## SAVOY CABBAGE PARCELS

*These cabbage parcels make an excellent accompaniment to barbecued pork or chicken.*

4 large Savoy or pointed green cabbage leaves
75 g (3 oz) butter
100 g (4 oz) leeks, thinly sliced
100 g (4 oz) carrots, peeled and coarsely grated
175 g (6 oz) cooked brown basmati rice
25 g (1 oz) pumpkin seeds, lightly toasted
30 ml (2 tbsp) chopped fresh tarragon
Salt and ground black pepper

Cut away the tough stalks from the cabbage leaves, then blanch the leaves in boiling, salted water for 1-2 minutes until they are just tender. Drain and refresh in cold water, then lay cabbage leaves on kitchen paper to dry them.

Melt 50 g (2 oz) of the butter in a pan, add the leeks and sauté for 3 minutes. Stir in the carrot and sauté for a further minute. Remove pan from the heat and stir in the rice, pumpkin seeds, tarragon and seasoning.

Lay a cabbage leaf on a large piece of foil and place one-quarter of the rice mixture in the centre. Fold the cabbage around the filling to form a parcel, dot with one-quarter of the remaining butter and fold up the foil to enclose the cabbage. Repeat with the remaining cabbage leaves and filling.

Cook the foil parcels on a prepared barbecue for 13-15 minutes, until the cabbage is tender and the filling heated through. SERVES 4

## VINE LEAVES WITH FETA, OLIVES & TOMATO

8 large vacuum-packed vine leaves
30 ml (2 tbsp) olive oil
100 g (4 oz) feta cheese, cut into small cubes
16 small black olives
8 cherry tomatoes, halved
8 sprigs fresh oregano
Ground black pepper
Cocktail sticks
Greek-style sesame bread, to serve (optional)

Rinse the vine leaves and dry them on kitchen paper. Lay them on a flat surface and brush each leaf with a little olive oil.

Divide the feta, black olives, tomatoes and oregano evenly between the leaves, placing them in the centre of each leaf. Grind over some black pepper and fold the leaves around the filling to enclose it completely. Secure the vine leaf parcels with cocktail sticks.

Brush the outside of the parcels with the remaining oil and cook them on a prepared barbecue for about 4-5 minutes, until the cheese has begun to melt. They do not need to be turned, but do keep the skewered side of the parcels upright, away from the coals.

Serve two vine leaves to each person. Peel away the leaves and eat the filling. The leaves are purely to enclose the filling and are not meant to be eaten. Serve with sesame bread, if desired.

SERVES 4 AS A STARTER

**RIGHT:** Vine Leaves with Feta, Olives & Tomato

## PATTY PAN, ONION & AUBERGINE KEBABS

16 small patty pan squash
8 baby aubergines, halved lengthways
8 baby onions, unpeeled
8 wooden or metal skewers

### MARINADE

60 ml (4 tbsp) chopped fresh coriander
120 ml (8 tbsp) olive oil
5 ml (1 tsp) garam masala
5 ml (1 tsp) dried chilli flakes
2 cloves garlic, crushed
Salt and ground black pepper

### BULGHUR WHEAT PILAF

225 g (8 oz) bulghur wheat
700 ml (1¼ pints) boiling vegetable stock
60 ml (4 tbsp) olive oil
1 onion, chopped
2 cloves garlic, crushed
5 ml (1 tsp) ground cumin
50 g (2 oz) raisins
60 ml (4 tbsp) coarsely chopped coriander
Salt and ground black pepper

Mix the marinade ingredients together in a large bowl. Boil the patty pan squash for 4 minutes, drain and add to the marinade, along with the aubergines. Boil the onions for 5 minutes, then drain, peel and halve them. Add the onions to the bowl of vegetables. Toss gently to coat evenly. Cover and refrigerate for 2 hours.

Make the pilaf. Soak the bulghur wheat in the boiling stock for about 40 minutes, until the grains have swelled and are tender. Drain well. Heat the oil in a saucepan and sauté the onion, garlic and cumin for 4 minutes until soft. Remove from the heat and stir in the bulghur wheat, raisins and coriander. Season the pilaf generously and set aside until required.

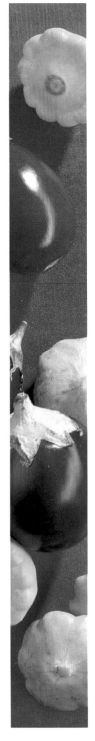

Thread the marinated vegetables evenly between the skewers, reserving the marinade for basting. Cook the kebabs on a prepared barbecue for about 10 minutes, turning and basting occasionally while cooking. Serve at once with the pilaf.  SERVES 4

## ORIENTAL TOFU SKEWERS

250 g (9 oz) tofu, cut into 16 cubes
1 large orange pepper, grilled, skinned and cut into 8 long strips
8 cherry tomatoes
75 g (3 oz) broccoli, divided into 8 florets
8 wooden or metal skewers
Noodles, to serve (optional)

### SESAME MARINADE

45 ml (3 tbsp) vegetable oil
15 ml (1 tbsp) sesame oil
15 ml (1 tbsp) soy sauce
5 ml (1 tsp) grated fresh root ginger
5 ml (1 tsp) sesame seeds
30 ml (2 tbsp) rice wine vinegar
1 spring onion, finely chopped

Mix the marinade ingredients together in a large bowl. Add the tofu cubes to the marinade, toss gently to coat, cover and refrigerate for 2 hours.

Remove the tofu from the marinade, reserving the remaining marinade for basting. Thread the tofu, pepper strips, tomatoes and broccoli on the skewers.

Cook the skewers on a prepared barbecue for 8-10 minutes, turning and basting them while cooking. Just before serving, pour any remaining marinade over the tofu skewers. Serve with noodles, if desired.

SERVES 4

**TOP AND BOTTOM:** Oriental Tofu Skewers
**CENTRE:** Patty Pan, Onion & Aubergine Kebabs

## FALAFEL PATTIES WITH YOGHURT & MINT DIP

30 ml (2 tbsp) vegetable oil
5 ml (1 tsp) cumin seeds
1 onion, finely chopped
2 cloves garlic, crushed
5 ml (1 tsp) chopped fresh green chilli
2.5 ml (½ tsp) turmeric
432-g (15-oz) can chick-peas, drained
Salt and ground black pepper
50 g (2 oz) fresh white breadcrumbs
1 egg, beaten
30 ml (2 tbsp) chopped fresh coriander
Flour for coating
Oil for brushing
A barbecue flat griddle plate or wire basket
for cooking
Lemon wedges and pitta bread, to serve

### YOGHURT AND MINT DIP

120 ml (8 tbsp) Greek-style yoghurt
60 ml (4 tbsp) chopped fresh mint
5 ml (1 tsp) lemon juice
Pinch of ground cumin
Salt and ground black pepper

Mix the ingredients for the dip together, cover and refrigerate until required.

Heat the vegetable oil in a frying pan, add cumin seeds, onion and garlic and sauté for 5 minutes. Add chilli and turmeric and cook for a further 2 minutes. Transfer the spice mixture to a food processor, add the chick-peas and seasoning, and blend briefly until the chick-peas are roughly mashed and combined with the spices.

Transfer to a bowl and add the breadcrumbs, egg and coriander. Mix to combine and divide into eight portions. With floured hands, shape into patties and refrigerate the falafel for about 4 hours.

Oil the griddle plate and heat on a prepared barbecue or, alternatively, place the falafel in a wire basket. Brush the falafel all over with oil and cook on the barbecue for 6-7 minutes on each side. Serve hot with the dip, lemon and pitta.　SERVES 4

## PEPPERS STUFFED WITH NUTTY RICE

4 medium red peppers
Oil for brushing

**NUTTY RICE**
225 g (8 oz) basmati rice
5 ml (1 tsp) saffron strands infused in
30 ml (2 tbsp) boiling water for 10 minutes
60 ml (4 tbsp) vegetable oil
1 red onion, thinly sliced
4 small cloves garlic, crushed
50 g (2 oz) pine nuts, toasted
25 g (1 oz) pistachio nuts, coarsely chopped
60 ml (4 tbsp) chopped fresh parsley
Salt and ground black pepper

Prepare the Nutty Rice. Cook the basmati rice in boiling, salted water, to which the saffron and its water has been added. The rice will take 8-10 minutes to cook. Drain and place the rice in a mixing bowl.

Heat the oil in a pan and sauté the onion and garlic for 2-3 minutes. Add to the rice, with the pine nuts, pistachios, parsley and seasoning. Toss to combine.

Halve the peppers lengthways and core and seed, leaving the stalks intact. Divide the Nutty Rice between the pepper halves. Lightly oil four large pieces of foil and place two pepper halves on each piece of foil. Fold to produce parcels and cook on a prepared barbecue for about 20 minutes, until the peppers are tender and the rice is hot.　SERVES 4

**RIGHT:** Falafel Patties with Yoghurt & Mint Dip

# MUSHROOM & MOZZARELLA BROCHETTES

*Rosemary branches can be used in this recipe to skewer the food. Choose long, mature branches and strip off the leaves, just leaving a few at the top. Soak them in cold water for 1 hour.*

16 fresh shiitake mushrooms, about 100 g (4 oz) in total weight
16 button mushrooms, about 225 g (8 oz) in total weight
16 mini mozzarella cheese balls
8 metal or rosemary branch skewers
Steamed cous-cous, to serve (optional)

### MARINADE
Zest and juice of 2 small lemons
30 ml (2 tbsp) olive oil
45 ml (3 tbsp) chopped fresh rosemary
10 ml (2 tsp) chilli oil
½ small fresh red chilli, seeded and finely chopped
½ small fresh green chilli, seeded and finely chopped
2 cloves garlic, crushed
Salt and ground black pepper

Mix the marinade ingredients together. Place the two types of mushrooms and the mini mozzarellas in a mixing bowl. Pour over the marinade and toss gently to coat evenly. Cover and refrigerate for 2 hours.

Remove the marinated mushrooms and cheese from the dish, reserving any remaining marinade for basting, and thread the mushrooms and cheese evenly between the skewers or rosemary branches.

Cook the brochettes on a prepared medium-hot barbecue for about 10 minutes, turning and basting them while cooking. Serve at once with steamed cous-cous, if desired.                  SERVES 4

# GOAT'S CHEESE, LEEK & WALNUT BRUSCHETTA

6 slices French bread, cut on an acute angle
45 ml (3 tbsp) olive oil
6 × 40-g (1½-oz) slices soft goat's cheese
Ground black pepper

### LEEK AND WALNUT TOPPING
30 ml (2 tbsp) olive oil
75 g (3 oz) leeks, thinly sliced
15 g (½ oz) walnuts, coarsely chopped
Salt and ground black pepper

Make the topping. Heat the oil in a saucepan and sauté the leeks for about 3 minutes until they are soft. Remove from the heat and stir in the remaining ingredients. Set aside until required.

Brush both sides of the sliced bread with 30 ml (2 tbsp) of the olive oil. Place the bread on the grill rack of a prepared barbecue and cook for 2-3 minutes, until toasted on one side. Do not toast the other side.

Remove from the barbecue and divide the Leek and Walnut Topping between the toasted sides of the bread slices. Top each with a piece of goat's cheese and drizzle with the remaining olive oil. Grind over some black pepper.

Return the bruschetta to the barbecue and cook for a further 3-4 minutes until the cheese begins to melt. Serve at once.                  SERVES 6 AS A STARTER

**LEFT AND BOTTOM:** Goat's Cheese, Leek & Walnut Bruschetta
**RIGHT:** Mushroom & Mozzarella Brochettes

# SWEET DESSERTS

*The recipes in this chapter allow you to extend your barbecue meal to the last course (provided that the coals have been tended so they are still glowing). Fruits lend themselves to barbecuing, as they cook quickly and combine well with other flavours. Barbecued bananas are a classic favourite and here made more special by adding a maple syrup and pecan nut sauce. Tamarillos with Brown Sugar are extremely easy to prepare, yet produce a delicious and unusual dessert. For a more sophisticated dish, try Almond-stuffed Medjool Dates, which are steeped in cinnamon and brandy.*

## BANANAS WITH MAPLE SYRUP & PECAN NUTS

50 g (2 oz) pecan nuts, coarsely chopped
90 ml (6 tbsp) maple syrup
4 bananas
Vanilla or rum-and-raisin ice cream, to serve

Place the chopped pecans and maple syrup in a small saucepan and set aside until required.

Cook the whole bananas in their skins on a prepared barbecue for 12-15 minutes, until the skins are completely black and the bananas are soft.

Just before serving, gently warm the pecan nuts and maple syrup. To serve, remove the bananas from their skins and top with the warm nutty syrup and scoops of ice cream.                                     SERVES 4

## FRUIT SKEWERS WITH CHOCOLATE-NUT SAUCE

12 strawberries
6 apricots, halved
3 pears, peeled and cut into quarters
30 ml (2 tbsp) caster sugar
6 wooden or metal skewers

### CHOCOLATE-NUT SAUCE

100 g (4 oz) milk chocolate, chopped
150 ml (¼ pint) single cream
6 marshmallows, chopped
25 g (1 oz) skinless hazelnuts, toasted and chopped

Make the sauce by melting the chocolate, cream and marshmallows gently, stirring constantly. Then whisk to produce a smooth sauce and boil for 2 minutes to thicken. Stir in the nuts and set the sauce aside.

Place the fruit in a bowl, sprinkle over the caster sugar and toss gently to coat. Divide the fruit between the skewers.

Place the fruit skewers on a prepared barbecue and cook them for 5-6 minutes, turning frequently, until the fruit is warmed through. Serve the skewers at once with the Chocolate-Nut Sauce passed separately for dipping.                                     SERVES 6

**RIGHT:** Fruit Skewers with Chocolate-Nut Sauce

## EXOTIC FRUIT WITH PASSIONFRUIT DIP

I small ripe pawpaw, cut into 4 thick slices with
seeds removed
I small ripe mango, cut into quarters around
the stone
2 bananas, unpeeled and halved lengthways
2 thick slices pineapple, halved
50 g (2 oz) unsalted butter, melted
10 ml (2 tsp) sifted icing sugar

### PASSIONFRUIT DIP
200 ml (7 fl oz) crème fraîche
15 ml (1 tbsp) sifted icing sugar
Pulp and juice of 3 passionfruit
Mint sprigs, to decorate

Mix the ingredients for the dip together in a bowl.
Cover and refrigerate until required.

Place all the fruit on a large tray. Mix together the
melted butter and icing sugar, and brush the mixture
all over the fruit. Cook all the fruit on a prepared
barbecue, turning the pawpaw, mango and pineapple
over occasionally until they begin to caramelize. The
mango, pineapple and bananas will take about 6
minutes to cook, and the pawpaw about 4 minutes.
Garnish with mint and serve the fruit with the dip.

SERVES 4

## PEACH & ALMOND DESSERT WITH AMARETTO

50 g (2 oz) Madeira cake, crumbled
6 amaretti biscuits, coarsely crushed
60 ml (4 tbsp) Amaretto liqueur
4 ripe peaches, halved with stones removed
25 g (1 oz) flaked almonds, toasted
120 ml (8 tbsp) freshly squeezed orange juice
Mascarpone cheese, to serve

Mix the Madeira cake, amaretti biscuits and half the
Amaretto liqueur together in a bowl. Divide the mixture between the hollows of the peaches. Sprinkle a
few flaked almonds on to each peach half.

Mix the remaining Amaretto liqueur and the orange
juice together. Place two peach halves on a large piece
of foil. Spoon over one-quarter of the orange juice
mixture and fold over the foil to make a parcel. Repeat
with the remaining peaches to produce four parcels.

Cook the peach parcels on a prepared barbecue for
about 10 minutes, until they are tender and warmed
through. Serve with mascarpone cheese.   SERVES 4

**TOP:** Peach & Almond Dessert with Amaretto
**BOTTOM:** Exotic Fruit with Passionfruit Dip

## ALMOND-STUFFED MEDJOOL DATES

12 large fresh Medjool dates
75 g (3 oz) blanched almonds, toasted
30 ml (2 tbsp) mascarpone cheese or cream cheese
60 ml (4 tbsp) brandy
2 cinnamon sticks, broken in half
30 ml (2 tbsp) soft brown sugar
60 ml (4 tbsp) freshly squeezed orange juice
Greek yoghurt, to serve (optional)

Make a slit in the side of each date and remove and discard the stones.

Reserve 12 whole blanched almonds and chop the rest finely. Place them in a bowl and add the mascarpone cheese and half the brandy. Mix well to combine and fill the dates with the mixture, adding a whole almond to each cavity.

Place six dates on a large piece of foil and place a cinnamon stick on the foil with the dates. Mix the remaining brandy, brown sugar and orange juice together. Spoon half of the mixture over the dates. Wrap up the foil to produce a parcel. Repeat with the remaining dates, cinnamon and orange juice mixture.

Cook the foil parcels on a prepared barbecue for about 10 minutes, until the dates are tender and warmed through. Serve with yoghurt, if desired.

SERVES 4

## TAMARILLOS WITH BROWN SUGAR

4 ripe tamarillos (tree tomatoes)
45 ml (3 tbsp) Demerara sugar
Vanilla ice cream, to serve

Halve the tamarillos and place two halves on a piece of foil. Sprinkle with one-quarter of the Demerara sugar and fold the foil over to produce a parcel. Repeat with the remaining tamarillos and sugar to produce four individual parcels.

Cook the tamarillo parcels on a prepared barbecue for about 10 minutes, until they are warmed through and the sugar has melted. Serve at once with scoops of vanilla ice cream.

SERVES 4

**TOP LEFT:** Tamarillos with Brown Sugar
**BOTTOM:** Almond-stuffed Medjool Dates

# ACCOMPANIMENTS

The Collection of recipes in this chapter will help you provide a complete barbecue meal. Some of the accompaniments, such as Skewered New Potatoes and Olive, Basil & Parmesan Ciabatta, are actually cooked on the grill. Other recipes include rice and salad dishes, muffins and the classic Chilli Beans. Although these are not cooked on the grill, they are quick and easy to prepare an make good accompaniments to many of the recipes in this section.

## JASMINE & SESAME RICE

225 g (8 oz) Thai jasmine rice or fragrant rice
5 ml (1 tsp) sesame oil
30 ml (2 tbsp) sesame seeds, toasted
4 spring onions, finely chopped
60 ml (4 tbsp) chopped fresh coriander
10 ml (2 tsp) lime juice
Salt and ground black pepper

Cook the rice in boiling, salted water for about 10 minutes, or until it is tender. Drain and transfer the rice to a large bowl.

Add the remaining ingredients to the warm rice and stir gently to mix. Taste and adjust seasoning, if necessary, and serve at once. SERVES 4

## SPICY RICE

225 g (8 oz) mixed wild and long-grain rice
45 ml (3 tbsp) olive oil
3 cloves garlic, crushed
5 ml (1 tsp) dried chilli flakes
45 ml (3 tbsp) chopped fresh parsley
175 g (6 oz) sweetcorn kernels
Salt and ground black pepper

Cook the rice in boiling, salted water for about 10 minutes, or until the rice is tender. Drain and set it aside. Heat the oil in a saucepan and cook the garlic for 2 minutes. Add the chilli flakes and cook for a further 30 seconds. Stir the rice into the cooked garlic and chilli, along with the parsley, sweetcorn and seasoning. SERVES 4

## RICE & PEAS

30 ml (2 tbsp) vegetable oil
I onion, thinly sliced
100 g (4 oz) creamed coconut, dissolved in
600 ml (1 pint) boiling water
600 ml (1 pint) vegetable stock
350 g (12 oz) long-grain rice
I fresh red chilli, seeded and finely chopped
30 ml (2 tbsp) chopped fresh thyme
Salt and ground black pepper
150 g (5 oz) canned red kidney beans, rinsed
15 ml (1 tbsp) toasted desiccated coconut, to garnish
Thyme sprigs, to garnish

Heat the oil in a saucepan, add the onion and sauté for 5 minutes until golden. Add the coconut with its water, the stock, rice, chilli, thyme and seasoning to the pan. Cover the pan and simmer for 20 minutes, until the rice grains have swelled and most of the liquid has been absorbed.

Uncover the pan, stir the kidney beans into the rice and cook for a further 8-10 minutes, until the rice is tender and all the liquid has been absorbed. Garnish with toasted coconut and thyme and serve at once. SERVES 6

**TOP:** Jasmine & Sesame Rice
**BOTTOM:** Rice & Peas

## CHILLI BEANS

45 ml (3 tbsp) vegetable oil
I medium onion, chopped
2 cloves garlic, crushed
10-15 ml (2-3 tsp) hot chilli powder
5 ml (I tsp) cumin seeds
397-g (14-oz) can chopped tomatoes
150 ml (¼ pint) red wine
30 ml (2 tbsp) tomato purée
20 ml (4 tsp) molasses or treacle
432-g (15-oz) can red kidney beans, drained
and rinsed
432-g (15-oz) can black-eyed beans, drained
and rinsed
150 ml (¼ pint) water
Salt and ground black pepper
45 ml (3 tbsp) chopped fresh oregano

Heat the oil in a large saucepan, add the onion and garlic, and sauté for 3 minutes. Stir in the chilli and cumin and cook for a further minute.

Add the chopped tomatoes, wine, tomato purée and molasses, and simmer for 10 minutes. Add the two types of beans and the water. Season the chilli, cover and cook for a further 20 minutes. Stir in the oregano, taste and adjust seasoning, if necessary, and cook for a further 4-5 minutes. Serve the chilli beans hot as an accompaniment to barbecued potatoes, burgers or sausages. SERVES 6

## SKEWERED NEW POTATOES

32 baby new potatoes, about 700 g (1½ lb) in
total weight
60 ml (4 tbsp) olive oil
Sea salt and ground black pepper
8 wooden skewers, soaked in cold water for
2 hours

### HERB BUTTER
75 g (3 oz) butter, softened
30 ml (2 tbsp) chopped fresh herbs of your choice
Salt and ground black pepper

Scrub the potatoes and cook them in boiling, salted water for about 12 minutes or until tender.

Drain the potatoes and, while they are still warm, toss with the olive oil and plenty of salt and pepper. Thread four potatoes on to each skewer and set aside until required.

Mix the ingredients for the Herb Butter together. Place the butter in a sausage shape on a piece of greaseproof paper or cling film and roll up to produce a cylinder. Refrigerate the butter until it becomes firm enough to slice.

Cook the potatoes on a prepared barbecue for 12-15 minutes, turning them frequently. Serve hot with the Herb Butter. SERVES 8

**RIGHT:** Chilli Beans

## GRILLED PEPPER & PASTA SALAD

175 g (6 oz) dried pasta shapes
4 halves sun-dried tomatoes in oil, drained and sliced
1 yellow pepper, grilled, skinned and sliced into strips
1 red pepper, grilled, skinned and sliced into strips
15 ml (1 tbsp) chopped fresh oregano
15 ml (1 tbsp) chopped fresh thyme

### TAPENADE DRESSING

45 ml (3 tbsp) extra virgin olive oil
15 ml (1 tbsp) balsamic vinegar
1 clove garlic, crushed
5 ml (1 tsp) black olive tapenade
Salt and ground black pepper

Place the ingredients for the dressing in a screw-topped jar and shake well to combine. Taste and adjust seasoning, if necessary. Set aside until required.

Cook the pasta in boiling, salted water for 12-15 minutes until it is tender. Drain and transfer the pasta to a large bowl. Pour over the dressing and add the remaining ingredients. Toss to combine. If time permits, leave the salad to stand for 1 hour before serving to allow the flavours to develop. SERVES 4

## CRISP GREEN SALAD

175 g (6 oz) mixed crisp lettuce leaves, such as Cos, iceberg and frisée, washed and torn into bite-sized pieces
2 sticks celery, sliced on the diagonal
1 small avocado, peeled, stoned and chopped
2 spring onions, sliced
75 g (3 oz) cucumber, chopped
50 g (2 oz) cashew nuts, toasted

### CASHEW NUT DRESSING

75 g (3 oz) cashew nuts, toasted
90 ml (6 tbsp) sunflower oil
45 ml (3 tbsp) cider vinegar
2.5 ml (½ tsp) soft brown sugar
Salt and ground black pepper

Make the dressing. Place the cashew nuts in a food processor and grind coarsely. Add the oil, vinegar, sugar and seasoning and blend briefly to produce a thick, nutty dressing.

Place the prepared salad ingredients in a large bowl. Just before serving, pour over the dressing and toss gently to combine. Serve at once. SERVES 4-6

**TOP:** Crisp Green Salad
**BOTTOM:** Grilled Pepper & Pasta Salad

# CORNMEAL MUFFINS

150 g (5 oz) coarse cornmeal
75 g (3 oz) self-raising flour
5 ml (1 tsp) baking powder
Pinch of salt
50 g (2 oz) butter
150 ml (¼ pint) milk
1 large egg, beaten
Butter for greasing

Preheat the oven to 200°C (400°F, Gas mark 6). Sift together the cornmeal, flour, baking powder and salt. Melt the butter in a small pan, and stir the milk and beaten egg into the melted butter.

Make a well in the centre of the sifted dry ingredients. Pour in the liquid mixture and beat together to produce a smooth batter.

Grease eight muffin tins and divide the mixture between the tins. Bake in the oven for 18-20 minutes until risen and golden. Allow the muffins to cool in the tins before removing them.    MAKES 8 MUFFINS

### BASIL AND PARMESAN MUFFINS

Add 16 chopped green olives, 12 coarsely chopped basil leaves and 60 ml (4 tbsp) grated Parmesan cheese to the prepared muffin batter. Sprinkle 30 ml (2 tbsp) grated Parmesan over the muffins once they are in the tins, and bake as described in the main recipe.

### HERB MUFFINS

Add 60 ml (4 tbsp) chopped fresh herbs of your choice to the prepared muffin batter, then bake as described in the main recipe.

### CHEESE MUFFINS

Add 50 g (2 oz) grated Gruyère cheese to the prepared muffin batter. Spoon the mixture into tins and sprinkle with an additional 50 g (2 oz) grated Gruyère. Bake as described in the main recipe.

# OLIVE, BASIL & PARMESAN CIABATTA

1 loaf ciabatta bread
100 g (4 oz) butter, softened
6 stuffed green olives, finely chopped
90 ml (6 tbsp) grated Parmesan cheese
10 large basil leaves, torn
Salt and ground black pepper

Cut slices in the ciabatta loaf, cutting almost through to the base. Mix the butter, olives, Parmesan, basil and salt and pepper together. Spread the flavoured butter liberally on the cut slices of the ciabatta. Wrap the loaf in foil and place it on one side of a prepared barbecue for 20-30 minutes, until the butter has melted and the bread is hot. Serve at once.    MAKES 1 LOAF

# GARLIC & SUN-DRIED TOMATO CIABATTA

1 loaf ciabatta bread
100 g (4 oz) butter, softened
20 ml (4 tsp) sun-dried tomato paste
5 ml (1 tsp) fennel seeds
2 large cloves garlic, crushed
Salt and ground black pepper

Cut slices in the ciabatta loaf, as described in the recipe above. Mix the remaining ingredients together, then prepare and cook the bread as described above.

MAKES 1 LOAF

**TOP:** Cornmeal Muffins
**BOTTOM:** Garlic & Sun-dried Tomato Ciabatta

# INDEX